# I HOPE MY CORPSE GIVES YOU THE PLAGUE: MY LIFE IN THE BUSH ERA OF GHOSTS

Also by Adam Engel

*Topiary: A Novel* (2009) (as A. Stephen Engel)

# I HOPE MY CORPSE GIVES YOU THE PLAGUE: MY LIFE IN THE BUSH ERA OF GHOSTS

BY

ADAM ENGEL

THE OLIVER ARTS & OPEN PRESS

Library of Congress Cataloguing-in-Publication Data
Engel, Adam,. 1965-
I Hope My Corpse Gives You the Plague:
My Life in the Bush Era of Ghosts

ISBN: 978-0-9819891-9-8

The Oliver Arts & Open Press
2578 Broadway, Suite #102
New York, NY 10025
http://www.oliveropenpress.com

# ACKNOWLEDGEMENTS

These essays previously appeared, sometimes in altered form, on one or more of the following websites: *Counterpunch.org*; *Countercurrents.org*; *Dissident Voice.org*; *Online Journal.com*; *Strike-the-Root.com*; *LewRockwell.com*; *PressAction.com*, and others.

I wish to express my gratitude for the innovation and courage of the editors Jeffrey St. Claire of *Counterpunch*; Bev Conover of *Online Journal*; Sunil Sharma, Kim Peterson, and Joshua Frank of *Dissident Voice*; Rob of *Strike-the-Root*; Lew Rockwell of *Lew Rockwell.com*; The Editors at *Countercurrents.org*; and Mark Hand of *Press Action* for publishing not only these essays, but thousands like them each year, giving voice to hundreds of authors who would otherwise never see print, being ignored by the "Official Media."

Day after day, week after week, year after year, these sites and others like them offer venues for writers, scholars, journalists and activists to speak truth to Power. It's true that Power couldn't give a damn. But many people crushed by that same power find ideas on these web sites worth living and dying for.

AE

*For my nephew, Benjamin.*
*May he grow up in a world in which there's nothing particularly urgent to write about*

# CONTENTS

# EDITOR'S FOREWORD

They won't recognize its title, but many readers coming to this book *will* recognize its author's name and also a fair number of the essays contained inside. Those are the facts. A story—an important one—lies behind them.

From summer 2002 until spring 2005 or so, Adam Engel became a highly regarded and widely known writer thanks to his many brilliantly satiric essays that appeared with gratifying regularity on some of the internet's most influential political web sites. These pieces were extraordinary and unique. They were irrepressibly impassioned and stupendously mordant at one and the same time. They were anchored in the personal while their subjects were as big as nations. They were clock-stopping, head-spinning, hilarious, absolutely outraged, deep in their bite, and so deftly written and conceived as almost to require a new school of criticism just to describe them.

And then they stopped. Except for a straggler or two—you'll find those toward the end of this volume—they disappeared. And that's where the story lies.

Not long ago, Adam told me that he quit the pieces because it "didn't seem to matter any more." Hardly an accident that that's the way it seemed to him just *then*—right after the second stolen national election in a row, right after the return to office of an administration whose business and purpose were to continue as the criminal slayers of peoples, of cultures, of nations, and, certainly, of dignities and freedoms.

For Adam Engel, who for those three years had been our Jonathan Swift and Samuel Beckett rolled together, it was too despairing for words—too despairing for words to seem to matter any more.

What brought him back is something that only he can explain. But the fact is that he never really did stop writing, but he simply stopped *publishing*. It was almost as if in so putrefied and diseased a world as the Bushiscti and their predecessors had made of *our* world, there could maybe still be meaning in words—but only so long as they remained *silent*. After all, Beckett himself moved steadily toward silence. And there may be more in Hamlet's "The rest is silence" than in all the other of his words put together. Gertrude Stein—a revered model of Adam Engel's—moved toward silence, and so did the Language School of poets, whom Engel writes about in his essay called "Radical Language." Like the nation, language itself had been made purulent and diseased and therefore had grown into something that must be escaped *from*. In "Radical Language," Engel writes: "Language has been so debased by media that even in so-called 'high art' (poetry, drama) sentences that one might easily hear spoken on Oprah or some other 'real people' show, or sit-coms, has been 'current' for the past 20 years."

Language can be poisonous stuff, and it's been made only more poisonous in proportion to the purulence, decay, and moral rot of the society that uses it. Here's Engel again: "Politically, poems and novels written in 'regular' language are using the language that injected racism, sexism, capitalism and nearly everything we know into our brains, where language either is thought or [else] influences thought."

The depth of Adam Engel's literary, cultural, and political thinking may have led him to silence, but—though the abandoned readers of his political satire may not have known it—he was much too talented and cunning to let silence defeat him. He turned the tables on it. And he did that by writing the closest thing to a "silent novel" that any American has ever written except perhaps for Stein herself, in *The Making of Americans*.

Out of ten thousand sheets of unpublished "writing"—of "silent" writing—Engel distilled and crafted what came to be known as *Topiary: A Novel*, brought out in 2009 by The Oliver Arts & Open Press.

In an interview[1] with the author Douglas Valentine, Engel said a number of things about words and language, and about the relation they have to the diseased and morally bankrupt society they exist inside of. An example:

---

[1] http://www.ericlarsen.info/2009.OLIVER.5.1.3.Interview.A.S.Engel.pdf

**Douglas Valentine:** You've talked a lot about language and I'd like to talk more and more about it, but I think we should talk about the shape and depth of the novel also. But first, before leaving words, here's a sentence, or a phrase. that I typed out from the book, and it goes, "Starved for sanity." Very well done! Another is, "get Word to public." I should mention that the character in the book had an earlier life as an ad agency writer, and his reminiscence here leads him to think that "word was product." Is the book in some degree saying that word is "product" and thus worthless unless a person can rescue it and make it sacred again?

**Adam Engel:** Look, the heart that beats in the breast of this book is Gertrude Stein. And you talk about prose, poetry, there's hardly any difference, and Stein never had a story except *The Autobiography of Alice B. Toklas*, which was really done for money, "Melanctha" in *Three Lives*... and some other early stuff, but otherwise, she never even had anything published by people, or whatever the publishers are, until she was dead, long dead and gone. However, she did realize that words were sacred, yet grammar was not. And she actually, in her *How to Write*, which is not what you would think—if you wanted to learn how to write "stories" and you looked in that book you'd be freaked out because it's in her language. But in *How to Write*, she has a chapter called "Arthur A. Grammar" and she just messes with grammar and sentences and—she uses verbs, gets rid of as many modifiers as she can because verbs are action, life. Actually, in *Topiary* I did just the opposite. I got rid of as many verbs and adverbs as I could, just to, you know, signify a kind of death, a wasteland, a world of things, where even words are now things.

How many American writers today would even think of such ideas—"words were sacred, yet grammar was not"—let alone care about them powerfully? How many American writers today would fall silent, whether in grief, rage, or impotence, because of the loss of that sacredness, the banalizing and commoditizing of it until the sacredness was drained away and words themselves had become strengthless and passive, reduced into "things," had become "product"?

The deftness, intensity, depth, and moral passion in Adam Engel's essays—and in his fiction—will let readers know that these questions, and more, are all "in there." Listen carefully. And if it comes to pass that he stops writing, or publishing, the way he did five years ago—well, then listen even more carefully than you did before, because what he'll be saying then will be far, far more important than ever.

EL

# I HOPE MY CORPSE GIVES YOU THE PLAGUE: MY LIFE IN THE BUSH ERA OF GHOSTS

# ARBEIT MACHT FREI

"...their screams linger 13 years..."
—Barbara Mor

One of the Dukes of NYC, either Giuliani or Bloomberg, said a few days ago something to the effect that those who forget George Bush are doomed to repeat him. No, no, it was those who DON'T VOTE FOR BUSH are willfully forgetting the heroes of 9/11. Look at me, I forgot whose quote I'm paraphrasing. Actually, I just have difficulty telling the two apart. I know that both are furiously against smoking, though one, Giuliani, I think, thinks it's okay as long as you're smoking a cigar in his friend's chic bar and the other one, Bloomberg, I think, believes all smoking should be banned except for Marijuana and only if the pot is smoked by him. The rest of us clowns get a fine or jail-time, depending on the size of our stash. Regardless of who impugned the jingoism of anyone who happens to willfully forget to vote for Bush, I'm pretty sure they're on the same page in terms of being willing to remember. After all, forgetting George Bush is like forgetting the WTC tragedy because Bush and Terrorism have become synonymous. So closely linked with the events of 9/11 is our unelected Commandant in Chief, that SOME people believe he knew more about the attacks than MOST would want to believe. SOME people believe George Bush created heroes, or at least knew they'd be created, in advance of their brief fiery heroism and horrific deaths.

I was almost a hero, once. Almost.

Early summer of 2001 I was hustling for the last shards of the dotcom boom and secured an interview with a banking corporation that bears the name of a famous American Robber Baron who sowed the seeds of his first fortune on the blood-filth of the Civil War. He sold defective arms to Union Soldiers, (or was it Confederate soldiers? Possibly both). Some called this Johnny-Bad-Apple-Seed a war profiteer; others said he was merely planting heroes.

It was supposed to be a three-to-six-month gig writing ad-copy, business documents, executive speeches and other corporate propaganda. Thing was, they wanted me to wear a suit and tie. I told the woman at Human Resources that I didn't sport such garb, particularly not in hot weather. Sorry, no suit, no gig, she said politely.

So I missed the opportunity to work in the Word Trade Center offices of this particular establishment on September 11, 2001. Had I not been so damn stubborn and uppity, I would have been a hero for sure. Like that nice woman from Human Resources, may she rest in peace.

Now, I know all that crap about a hero ain't nuthin' but a side of cole-slaw all mushy white slimy gives you gas and blah, blah, blah; and it's true that I don't know much about firemen and EMTs but what I see on the News; and my only real experience with the men in blue is watching them harass young black and Hispanic males in the streets and subways and the occasional news story about some bad apples who—oops!—mistake a wallet for a bazooka and empty 41 slugs into some kid in front of his own home; but really the "men and women in uniform"—cops, firemen, EMTs etc.—who rushed toward the burning towers exhibited courage, self-sacrifice, compassion and all the virtues we associate with the word "hero."

Then again, such people do this for a living. I assume it's part of their job description. They, the ones who are true to their calling, risk their lives often. So why is the fireman who rushed into a burning building on September 10th any less a hero than his colleague who got caught beneath the rubble on September 11th? Why haven't the guys who died saving folks from fires before September 11th not become a National Fetish portrayed on postage stamps, raising the flag like the Marines at Iwo Jima, or displayed in life-sized corporate-sponsored posters all over NYC, or feted like celebrities of lesser worth but more renown on splashy tabloid covers?

Could it be that it's time for We the People to grow accustomed to praising—and mourning—men and women in uniform? With corporate sponsors, yet. Graphic artists doing their best Norman Rockwell to portray the generic, multi-ethnic "EMT-COP-FIREMAN" in bold colors beneath a tactfully understated corporate logo. Anybody read Gogol's Dead Souls? Interesting book.

## Vampire Ghouls from Planet X

Okay, so let's say the men and women in uniform got the recognition they deserve. Are they the only "heroes" of this sad tale, just because rabble rousing, publicity-hunting, vile, hate-filled twigs like George "I-Fought-the Law-And-My-Paw-Won" Bush, and Rudy "Two-timing Man of the Year" Giuliani, (who built his tax-payer funded security bunker INSIDE the WTC; no Odysseus he; and played hide-the-pickle with his "female associate" while his wife and kids watched it all on television INSIDE tax-payer funded Gracie Mansion—again, no Odysseus, he) say they are?

Boy, was that Giuliani brave when he stood in front of the cameras and assured us "I'm okay, you're okay—if not, we'll set up some kind of fund for your family or something." And darn, was Emperor

Bush tough on terrorism aboard Air Force One, or in Cheney's Bunker, or wherever the hell he was while his beloved men and woman in uniform were dying like heroes.

No way. I'm not buying. Not this time.

I give all the credit due to the cops, firefighters and others who risked and/or lost their lives trying to save the victims of that heinous attack; but I'm not gonna fall for the propaganda of these virulent soul-sucking vampires Bush and Giuliani. And Bloomberg, who won't allow adults over twenty-one to smoke in bars, or worse, won't allow adults over 21 who own bars let their paying customers smoke in their private establishments. Let's see, when did I first encounter the phenomenon of Megaphone-At-The-Microphone? Oh yes, 1992 it was. A mass rally of off-duty out-of-uniform (but still heroic?) cops protesting for better pay, benefits, and working conditions. Nothing wrong with that. Except many of these cops were drunk, armed, swigging beer, and shouting racial epithets about their boss, Mayor David Dinkins. And how did challenger Rudy rise to that occasion? Exhort the unruly drunks to go home, sleep it off and start a new rally (sans firearms) in the morning? Oh, no. He speechified, riled 'em up, made 'em hungry for action. Maybe he was just being a smart politician. That mad trip to the microphone in 1992 didn't hurt his campaign any; and that somber shtick before the microphones on 9/11/2001 turned him into a National hero (there, I said it. Happy now? He's a 'hero') and *Time Magazine*'s Man of the Year. What the HELL did he do that day besides talk tough into a microphone? Joey Ramone should have been Man of the Year for his stalwart performance at CBGB's circa 1976.

As for George, certain allegations made by Gore Vidal and others that he knew more about the imminence of the WTC attacks than one would ever want to believe are still debatable (and should damn well be debated), but NOBODY'S gonna tell me that his fellow spoiled brat millionaire's son and fellow life-abuser Bin Laden (more on that criminal later) didn't give George the greatest gift this man, who's been given gifts a-plenty all his life, has ever received—with the possible exception of the Supreme Court's generous donation of the U.S. Presidency.

But enough about these ghouls—they're giving me the chills. Let's talk about some real people. The men and women in uniform. No, not the cops and firemen this time. I'm talking about the men in suits and women in skirts and blouses and what not. The kind of uniform I wouldn't wear, which is why I'm just an almost-hero instead of a real one.

## Close to Home

Well, I hate to brag, but even though I'm not a hero, I happened to go to high school with one. I didn't now him all that well. But I remember him in his flannel shirt, unbuttoned and untucked, a black concert t-shirt underneath. Skinny guy. Quiet. Seventeen, still, in my brain. Again, I don't mean to brag, but with all these PATRIOTS waving their flags and whoopin' it up for war with terrorism, I figure I've as much right as anyone to wanna kill terrorism, I mean, to grab terrorism by the throat and kick its craven balls in and punch it in the mouth and shove it down the stairs and, and—actually, there's someone else who might want to kick terrorism's plastique ass even more than I do: my wife. You see, one of HER high school friends was also a hero. Grace, her name was. A great big hero, who left behind a daughter. Unlike my hero, who was really only an acquaintance, Grace was a dear friend of my wife's. Which was probably why my wife just sat there dumbfounded, crying, when we heard the news on the radio (okay, so we didn't have a TV at the time, but we can still be PATRIOTS, can't we?). Grace had been a waitress for a long time while she was supporting her daughter and going to school and she considered herself lucky to have worked her way up to a white collar position in a cubicle in a famous skyscraper so she could construct a richer existence for her kid.

So, in honor of my high school hero and Grace, and all the other folks who wore the uniform I didn't have the guts to wear myself, I'm gonna play PRETEND. Imagine I really was a hero. Imagine I took that hack writing job and woke up real, real early so as to beat the mad rush of potential heroes to the subway (a potential target) so I could maybe catch some light and air before ascending to my cell—uh, I mean cubicle—in an office suite high above the maddening crowd. Or better yet, let's put you in the hero's seat. Let's pretend YOU are

ME pretending to be a hero (due to my embarrassingly sparse imagination, we'll have to make you a corporate propaganda hack; it's all I know).

## Morning in America

Okay. Here we go. You hate your work (obviously, or you wouldn't be throwing away money on IRA's, 401(K)s and other scams; in fact, you don't even have real work; what you have, my poor hero-to-be, is a JOB). You despise your boss, your "corporate family," the cheery company news-letter you helped fabricate, your co-workers paranoid about down-sizing (little do they know HOW down-sized), your nine-to-five (six, seven really) life, so called.

But there are little things: you have your Starbucks coffee and your raisin bran muffin, and since it's your habit to come so damn early so as to avoid the proverbial "rush hour" and maybe get your mental shit together for the coming day, you can enjoy some preparatory peace and solitude.

You pass the shame-faced smokers outside the building. Smoking's frowned upon—hell, we don't wanna pollute the pristine air of NYC or anything—but you've got a full day's stash of mint-flavored Nicorette gum. The supersonic elevator takes you to your dreaded destination. The speed and altitude cause your ears to pop; the gum helps somewhat.

For whatever reason, you feel kind of okay. Secure, in fact. Perhaps it's the familiarity of the office, the routine. Or maybe it's the techno-regal power of your surroundings: this big-assed skyscraper made of stone and steel and heavy glass. The World Goddamned Trade Center. You've aced the commute and you're in your home-away-from-home, with time to kill before you have to pretend to do whatever you're being paid to pretend to do.

You reach your cubicle, drape your jacket over your chair, log on to your machine. Check your email and internal memos. Surf the Web. You think: what the hell am I doing here? If you're ME, you are writing copy or business reports or executive speeches or some such poppycock, which will take you an hour and a half, maybe two hours, then you have the hassle of looking busy—read left/progressive websites; detonate your special panic-button-instant-screen-saver if a "boss" or snitch strolls by—until five or six or whenever it won't be too conspicuous to make your get-away. Unless some asshole calls a late meeting—not necessarily a bad thing if it lets everyone look busy—you'll spend the day reading online essays and articles that will make you even more pissed off about your. . .uh. . .situation, than you already were.

On the other hand, if you're neither me nor you, but my wife's friend, Grace, you'll gaze at the photo of your little girl pasted to the wall of your cell—oops again!—I mean, cubicle, and realize how LUCKY you are to have put yourself through school waiting tables and taking care of your baby and paying for day-care, the apartment, food, clothes, healthcare, and climbed to the esteemed position of white collar drudge, so you better quit yer belly-aching and thank God Almighty you attained the American dream of a better future for your kid (and fuck that global warming crap, they'll fix it). You made it, you dreamed it and it became so, like the college advertisements said you would. So what's the problem (besides your monstrous debt to Student Loans Inc.)?

But enough about ungrateful Grace. Let's talk about me and you, or rather, me as you.

The coffee and bran muffin have done their work, so you take your copy of Chalmers Johnson's Blow Back and head for the can. Scrubbed sparkling fresh so early in the AM. Toilet virgin clean. You open to some heinous atrocity—the book is full of 'em—and simultaneously unknot your sphincter and your tie.

Suddenly, KABOOM. Lights out. People screaming. Sirens sirening. You can't move. You're buried in debris, your legs are crushed to powder. You can't feel them anyway because a big chunk of something snapped your spinal chord like celery. You know it's probably THE END, whatever the hell happened, but if, for argument's sake, you're ME, you know damn well what happened—didn't it ALMOST happen in '93?—and it has more than a little to do with "Blow Back." "Stupid," you think to yourself and of yourself. "Why didn't I take that gig writing Unix text manuals?"

But maybe, if you're Grace, you didn't really have a choice.

You think you might want to call your wife on your cell-phone, but you left it in your coat pocket in your cubicle. You're not in your safe little cubicle now, but your tile-and-porcelain tomb. Anyway, that's not your style, making a call like that. Too painful. Too futile. Why make this nightmare even worse than it is?

But if you're Grace, you probably want to leave a "good-bye" message for your little girl. You probably—no. I don't know about YOU, but I can't go on imagining kindly, stressed out, Grace, living loving mom, not yet 40, dying alone and broken in the pitch-black wreckage of an office toilet. In a building that's about to collapse into a heap of ash. Better it were ME. Or YOU.

## Say Goodnight, Grace

I'm pretty sure only heroes are supposed to speak these days, but they've been strangely silent. Possibly cause they're dead, and nobody wants to hear from their desperate bereaved (like, uh... Grace's daughter). They might ask for something. Compensation. Understanding. Peace of Mind.

But, me being an almost-hero and all, I'd like to address the only heroes who seem to have survived this mess with their faculties—such as they are—intact:

I have nothing but contempt for you, Rudy, and whatever hack you hired to ghost your self-aggrandizing auto-mythography. Unlike Grace, I'm sure you're no hero to the kids YOU left behind.

And George, Governor Death, President selected by a narrow margin of 5 to 4, man-child who's always been given everything and always managed to wreck it all, your nihilistic, narcissistic, narrow mind is rivaled on this sad planet only by your brother spoiled brat son of Thanatos, Bin Laden. You remember Osama, don't you? I know he's not all that important now, what with the Iraqi debacle threatening to—well, nothing really; people just don't seem to care. You're still as popular as you were in college. But really, George, treating Osama like he's nothing but a fanatical mass-murderer and not the scourge of Western Civilization the poor lad wants so desperately to be just won't do. After all, the Bin Ladens of Saudi Arabia are old family friends. And business associates. Just ask Poppy.

## Say Goodnight, Grace

# UNCLE SAM IS YOU
# A FIELD GUIDE TO BOOBUS AMERICANUS

Bloated and paranoid addicts of sugar, salt, lard, beer, nicotine, aspartame and MSG—Oh, Boobus Americanus, carnivorous sheep, slaughtering and led to slaughter—Uncle Sam is YOU!

Fighting, fighting, fighting. Against who? Has any "foreign enemy" ever tried to mess with my freedoms? Any man, woman, or child from the Mid-East (or France) ever once caused me grief and aggravation by obliterating people, forests, cities in my name while simultaneously snooping on me, stripping me of my "cherished freedoms" all on my dumb tax-payer dime? No way. Never ever. It's YOU, Jackson. It's always been YOU. THE MAN says jump and YOU jump. THE MAN says "Wreck the joint" and YOU start smashing everything in sight, and leave me holding the bag.

I can't, I won't, even blame "America," for what is a nation but a fiction, a set of laws agreed upon by its people, in a democracy, or enforced by its elite, as in whatever we have now? America might not be such a bad place if YOU had stood up to the MAN instead of running to fight every war HE gets himself into, waving HIS symbols, hating HIS enemies even if formerly they were HIS friends, even if his enemy is YOU. That's the deal isn't it? YOU'LL do anything HE says, so long as the enemy isn't YOU.

And why? Cause it's "YOUR" country? It is not YOUR country, it hasn't been for years (if it ever was), and YOU know it. Even so. If a band of thieves broke into YOUR house and wrecked the place and abused YOUR children would YOU excuse them because they did it all in "YOUR" home? When they decide to do the same thing to some poor family two blocks away, a family YOU'VE never met, a family YOU have nothing to do with, will YOU go along with them on their terror-fest because the idea was hatched in "YOUR" home? Do I have to push the analogy further or do YOU get the point? I know YOU'RE not big on subtlety, but this seems pretty cut and dried.

YOU are an ignorant, violent, boorish people addicted to bad food and overpriced drugs. I know, I know: It's the Media, the Corporations, the Government, the evil gnomes from outer space. Well, maybe if YOU hadn't been so dazed and confused we wouldn't be in this mess. What kind of power would a first rate third-rate moron like Dubya possibly have over a free and informed populace that would demand the truth from ALL media sources and probably wouldn't care to buy ninety percent of the junk the "all-powerful" Corporations sell daily by the Garbage Bag-full? Such a people would never buy the idea that a legal fiction had the "rights" of an individual person (whoever thought that one up deserves to be dictator, as opposed to Il Dufus, who merely stumbled into the job).

Don't gimme that crap that YOU don't know about the thousands slaughtered for no damn good reason in Afghanistan, Iraq, Palestine just cause YOU didn't see the corpses in the *New York Times* or YOUR local gazette. YOU saw the photos of cruise missiles smashing into cities. Think Uncle Sam's gonna waste millions in hardware to smoke empty buildings?

"We" did it all for the thousands killed in the WTC. Oh really? Then why aren't "we" clamoring for an investigation into just who did all that killing. I grew up with someone who died there, as did my wife. And I smelled the burning from my west side apartment. YOU didn't. Yet YOU wave yer little flags like when teacher told YOU to in the fifth grade about how grand it all was. Send teenagers who should be living life and studying it instead of destroying it thousands of miles away to kill other teenagers and teenagers' children just so YOU can feel safe in your twice mortgaged shit-box of a house, so you can march off to your corporate cubicle, if you have one?

That "it's not the American people's fault, it's their government's" line wore thin years ago. Isn't this supposed to be a government "of the people, by the people and for the people?" Then how do we point the finger at the government if the government is us? Of course, it's not us, not even remotely so, but that doesn't excuse YOU for pretending that it is. There's the "evil," as Dubya, who wrenched that term back from the 19th century, might say. Pretending that "we" are all in this together. "United We Stand." Isn't that what the corporate sponsored billboards and banners say?

So, what to do.

Nothing. Shut yer yap, if YOU know what's good for ya. Eat yer Beef-a-Roni. Suck yer Bud. Chew yer corporate cud, crud, crude, cruel, crucifixion of the real. What's on TV? I hear they're making last week into a movie. Or was it next week, or the week before? Well anyhow, one of these weeks is going to be coming to a theater near YOU. Then on video. They signed Today and Tomorrow to play the leads. Yesterday's in it too, but YOU know how it is in show biz once you're 24 hours old. The roles stop comin.' Gotta get what you can. Supporting character's not bad. As Boris Karloff once said, "A Yesterday is a working Day." Something like that. Remember Boris? The guy whose make-up informed YOUR nightmare visions of Frankenstein's monster (that's Mr. Frankenstein, to YOU, Jackson). Speaking of Frankenstein. . .oh, never mind.

Peek-a-boo. I see YOU. Eating snacks before the telly. Man on the screen says,

"We like you."

Astounded, mouth full of chewy goodness, YOU gurgle,

"You like ...me?"

"We love you. Very much."

"Love. Loooovvvvve. Love ME?"

"We've always loved you."

"Love. Gooooooooood. Love good."

"But there are people who want to hurt us."

"Hurt...you?"

"If they hurt us, who will love you?"

"Love. Good. No hurt. No hurt you!"

"You wouldn't want bad people to hurt us, would you?"

"Bad. Bad. No hurt. Love."

"You'll protect us, won't you?"

"Me. Protect. You. You me protect. No hurt love. Kill. Kill. KILL!"

And so on. YOU'VE been through it all before, I'm sure. And it's a good thing, a noble thing, that YOU want to protect the guys on TV who appear to love YOU, beasts that YOU are. But let's be clear. What do I get outta this? I'm not the guys on TV. In fact, I hate the guys on TV. It's not me they claim to love, but YOU. And to be honest, I'm not alone. There are almost six billion of us, and we hate those guys on TV.

So, it comes down to this. It's us against YOU, whoever YOU are, and the Guys on TV. I refuse to take any blame for all this. I've been fighting YOU since Reagan. True, I should have done more to protest the First Gulf Massacre, but it was such a tidal wave of YOU, YOU everywhere waving yer little flags. And it seemed to be over pretty quick—until the sanctions.

YOU are a danger to myself and others. Think about it. Think THE

MAN would have any power whatsoever without YOU? Who's he gonna get to do HIS dirty work, me? But with YOU and your unquestioning obedience HE's got Auschwitz, the Gulag, Hiroshima, Vietnam, Iraq and all sorts of global chess games—and guess who's the pawn? I mean, YOU put Hitler into power. True, YOU and your kids ended up cannon fodder ten years later and had your cities bombed, but I ended up in concentration camps (and I'm not just talking about Jews and Gypsies, but Communists, Anarchists, Conscientious objectors, clergymen, intellectuals, dissidents, in short all the folks who are what YOU are not: Free.)

I guess, ultimately, it's YOUR cowardice that gets me the most. I don't honestly believe YOU'RE stupid—willfully ignorant, yes, but not stupid. YOU'LL just do anything, ANYTHING to anyone to save your pasty skin. Be honest: YOU'RE terrified; hence, the "war on terror." YOU hope maybe THE MAN will make fear go away? The fear that began when Daddy...uh, let's not go there. Suffice it to say that THE MAN controls YOU through fear—and that's a lot more powerful than Stupidity.

Anyway, YOU and I are through. There's nothing left between us. As Michael Corleone said to his weak, stupid, cowardly brother Fredo, "You're nothing to me now. You're not a brother, you're not a friend..."

Yes, I believe in what the founding fathers said about the peoples' right to dissolve a government that turns on them. And hell yeah I believe in the Second Amendment, though unfortunately, with a mega Trillion Military built on "the American people's tax dollars," the opportunity to form a "well-regulated militia" to protect myself and others against the tyranny YOU support is long past.

But don't worry. I'll think of something. Me and the other five billion some-odd other folks who want to save the world from YOU.

**Adam Engel** is not YOUR "countryman" or "fellow citizen." He'd feel safer confronting a real enemy, with or without arms, than a mob of rats like YOU (patriots seldom travel alone, eh?) with YOUR symbols and "United We Stand" yackety yak one Nation under a vengeful, psycho-god in love with DEATH go tell it to Dubya and Perle and the Gang. Johnsons and other Free People can contact Engel at bartlebysamsa65@gmail.com. No patriotic SPAM or pre-fab slogans, please.

# ABRAHAM & SONS, LLP

Okay, see I'm trying to figure out why half the world's population still believes in angry sky gods who HATE PEOPLE (especially women). This much I got: Jews tried to ruin all the fun in the ancient world (they sure tried to ruin my fun as a kid) by slaughtering anyone who wouldn't kiss the spacious yet invisible tuchass of Yahweh. Then Jesus came along and tried to loosen things up—not too much, but enough—but the Rabbis fingered him to the Romans (Americans in sandals) who nailed him to a cross to show the world, ancient and modern, that that's what everybody who tried to live his own life was in for: Pain, pain and more pain (Forgive them, Pops, they knew not what they did? Damn straight they did!). But just because the West has been so barbarically cruel and despotic to the Islamic world for the past two centuries (and during the Great Crusades), it doesn't make Islam any better or worse than the previous two nightmares. I'd say they're on equal footing.

Truly, I can't tell the damn difference between Judaism and Islam, and I'm Jewish, or so they tell me, that is, my parents were Jewish so that makes me Jewish? But what if my parents were hockey fans, would that make me too a hockey fan? No, the Germans came up with that one, the ethnicity of Judaism. In essence they're saying Moses didn't make you Jewish, Hitler did, and both the Zionists and the Nazis agree on this as they do on so many things, such as "racial" purity by virtue of intra-marriage.

"What's the greatest gift, I mean the GREATEST gift god gave to the Jewish people?" a rabbi once asked me with a smug smile. "The Catskills?" I replied. "NO! Idiot. The gift of marriage. That Jews may marry other Jews and the race may prosper." "But I didn't marry a Jew. I'm not even a Jew myself if believing in Yahweh and all his nasty works—beating on those poor desert folks to get his kicks—means being Jewish. Why didn't he pick on someone his own size?" "There was nobody his size. Anyway, you married a shiksa? Then you're completing the work that Hitler started." "Whoa. Now hold on there, mein yiddisher hombre. You mean that me, little ol' me with my diddly little human life expectancy of three score and ten plus or minus a few for smoking cigars—I don't inhale—should be compared to Hitler, a man responsible for murdering eleven million people in concentration camps, six million of them Jewish, and causing a world war that resulted in a body count of about 40 million, simply because I chose to spend the rest of my life, such as it is, with the one person on this planet I truly love?" "Darn tootin'," said the rabbi. He proceeded to go on about the sins of assimilation by celebrity Jews such as Woody Allen (still a "good guy" at the time; playing Mr. Bumble to Mia Farrow's mother Theresa), etc. That's where I caught him. "But," I said, "What was Woody Allen's greatest gift to the Jews?" The Chief rabbi and his fellow lesser rabbis scratched their beards, then shrugged their shoulders. "He didn't marry a Shiksa! He only lives with one."

The women in the kitchen, doing the dishes, laughed at this, and that was the end of my welcome, because women, among all these fundamentalist types—Jewish, Christian, Muslim or Hare Krishna—are not permitted to laugh, especially not at the joke of a wise-ass stranger. I could spend a lifetime going on about the Jews, but that would offend the Christians, who are equally ridiculous. It's kind of funny we have the most illiterate "industrialized" nation on one hand, but also the most religious. I mean, isn't all religion just literary criticism? Bad literary criticism, but Lit-Crit nonetheless. Don't they call both Fundamentalist Christians and Jews "people of the book"? I mean the Fundamentalist Christians are always going around thumping their bibles (it's a bit of a schlep to carry around a Torah, much less pound one, so Jews don't get much thumping done) and talking about "Chronicles verse 4 word six letter 3" or some shit like that? Who knows? Maybe they just memorize that stuff from church on Sundays. Maybe they don't actually read their bibles—all that sex and violence might freak them out of their polyester garb—just thump them. Now the Old Testament was relentlessly long and boring, and the New Testament was just boring, but mercifully short (probably the reason there're so many more Christians than Jews), so I just haven't yet been able to bring myself to read the Koran. I can't say much about Islam other than that it looks to me a whole lot like Orthodox Judaism, what with the praying several times a day to a single super pissed off god who hates women even though, technically, by creating men, women created Him and the women's gods were around for about 200,000 years of human evolution and Allah and his buddies Christ and Yahweh have only been around for a few millennia and LOOK AT THE DAMAGE THEY'VE DONE.

Not only has the Christian world gone through Crusades, Inquisitions and two world wars, during the course of one of which they murdered nearly all of Europe's Jews, but then the Jews themselves went out and kicked the Palestinians off their land (allegedly promised to them by Yahweh, but only after they got rid of the Canaanites. Find me a Canaanite and I'll show you the Mother Of All Lawsuits), but the Muslims weren't much better, spreading their religion, like the Christians, by the sword (the Jews didn't spread their religion because people have enough problems with their own religions, the last thing they need is kosher wine and heavy black cassocks in the summer; but also it's supposed to be like a special club, the "Chosen People," sort of like the Skull and Bones among the Big three Abrahamic hustles). So now we have the Israelis or Zionists—not a religion, really, then again, neither am I, yet we both fall under the category of "Jews"—torturing and murdering the Palestinians for the OTHER half of the land they took but didn't officially get until they did what any other Nation among Nations would do: Stole it by force. The Moslems are pissed off at this, but more pissed off at the West in general for exploiting them for their oil, but unfortunately for them (and fortunately for us?) their leaders are either super fundamentalists whackos, corrupt Military Dictators, Billionaire Monarchs, or merely Whichever-Way-The-Sirocco-Blows politicians who just don't have the firepower to take on the west, so they have to wheel and deal with Washington and hope their people don't rise up and storm the palace, like in Iran. And finally we have the West itself, or more specifically the "last Super Power" which is—and let's cut that Judeo Christian crap—a Christian nation run by Fundamentalist Christians who want all the Jews to gather in Palestine so Christ can come and either convert or kill them (but what's he gonna convert them to, Reform Judaism?), and the whacko Zionist court Jews, lobbyists and AIPACers who'll gladly go along with their Armageddon trip so long as they "restructure" the Mid-East (you know, minor alterations, like erasing Afghanistan and Iraq) to make the world "safe" for Israel, which seems pretty safe considering its obviously well-equipped army and "secret" stash of nukes. But then, those Palestinian kids sure have good aim with rocks and plenty of suicide bombers to blow themselves up in pizza parlors as gifts to the IDF, who can then ask for even more weapons from the United States and receive them (kinda like the 9/11 tragedy was such a boon to Bush, Inc., because all clods have silver lined spoons in their mouths or some old cliché). But what has this to do with life and death in the cosmos? Not much. Religion is just literary criticism, like I said, and anyone who's suffered through a Ph.D. in English knows there ain't no spirituality in that. In fact, no matter who wins, it seems women are the losers 'cause all these religions are merely patriarchal reactions to tens if not hundreds of thousands of years of peace and harmony and human evolution under matriarchal societies, who worshipped Goddesses and ate of the Tree and thought sex was celebratory, not sinful, without being TOO literal: They knew what they were really worshipping was Life and Earth's power to generate more life, but that don't mean bupkis if you're a Jew or Christian or Muslim waiting for your pie in the sky from your version of an ancient Sumerian sky god (and a pie in the face for the "infidels").

So relax, enjoy. Like all schools of criticism, these dusty old turkeys are gonna end soon. Not with a whimper, but a BIG BANG. Hey! Isn't that how it all began? That is, according to Science, the newest "religion."

## An American Tale

Your grandmother, born to slavery, married a full-blood Mohawk who'd served as a scout, cook, and gravedigger for the Union Army.

Your father died during his first week in the first War to End All Wars, which was about to end anyway. Your mother named you Dread, after Dred Scott and the pain of life.

When you were four years old your mother married Kurt, who wore a suit, made money, and let you call him "Dad." When you were eight, Kurt and your mother had your little brother, Manley. The Depression came. Kurt stopped wearing a suit, stopped making money, started drinking. He smelled bad and beat on you, Manley, and especially your mother. You weren't too upset when Kurt was stabbed to death in a poker game.

It fell upon you and your mother to bring in money. You worked odd jobs for whatever legitimate businesses would hire you, usually for the day, served as a "mule" for drug dealers, stole whatever food and necessities you needed to get by. Your mother took in white people's laundry until your brother was old enough to spend the days with other children—their crowded street games a security tactic; in unity, strength—and the nights with you. She then stayed overnight six days a week cleaning a white family's house and raising their kids.

You swept roads and streets under the WPA program then managed to survive the second War to End all Wars from Pearl Harbor to Nagasaki, cleaning and cooking for white officers, at first, then fighting German white people overseas.

After the war you were hired to cook for the same Harlem restaurant you'd work for for the next forty years (even when it became an "institution," serving soul food to white Columbia students, poets, and professors, and downtown artists and musicians from the late 50s to early 70s when the clientèle became black again).

After the war you married a young teacher named Sara, who bore your first son exactly five years after Hiroshima and a few months before your little brother Manley was killed in Korea.

Your first son, Blake, was killed in Vietnam; your wife grew ill. Though your second son, Michael, came back physically unharmed, the war had done things to his head. During his short migration from prescription painkillers provided by the VA for the pain in his head, to sniffing, then shooting heroin, his girlfriend had two beautiful daughters by him, one a straight A student, the younger one not brilliant but bright enough to become a nurse. She cared for your wife, who died without health insurance, leaving you alone, sad, angry and confused. Your older granddaughter went to Harvard to study Law, and the nurse went into the Army to pay them back for putting her through school.

There weren't many wounded Americans in this first war against Saddam, and most of the Iraqis were killed by planes and helicopters well before she reached them. She came home to work in a VA hospital. She had a child with a Drinker.

You knew enough about drinkers to predict the beatings she and the child would receive, but you could not predict the illness that forced her from her the Army, her job, and made her weak and tired of life at age 23 (the Drinker left when she could no longer support him). Her sister, a lawyer now, sent money, and you helped by renting two rooms of the apartment you'd spent your life in to two men your age. You quit the restaurant to spend the days looking after the baby until he was old enough for school.

Your grand-daughter the lawyer wrote letters asking why the Army would not admit to any such thing as Gulf War Syndrome or pay those who suffered from it, like her sister, disability or retribution or something. The Army answered all of her letters politely by saying nothing.

Meanwhile, your great-grandson, who could no longer be contained in the house by you or his sick mother, joined a gang, and in a few years was arrested for activities involving the gang, activities which could not be proved, but, as the boy sharply noted, he was ultimately guilty of being part of a huge gang called "N—." He had a quick wit, but the authorities narrowed his life to two choices: Jail or the Marines. He chose to be shipped off to Iraq, where his mother had gotten sick, and he was killed.

You and your grand-daughter, the lawyer, took his body from the secretive military and had it buried and services performed. His mother was too weak, sick, stricken to attend.

So here you are, 89 years old on this hot May afternoon, on your way to the apartment of a guy known as "Medicine Man" for making two or three trips a week to Canada—depending on demand—for groups of mostly older folks who pay him to pick up their medicines cheap. Even with the sizable cut he takes, its cheaper than buying it from the supermarket drugstore and pharmacy chains.

You are approached by two young white men—late twenties—in expensive suits and corporate hair-cuts.

"Hey nigga! Hey dude!"

Your anger like a bullet ricochets off the walls of your skull.

Then you notice their Columbia class rings, six years old. They must have come back to the alma mater to celebrate the current graduation or get together with old Frat brothers or who the hell knows what. Booze on their breath, fear in their eyes. Must have learned that talk from the rap albums they'd been listening to since high school. Drank too much and crossed the park for weed. Liquid courage dare cross Morning Side Park like in the Old Days, before the suits and haircuts and graduation rings. Before whatever cubicles imprisoned them. You want to punch their pink faces to pulp and explain to them that the "N-word" is no longer allowed to leave white mouths, for it was seized by black people long ago. Instead, you laugh out loud, for the first time in what seems many years.

Here, in America, Land of the Free, two young, clean-cut white men in expensive suits and Ivy League rings have to skulk around the region of their worst nightmares, a hot day in Harlem full of the angry black folk their parents and schools and TV programs had warned them about all their soft lives, just to buy a bag of herb. Weed. Dried up leaves of hemp.

"God Bless America," you say as you brush past them on your way to "Medicine Man."

"Hey, wait a minute," they call after you. "Sir? Sir? We just wanna score a coupla joints. Sir?"

"I don't smoke," you call over your shoulder. "Bad for your health. Like being white and racist on 119th and Lex."

# THE ARMAGEDDON JAMBOREE! DANCE, PUPPETS OF WELTSCHMERZ, DANCE!

> Jazz Owl: "I wanna sing—a, about the moon—a and the June—a and the Spring—a!"
> Church Owl: "Stop! Enough is too much! "
>
> —from some old cartoon I forgot who made it (Warner Brothers?) let 'em sue me.

Fairies, Angels, and UFOs will come, and god and goddess too (he'll come like Gary Cooper in a tux and she in sequins like Marlene Dietrich—or is it the other way?), so loud was the Rock N' Roll of LIFE, so ineffective, but fun anyway to make some noise and dance. We'll dance on their graves and on our own; we'll clang our pots and smoke them; we'll amplify our ukuleles, bang the ear-drums slowly, meltdown decibel boom or bust and

WELCOME TO THE WOODSTOCK, D.C. ARMAGEDDON JAMBOREE!

Greed, fear, and Muzak be damned! We'll have a blast (no pun intended), and know this doesn't have to be, this Thanatos Waltz, although it is and was and ever always puff of us poof of us bodies in time to be forgotten.

Oh well. Big deal. Shut up. Dance. Dance or die. Dance and die. Don't matter: Do the bunny hop hustle bump and grind jitterbug Charleston go go go, L'il sister, show yer hoochie koochie cuckoo shoes nude to the waist oh darlin' lemme part yer beet curtains it's only for one night a life without consequence, a Dance without permit.

Pick an issue, any issue, the environment the economy the wars in Asia, Africa, South America, Middle East gangland drug land terror land if you don't think this is bats you're surely bats don't matter anyway bro' just dance!

And NO this DOES NOT HAVE TO BE!

Oh Puppets of Weltschmerz! Why must we cower before our deranged Fearer and his gas-bag gang of fools (surely they're out of their league and their minds)? Every one of them, like Mad Adolph, yearns to be Gott of his own psychotic Dämmerung. It does not HAVE to be, but verily, it will.

Soooooooooo—

Let the people converge (and dance). Set out on this vast night pilgrimage (and dance) to their own Capital (and dance), the seat of Democracy (and dance), the power node (and dance) the monad (and dance), Stonehenge on the Potomac and dance, dance, dance!

If it's gonna be The End let's be BAD CHILDREN and tootsie waggin' two-step shake them Botox baby, go go go!

Or maybe it won't be the end at all. Maybe this DOES NOT HAVE TO BE.

But this is so apocalyptic ain't no march on Washington 100,000 people and great speeches the beginning of something but then what? Malcolm X said THE MAN wanted every one of those folks outta town by sun down and sure enough every one of those folks was outta town by sundown what kind of deal is that as historian John Henrik Clarke said enough show biz enough celebrity speeches enough Million Man March (and no women) then back to the same old Nothing With Cream On Top nonsense...oh enough! Really enough. The world indeed was too much with us.

Sooooooooo—

dance dance dance! Americans, come out of your homes and walk (before you dance). Pack your backs and your papooses and your rations, whatever you can carry, this is not Exodus but In-To-Us we're all converging on the CENTER that's not even a state!

There's 280 million people in this country and every goddamn one of them has got to go to Washington and DANCE! What the hell they gonna do kill 280 million of us? And with what, Nukes? Bio weapons? This is the MAN'S town even if he is a Wall-flower, even if he skee-daddles like HE did during the 9/11/01 attacks, just gets in HIS plane and leaves. Even if the hallowed halls of Congress are empty—doesn't matter either way, does it? just more space to dance—nobody's gonna do anything to anyone because 280 million people won't even fit in D.C.—we'll be all over the place, massing upon Maryland, vexing Virginia, teeming o'er Tennessee. And nobody has to worry about going back to your jobs because your boss is comin' too if he knows what's good for him and that's not a threat it's an explanation: they're talking NUKES again, first strike, the whole shebang. This is absolutely outta control (don't even talk about the environment don't go there don't have time) and anyway, if all 280 million of us converge then who are the MIGHTY MILITARY MEN gonna be shootin,' their own families for gods sake?

"Biblical, epochal ...yeah, yeah, yeah" or whatever Gerry Garcia and the Beatles said at one time or another because THIS IS OUR CHANCE so let's dance the last dance in honor of Donna Summers and the leisure suit.

Oh, Citizens of Mexico, Canada, and anywhere else in the Americas, if you can make it across the border and I'm sure you will cause the cops'll have their hands full trying to get us the hell out of OUR capital city, YOU ARE INVITED.

We SHALL overcome by voting with our feet—thump, thump—by demanding to be seen and heard—thump, thump—by demanding EVERYTHING immediately and sooner, no refunds, and reminding the folks in power that they're not in power after all. We are.

Sooooooo—

shake yer booty, booby (an yer boobies too!), quake rattle rock and roll!

Look upon this dance, ye mousy, and DESPAIR!

**Adam Engel** is taking dance lessons. Anyone with decent tunes, or heavy-duty audio equipment and HUGE POWERFUL amps can contact bartlebysamsa65@gmail.com

# NO BLOOD FOR MARIJUANA IN IRAQ!

Man have I been stupid! Who knew that WINNING the War Against Iraq would mean LOSING the War Against Drugs! But now the weed's outta the bag, so to speak. Lemme 'splain:

I never bought the "No Blood for Oil" placards those government agents wave around at peace rallies or marching up and down like atavistic suffragettes in front of City Hall. No. I knew all along this war with Iraq was about good versus evil. No question about that. I just didn't know how evil the evil we were facing was...

Anybody take a gander at a SUPER FAMOUS MAINSTREAM NEWSMAG last week? What's on the cover of that fine journal of opinion (and cool pix)? You said it buddy: Marijuana.

Anybody rush through Port Authority in Manhattan last week and glance at the newsstand for all of three seconds, like I did, just long enough to read the cover of a RELATIVELY FAMOUS MONTHLY NEWSMAG, where it's implied, in BIG BLACK LETTERS that we, the people of the United States, must face the inevitable burden of Iraq becoming the 51st STATE after its ignominious military defeat?

Anybody put two and two together and not come out with five?

Exactly. This whole business with Iraq is about LEGALIZING MARIJUANA! Man, I knew that Saddam was a hustler, but I had no idea how deep his evil—oh, let's get off this pee-cee sissy-talk for a minute and stop apostrophizing or mentonymizing or whatever the hell you call it and tell it like it is—the evil of the IRAQI PEOPLE, the sheer cunning of this "PEOPLE"—really was!

At least half a million Iraqi children have conveniently died, according to Madeleine Albright in 1996 (knowing the malice of these Iraqis, dying on our dime, the figure has probably grown in leaps and bounds by now). What are these brats croaking from? Cancer, leukemia and other such maladies. Why? Cause of sanctions. Can't get chemotherapy. A nasty, but often effective therapy that makes you wanna puke. And what, according to some hippy liberal Doctors and do-gooders in California and other axes of evil can make someone on said therapy not wanna puke? Right again, buster: Marijuana!

It was so damn obvious, yet so subtle, that not even the right honorable President of the United States, a Yale graduate, could see through it. But there it is, plain as the ghost of Cheney's face: Iraq wants to become the 51st state and legalize Marijuana. God-damn those terrorist werewolves praying on decent American—

"We have nothing against the people of Iraq," my ass! We got a lot against 'em, if we just follow the damn logic for once and read between the lines:

1. Many of these Iraqis, both young and old, might possibly be in the process of dying from diseases caused by depleted uranium and various toxins used by the U.S. of A. while defending the fine City of Kuwait against Saddam's aggression in '91. So now, after defying our mandated on-site weapons searches for chemical weapons or whatever, they're begging us, the country with the finest medical care money can buy, for "chemical assistance" in the form of chemotherapy.

2. This "chemotherapy" has dual use capacity: keeps 'em alive and makes 'em wanna puke.

3. Smoking Marijuana, a known carcinogen and god knows what all, makes 'em feel like not puking. In fact, it might even make the little tykes hungry (at which point, of course, they'll be begging for food; our food).

4. In order to make Iraq the 51st state, we're gonna have to blast 'em into submission (doesn't have to be that way; they want it that way to get us hooked on marijuana!). We'll have to send our boys over (don't talk to me about no women in our armed forces; only American woman who died in the War of '91 was Meg Ryan, and she was FRAGGED) to shoot 'em and bomb 'em and spray 'em with more Depleted Uranium and more toxins, which will of course raise the cancer rate among children born and unborn (hope you voted only Pro-Life candidates, by the way) and you know what comes next. Yup. More whining and crying for chemotherapy, which leads directly to the abuse of marijuana! Not only that, they'll be pushing our boys in uniform to shoot marijuana, just like they did in Viet Nam, to get 'em hooked on the stuff and turn 'em into hippie dope fiends who'll be about as effective in a firefight as Alan Dershowitz

and just as freaky!

5. Here's the Clincher: We have a benevolent leader, god bless him, who believes in States Rights (especially if you're in the right state of rightness in the right states of Florida or Texas). If Iraq becomes the 51st state, and you know that's what they're planning, they'll have the right to vote like all the rest of us. Then, as everyone in the free world knows, they can do anything they damn well please, including—you guessed it—LEGALIZING MARIJUANA FOR MEDICINAL PURPOSES.

Now, I may be stupid, but I ain't dumb. I know all that fancy legal-medical talk about glaucoma and chemo-therapy and what not is just smoke screen for a particular, mind-altering smoke to waft into the nostrils of every susceptible American in its pungent path.

Iraq plans to become, via military conquest (paid for by U.S. dollars) and statehood, the Marijuana capital of the United States! The quarter million of our boys (and girls; won't do no fighting, but I hear the fellas like to grope 'em when native women ain't available) already there'll be shooting up pot, listening to Schubert, munching couscous, sipping bitter coffee at cut-rate prices (Conspiracy against Starbucks? Wouldn't rule out anything). And they won't want to come home and get regular jobs, or defend the Home Land from terrorists either. Why? Well, Duh! Because, if Iraq becomes the 51st state, as U.S. citizens, they WILL be home!

And there'll be worse to come. You thought Frisco in '67 was a scene? Iraq, the 51st state, will become the mother of all dope dens. We got several million John (and Joanna) Walker Lint-Traps, full of crazy ideas they caught in college, probably through computer viruses and such, just aching to get over to Iraq in search of, not of Allah, but cheap, potent ganja. We might lose yet another generation to sex, drugs and—well, not Rock 'n Roll exactly; probably worse: that spooky A-rab music you hear in the background of exotic porn videos.

Think I haven't done my research? Think I can't cite verifiable sources? Well, I happen to have a genuine Iraqi tied up right here in by basement (believe me it's not hard; you can order just about anything over the Web these days; of course, they sent me damaged goods: my Iraqi boy, Tariq, was, or says he was, wounded in a preliminary bombing sortie last month).

"Hey, Tariq."

"Yes sir. Please don't hit me sir. I, the pain—it hurts so. Please!"

"Relax. I ain't gonna hit you again. I just wanna ask you something. Do you or do you not want to shoot marijuana for your 'pain,' so called.

"Marijuana? For this pain? No sir. Not at all. Marijuana will do nothing for this pain. But if you please, sir. Please. A doctor. He can legally prescribe. Something for the pain. Please. How do you say in America, 'Percocet? Demerol? Morphine?"

AH HAH!

# NO BLOOD THE BOOBUS IN THE LIE, IF YOU REALLY WANT TO HEAR ABOUT IT. . .

Boobus Americanus wouldn't know himself if he sat beside his doppelgänger on a bus. Is this a problem, this chronic Zombie-ism?

Boobus Americanus woiks and woiks HARD. Whattya doin' Boobus? Woikin hard? "Woikin hard! Woikin, woikin." Busy, Boobus? "Busy, busy, busy. Woikin' hard, woikin' hard!" Well how 'bout this: You can lead a horse to water, but if you do, at least have the guts, compassion and decency to drown him when you get there.

Boobus at the gym, on the treadmill—fitting metaphor—gaze up at the one-eyed monster. CNN, Fox News, MTV, whatever. Hole in his head receives cathode blast of get-disease, get, get; spunk, smegma. Layers of scar-hardened cerebra Raw sores open to absorb, absorb; soak in, soak in. Sponge tissue. Quicker picker upper.

Ego Americanus is dead. Boobus individualus is dead. Boobus persona is dead. In their place? Boobus Americorpus, Incorporated, A Very Limited Liability Company (VLLC). Tax-free.

"Dead slugs leave no trails," sez Professor B. S. Americanus, Ph.D.

Boobus would be quite fortunate, both spiritually and materially—even now, Big Pharma greedily awaits his senescense—to get killed before he dies. But to live before he dies? That is too much.

Poor Boobus Americanus! His parents are perverts, derelicts, freaks. Papa Republican and Momma Democrat. Whenever Papa "gets his drink on," he thrashes Momma—and does unspeakable things to Boobus. Momma then both comforts Boobus and turns to him for succor. She confides in him, tells him "we're not gonna take anymore abuse," and brings him hope. But once Papa sobers up, or there's an "external threat" to the household, Momma stands by her man. Subsequently, they both beat on Boobus and send him to sleep in the woodshed. Without any health coverage or supper.

Boobus Americanus says, "Lot's of people actually made money during the last Great Depression. Why not this one? This new depression all the experts are talking about is gonna be my GREAT OPPORTUNITY!" That's the spirit, Boobus! Every man for himself. Unless it's tax-time, or war-time, or corporate-cutback time, in which case it's every man for THE MAN.

Perhaps the Greatest Icon in the Pantheon of Boobs is the late Evel Knievel. For he sacrificed his own flesh, blood, and just about every bone in his body, for the entertainment of his fellows. A true (RedWhiteAnd) Blue Celebrity. The only man born of woman who comes close to rivaling the Deus Americanus, Knievel, is the King Himself, Elvis, who couldn't play guitar nearly as well as the black musicians who invented him, nor compose music at all, but did sacrifice his body for the entertainment of his fellows, and unlike the Great Kneivel, or Bono (who's a Boobus, though not Americanus) could somewhat carry a tune.

Boobus Americanus is renowned for his sympathy. Not empathy, which entails the possession of some imagination, but sympathy. "Those poor little bastards!" says Boobus of the Iraqis, Afghanis, Serbians etc. etc. etc. his Nation has blown to bits. "I know. This year, we'll get the whole neighborhood together, and all the guys and gals at work, and use all our resources to put together an EXTREME Christmas Care Package. It'll be the bestest, most spectacular Christmas those little critters ever had!" But, Boobus, my dear fellow, most of these people don't even celebrate Christmas, one might point out. "That's the whole point, silly," Boobus will, of course, reply. "That's why WE'RE over there. To bring Democracy and Christmasize them!"

"Life and Death are REAL things. THIS is neither Life, nor Death. I want OUT," said Mrs. Americanus, before her lawyer filed the papers.

# COPY, ESCHER, BACH (YOU COPY?)

I've been educated in the finest Universities in preparation for this breakdown. Literate, patient, diligent. Fit for the cubicle. I will work hard for the Company. I will write winning copy. I won't get up to pee, on company time, unless I really have to go. I won't smoke. I'll sit staid before my monitor. Grim determination. Won't fidget. Write winning copy.

Advertisements, marketing, executive speeches and proposals. Inter-office memos. Company newsletters and PR.

I will rise with the sun. Better yet, I'll beat it. I will shower, shave and lower myself like a diver into my suit. I will travel by bus and by train to the tall building that contains my station. I will leave my cubicle, from time to time, to attend meetings. I will participate in the meetings like a team-player, an eager worker, who wishes to communicate his ideas to others, to share ideas with others, to interact and cooperate with others in their communal effort to get things done.

What is to be done? We must create messages. Mission statements. Slogans. We must convey Executive concepts in clear, friendly, and when appropriate, witty language.

Lunch. I'm not hungry. I want beer. But I will not drink beer. Might slow me down. Perhaps a roll or a bagel and a bottle of seltzer.

I am no longer young. No cigarettes in the stairwell. That's for kids. The go-getting, tireless young with their palm pilots and twelve hour days. Must I work twelve hour days? No. I will not work twelve hour days. I will work eight hours, like my predecessors. Still, with the commute, my day will amount to twelve hours. Eight hours in the cubicle, four hours on trains and buses.

But I will have my own station. A place to call home five (or more) days a week. How will I decorate this cubicle? With photographs of loved ones to remind me of...my reason for living? I love my wife. Perhaps, if we work hard, we will be able to afford children. I will place photographs of The Wife and Kids in the cubicle to remind me that the day will end, that I will be going home to loved ones.

I will work hard in my cubicle to help the Company earn value. But sitting all day, I might injure my back. Perhaps I will score a small amount of percocet from time to time. I will go home and do yoga. I will ride the stationary bike. I will meditate. If there is time left, I will try to write, though it will be difficult to pen my own ideas after typing the thoughts of the Company all day in my cubicle.

At last I will crawl into bed and read. But there won't be much time for reading, for I must fall asleep early so that I may rise early to begin the journey to my station. Also, if we do have children, when they are very young they will wake me in the night. As they develop, I must spend quality time with them so they don't feel neglected and grow up to be degenerates and cause me no end of grief in my declining years. Then again, these are my declining years, these years in the cubicle. How many have I left?

Maybe, after a time, if I write winning copy, the Company will move me to an office. My own office! In my office I will pace back and forth as I think hard for the Company. I must be creative and productive. After all, the Company allowed me my own office. They raised my salary. The health and well-being of my loved ones, the very roof over our heads, depends on the success of the Company, depends on my success within the Company.

But I will grow older, older, and the workers will grow younger and more vigorous. I will grow tired of pacing. I will lie down to rest on the nice couch in my office and snooze to Fugues and Cello Suites.

And then the vultures will descend. As they carry me away, I will remember life before the cubicle, a dream. I will remember memory itself, and desire. I will remember wanting. Nevertheless, I won't miss seeing when the vultures tear away my eyes. I won't miss knowing as they shuck my cranium like an oyster.

**Adam Engel** reads you. Reads you. Copy. Copy. Over and out. Copy to. Copy.

# I HOPE MY CORPSE GIVES YOU THE PLAGUE

"Ask not what your country can do for you. Ask not what you can do cause you've probably already done it your country thanks you very much. Ask nothing, and if you're lucky you shall receive nothing worse than nothing."

Well, why NOT ask what my country can do for me? Why not ask simply, what's in it for me?

What has America done for me lately, that big plot of land shared by 280,000,000 head trips, some minute percentage of which are somewhat similar to my own in some small way, but otherwise born to be programmed, propagandized, brain-washed about how god wanted us: manifest by god and destined by god to take god's country and everything in it, and every one, and do with them what we will?

Maybe I'd fight for the old neighborhood where I grew up. Or maybe I'd die to protect the 'hood. But even NYC is too big and complex—8,000,000 head trips. Might as well be 280,000,000 or 280 for all that "united we stand" bullshit.

How many people do I really stand united with? How many is it possible to stand united with? Certainly not 280,000,000. Only thing I have in common with most of them is I want to be left the hell alone. But that is the one impossibility in America, unless you happen to be very, very rich and connected to the kind of wealth that is not to be fucked with. The kind of wealth that frightens even government to stay at least 100 feet away at all times, to look at you with awe and defer to your superior collection of whatever stuff it is of value (another fiction) that you possess in obscene abundance—paper, metal, electronic pulses of on and off, one and zero.

"Stay away, I'm a wealthy man. Just stay away. Don't begrudge me my freedom."

Now there's a word you don't hear everyday. "Freedom." You can't possibly hear it, it's repeated so often it's part of the aural atmosphere. Freedom in the air, choking us like smog. Who needs this kind of "freedom" anyway, this gift to us from Uncle Sam for being such good children?

"Really you're lucky you weren't born in China or Somalia or some place REALLY bad..."

But am I? I mean, "Who says?"

We should be grateful that government officials, elected or selected, don't kill us or torture us or throw us away like garbage? Grateful that they're not—at least to white people—as vicious as some others (whom they nonetheless support with guns and butter)? Well then, my wife and kids should be grateful I don't beat them half as badly or as often as my neighbor next door beats his.

Freedom to work for a corporation, to be locked in a cubicle in the labyrinth of the great office on the thirty-somethingth floor. Working away at nothing particularly important, but it's the only way to get health insurance, and possibly money enough to live in your "own" apartment, if you're single, or share a decent apartment with your spouse and kids, provided they bring in money (these damn spoiled kids! in the good old days before child labor laws, kids were worth something, whether you were a farmer sending them to the fields or a shopkeeper making them sweep up or a factory worker begging The Big Boss hire your kids "oh PLEASE, master! they're all at least ten years old, the eldest almost thirteen.")

Went to the National Institute of Health (NIH) to become a guinea pig but thought to myself, "There's no national aspirin, there's no national penicillin, there's no national out patient clinic, hospital or anything else that might let people benefit from experiments done on yours truly."

So where is all this research data going? Who's benefiting from this NIH? I don't have to tell you to go to your Duane Read or Walgreen's or other National pharmacy chain to figure that out.

Anyway, back to the issue at hand: what has "my" country done for me lately?

Besides waste my most impressionable years drumming lies into my head?

Besides terrifying me with tales of nuclear menace and drudgery and breadlines and having to share apartments with strangers (!!!) and other horrors from them Commie Soviets who no longer exist, allegedly, because my tax money afforded Uncle Sam more missiles than "Collective Ownership" provided Uncle Misha?

Besides perpetual war for perpetual fleece, the mayhem and suffering that I am perpetually funding, thereby making me perpetually complicit to murder?

Besides making me "grateful" I was born with white skin and therefore not a congenital enemy of the state?

Besides making me an enemy of EVERYONE ELSE not lucky enough to have been born on this great chunk of stolen property?

Besides spending an incredible $400,000,000,000 of peoples' tax money on its war machine, and a fraction of that on feeding, clothing, housing educating and tending to the health of its citizens?

Besides being nothing but a legal fiction, created on and held together by a piece of paper, yet demanding that I love it and its corporations, which are not "which's" but "who's" and far more important than its people, for corporations are immortal and richer than god, who may not bless America, but certainly blesses Raytheon and Boeing?

Besides being nothing but a MERE fiction and demanding that I love it, not a LEGAL fiction, because it broke nearly every law written on the piece of paper that allegedly provided its life, its "constitution?"

Besides allowing me to follow the advice of a friend and take "Unemployment" when I was unemployed ("Hell, they took it from your paycheck these past fifteen years, it's your money," he said), and forcing me to undergo the humiliation of not serving a corporation, at least not the one that downsized me, and then...and then...double-dip TAXING me on these measly "benefits."

Besides telling lies, lies, lies everywhere and always, from the lie that it is anything more than a fiction (and not even a legal one) to the lie that it values me as a customer; therefore, I should love it.

I know, I know: "America, love it or leave it!" Well I'll leave it soon enough, Jackson, and YOU can pay the bill. I hope my corpse gives you the plague.

# CALL ME JOHNSON: STICKING UP TO THE JONESES

"To say someone is a Johnson means he keeps his word and honors his obligations. He's a good man to do business with and a good man to have on your team. He is not a malicious, snooping, interfering self-righteous trouble-making person. . . . A Johnson minds his own business. But he will help when help is needed. He doesn't stand by while someone is drowning or trapped in a wrecked car."

William S. Burroughs, "The Adding Machine"

William Burroughs, that nasty, ex-junky, queer (and what are YOU gonna do about it?), gun enthusiast and satirist, that—horror of horrors—FREE MAN, had a word for the decent, peace loving folk of the world. He called them Johnsons, or The Johnson Family, an expression he first encountered in a book, "You Can't Win," by Joe Black.

While Burroughs described what it means to be a Johnson quite well, he neglected to mention the other family in this Manichean contest: The Joneses.

You know the Joneses. Those folks who are always trying to keep up with each other and take each other out and lead you to the Kool-Aid.

Johnsons shut up and leave you alone unless you need a hand, unless anybody needs a hand and wants a hand. They'll help you out and then be on their way, not lingering to be congratulated, immortalized, PERSONified live on TV.

But a Jones'll stab you in the back until you're good and dead. Look in the US PATRIOT/TIPS stool pigeon registry and you'll find only the first-names are different; the last name's always "Jones." You usually won't find a Johnson on any list, certainly not a list belonging to a government. Johnsons stay under the radar but do the right thing.

Burroughs wrote, "The Johnson Family formulates a Manichean position where good and evil are in conflict and the outcome is at this point uncertain. It is not an eternal conflict, since one or the other must win a final victory. Which side are you on?"

I imagine if there was a religion for Johnsons it would be some variation of Zen, in which the only law, commandment or moral imperative would be to SIT DOWN and SHUT UP.

Joneses on the other hand comprise the extreme, fundamentalist, doctrinaire wing of almost all major religions—Judaism Christianity Islam Hinduism Buddhism Capitalism Communism etc.—and don't be fooled by any old Yarmulke or Collar or Turban or other disguise. They're looking for your money and your soul. They need your soul to make quota; they need your money to make their brother's wife (or son), and also to buy guns so other Joneses can kill each other in the name of their respective Jones morality, virtue and god.

Well I don't know about you, but my name is Johnson. "My people" are of no specific race, creed or ethnicity, though as a Johnson I always have and always will stand up to bigotry of any kind, nor do they belong to a specific Nation State. As a Johnson I try, to the best of my ability, to treat all world citizens as people, not the property of whatever government that claims to own them. No, there are as many Joneses among the Jews, Christians, Muslims and Hindus etc. as there are as there are among Americans, Chinese, Eskimos or any other religious group, ethnicity, nation state or category humans find themselves placed or born into.

So, when I first heard the words "NEVER AGAIN," I took them to mean never again. For anybody. It meant all Johnsons had to make sure "it" never happened again to anyone, ever. If there's one lesson we Johnson's learned from the Nazis it's to stop any Fascist Joneses in their tracks before the first Fascist Jones uniform comes back from the tailor. That means fighting all racism, "ethnism," sexism, homophobia, xenophobia, injustice and any Jones phobia or "ism" at all times, always, as much as is in our power to do so. Might not even have been a war or a Holocaust had some German Johnson interjected himself between Hitler and his first bedraggled, snarling audience and thrown a fat ripe tomato in his face. Imagine Adolph trying to look all mean and autocratic with tomato guts dripping from his Charlie Chaplin mustache...

I don't know about you, but I have no intention of being like the good German Joneses who said nothing while their Jewish German neighbors were shipped off standing-room-only on cattle cars to be slaughtered like... cattle... around 1941, nor do I want to be a good

American Jones who sat by all patriotic that same year as their Japanese-American neighbors were shipped off to a humiliating albeit not fatal "detention."

Never again means liberty and justice for all, all the time, always, the right to mind their own business and be left the hell alone, as Bill Burroughs might say. But those Joneses are cunning and you gotta watch 'em. Seems like right now, while Dubya Jones has filled his cabinet with African-American Joneses, Jewish American Joneses, female Joneses and every color shape and size of Joneses imaginable, there's a stink of "It's happening, It Will Happen" rising from the Dubya Jones Administration and all those sniveling shit-bird Joneses in Congress.

Seems like there's trouble in the making for all of us, but Arab Americans in particular or anyone who looks like one (a Jones can't tell the difference between an Arab Christian, a Pakistani Moslem, an Indian Hindu, or an Iranian Jew and pretty much doesn't give a damn).

This could just be a shiver I'm feeling in these old, arthritic Johnson bones, but it seems to me that even "Arab-looking" Americans who wrap themselves in the flag doesn't work; the Flag may be said to carry Potent Magic these days, but it still ain't bullet proof—seem a little less, shall we say, "free" than they had been, a little less "safe," a little less "American."

Seems like the Joneses are up to nasty, nasty, nasty. Again.

Maybe, me being a Jewish-American-born Johnson, and made not a little suspicious of Jones nature by the Holocaust and other Jonesian monstrosities, I'm being paranoid. But as Burroughs said, "A paranoid is someone who knows a little bit about what's going on."

Well, whatever I know or don't know, I'll be damned if I'll sit back like a "good German" or "good American" Jones if it ever comes to watching my Arab-American or any other neighbors "held indefinitely" for questioning due to suspicion of "Terrorism-By-Default" or whatever the Joneses might come up with. Never again, as I said, means never again, not here, not anywhere. Never again means standing up like a Johnson, immediately, to let those Joneses know that NOBODY'S life is cheap.

I believe we Johnsons outnumber the Joneses by orders of magnitude on this planet, so if we each do our bit maybe we can accomplish something, or at least stop the Joneses from doing any more harm than they've already done. If you look around—anywhere, from your own neighborhood that's unseasonably warm AGAIN this year to the spooks on TV spooking your kids into thinking god himself was a Jones and this is his will—you'll see how much considerable harm the Joneses have done to this world already.

The world is never gonna be safe for anybody until Johnsons make it safe for everybody.

You can pretend the Johnsons are naive, idealistic, that they don't understand the hard realities of religion, patriotism, racial identity, class, money, snack food, whatever. But again, look at the world around you with its toxic water, rotten-egg-sperm asthma-air and grim, grim future. Blood all over the place it makes me sick. Look at "your own people," whoever they are. Do they and they alone have your interests in mind? Are your children their children, or merely their clay and fodder? Are they really your people, after all? Or more Joneses, leading you and the rest of the herd to yet another vat of poison Kool-aid?

No. No way. Not this time.

My people are the Johnsons.

# WALTER THE WEATHERMAN WAITS FOR GOD

So I'm in the same fetal position I'd crouched in 30 years ago, only it isn't *Time*'s or *Newsweek*'s or CBSNBSABC news' fault, but Walter the Weatherman's. Crazy Walter the Weatherman ten years old. Baby-sitting the lad as a favor to his mom, who left him in my less-than-capable hands so she could work an extra shift. Christmas and all—she's usually a prudent woman, but you know how things go and go and go until you're in sizeable debt to those nice banks and credit card companies who send you checks for loads and loads of Holiday shopping liquidity this joyous time of year; but that's not relevant to the weather. Is it?

Not relevant to why me and Walter cower under cob-webby stairs in the cold damp basement, waiting for THE END.

Anyway: Walter. Knows all about The Weather. His mother told me about how she bought him some kind of contraption lets him monitor the weather from his bedroom window. New fangled high tech barometer or something. But he's also tuned in to all the weather stations on cable and a dozen sites on the Net.

Finally, the mother told me, she had to monitor his access, put in one of those chips that Clintonistas got all hot 'n bothered about (and I'm sure the Bush-men would be spraying their shorts too if they had testicles) in his computer or his head. Or maybe it was some "Save The Children" software provided by her snoopy ISP. Whatever, she cut him off. Not completely. Just put him under probationary Parental Guidance till he learned to handle his obsessions or the Ritalin kicked in.

"But it's good for a boy his age to have a hobby," his mother said. "If Walter doesn't grow up to be a meteorologist, well, I don't know WHAT."

Well I can think of a few things. Turns out his bright young mind is a bit too inexperienced to distinguish between storms and tornadoes. Every time he hears a report of a storm coming he runs down to the basement and hides under the stairs. Thinks a twister's on its way to carry him to Munchkin land.

My reaction to this briefing the mother gave me as she filled her thermos with black, black coffee and fixed the name-tag on her uniform was to think (to myself), "this kid's got god on the brain he's using the technology set before him to monitor the wrath of god the great mind of nature or the cosmos, not the crap they feed him in church or temple whatever religious hustle his mother's affiliated with, some clergyman on the take jabbering about how 2000 years ago God or one of his harassed secretaries, scribbling prophesy for three shekels a day, wrote this or that and therefore DISASTER is going to occur in Jerusalem or Bethlehem or some other place about as meaningful to Walter the Weatherman as Pepperidge, Ohio—unless one factors in deviate precipitation patterns or temperatures of abnormally high or low degree."

I thought of the young Einstein breaking his watch so he could see how Time really worked, or ten-year-old Percy Shelley leading his sisters in rebellion against the established order of DADDY'S HOUSE before they shipped him off in chains to Eton. Harmless enough. Though little Einstein, according to the folklore, seemed to be motivated by curiosity rather than fear, and Shelley (well, god knows what HE was thinking about).

But Einstein didn't have asthma or receive daily updates of melting polar caps and perverse migration patterns and other behavioral freak-outs of fish, fowl and all manner of creepy-crawlers and flying things. Einstein didn't have so called "meteorologists" (weathermen, usually overweight, buffoonish, ex-food critics in Network insignia sports jackets) telling him it's going to be one helluva beautiful day with the Sun out and children playing and smiley faces all over his map of the US, only it's December and this shouldn't be happening; the smiley faces should at least be wearing hats and scarves. But often there's a sad crying face on the map, which means it's raining or going to rain, possibly for days on end, which again wouldn't be such a bad thing except I remember last year (Fall 2001-June 2002) it was "November"—dreary rainy blah—from October to late May; then it was August—sticky gray-rown heat-mare—from early June until October. Luckily, it became November in November this year of somebody's lord, 2002, and it's even behaving like December in

December. We had a "white Christmas," albeit the whitest damn Christmas since 1969. Of course, it could all just be a fluke or... well do I really have to go over the same old shit everybody outside the Bush Administration knows backwards and forwards as they fill up their SUVs and prepare to "take out Saddam" and whoever else for more black gold?

No wonder Walter's so messed up. He's studying a "science," in his own child's way, only to learn, as he becomes more adept and involved, that either the science that so captivates him is a lie, or if the measurements are "accurate," there's no precedent for this kind of information, there's no real pattern here except the kind of pattern ten-year-old brains aren't yet wired to detect: CHAOS, DOOM, MEGA-DEATH.

Hell, I'd have headed for the basement too. In fact I did, and I was even younger. Eight, nine. Only I wasn't hiding from the Weather, we had "regular weather" back then, I was hiding from the Russians, whose super duper commie firepower, Time, Newsweek and CBSNBCABC told me, was going to fall soundless from the sky and blast me and everyone and everything I ever knew and loved to dust and ashes: a brief, drunken episode in the Cosmic Memory. Best forgotten, actually. Never happened. Planet? What planet? I don't remember any planet. Bluish-green, you say? Nope. Sorry, Bud, never seen it.

Poor Walter the Weatherman. His mother never should have let him tune in, in the first place. Then again, these things can't be helped. Sooner or later, even the youngest, most innocent among us are going to find out the TRUTH, or some small part of it, even if they can't put all the pieces together, or understand much of what they do compile. Whatever message they manage to decode is going to tell them things that'll drive them screaming to the basement, arms over knees in free-form "Duck and Cover" crouch, asking whatever "god" there is out there to please, please, please go away and leave them and those they love the hell alone.

"It's not god," I told Walter, passing him a bag of chips. "It's THE MAN. He likes to fuck us up then blame god. Not the 'it' or 'energy' of Creation, but some vengeful, implacable, doom-fanatic god made in His image. Understand, little amigo? THE MAN is in your head and you gotta, like, EXPECTORATE him immediately, if not sooner. You 'grock' me there, pal?"

"Tornado. Bad Twister. Stay still," said Walter. "Don't talk. Don't move. Shhhh."

I'm not as young as I used to be. My back hurts. I hate to mess with the kid's hobby, but I'm gonna have to get out from this cramped position under the stairs in this cold basement and walk like a FREE

MAN and get some FRESH AIR. These are children's games, after all, best played by children.

**Adam Engel** and Walter the Weatherman are still under the basement stairs. Fortunately, Walter never goes anywhere, not even the basement, without a laptop and wireless modem. They can be reached—good news only, please—at bartlebysamsa65@hotmail.com

# CRUMBLECAKE AND FISH

Christmas. Crumblecake and Fish. At least that's what I thought they said, though on the table was roast beef, chocolate cake and various pastries, none of them crumbly. No crumblecake. No fish.

RelativeShe and RelativeHe had watched a show about Crumblecake and Fish on some mainstream news show. Crumblecake and Fish is a company that specializes in clothing meant for white people, RelativeHe explained.

"What white people," I asked. "How can you specialize in clothing for white people and not yellow or brown people?"

"Well, yeah," both RelativeHe and RelativeShe agreed—especially since RelativeShe is not white at all, but yellow or Korean or whatever you want to call this arbitrary junk genetic distinction between human hues.

"What about me?" I asked.

"No, definitely not your kind of white people," they agreed.

"So shouldn't I be wearing clothes made for black people?"

"I don't know, I don't think they make clothing just for black people. Anyway if they did, it wouldn't look right on you," said RelativeShe.

"Why not?"

"Because nothing looks good on you. You're a sartorial anomaly," said RelativeShe.

"Oh yeah, true. But getting back to the clothing made for white people...

"Well, not All white people," sniffed RelativeHe.

"I would think not, because a lot of people I know wear clothing designed for black people even though most black people stopped wearing that stuff years ago," I said.

"You're confusing the issue," said RelativeShe.

"I'm just trying to understand how you can make clothing for white people and not for black people, I mean—"

"Okay, okay—rich white people," said RelativeHe.

"Oh, now I get it. So if a Rich Black Guy like Bill Cosby—"

"Exactly. Bill Cosby could wear their clothes but most black people wouldn't look good in them," said RelativeHe.

"Bill Cosby's no Denzel Washington," I said.

"Well, Denzel could wear these clothes too," said RelativeHe.

"But they're both black I thought you meant—"

"You know what we mean," snapped RelativeShe. "We mean regular black people wouldn't shop for this company's line."

"Because regular black people think these clothes are ugly? I sure do. I think—"

"No, because regular black people can't afford them," said RelativeHe.

"Okay, so this company specializes in clothing only Rich White People could buy even if they're black?" I said.

"Exactly," said RelativeHe.

"So, what's the problem?" I asked.

"Well, since they focus on clothing for white people—" began RelativeHe.

"— and rich black people," I added

"Yeah right," RelativeHe was growing annoyed. "Because they focus on this kind of product, they only hire white people."

"Rich White People?" I asked.

"Don't be stupid. Why would a rich white person want one of their jobs?" said RelativeShe.

"What about executives?" I asked.

"Okay, executives," agreed RelativeShe.

"But there are no rich black executives of this company," I said.

"Exactly," said RelativeShe. "Which makes sense, because they specialize in—"

"But you just said rich black people would wear their stuff, so I don't understand—"

"It doesn't matter what you understand," huffed RelativeHe. "There are no black people, rich poor or middle class in this company. Period."

"Isn't that illegal?" I asked.

"That's what a bunch of people are crying about, even people who don't work for the company and never plan on working for the company, just on making trouble," said RelativeHe.

"Well the black folks who sat down at that lunch counter at Woolworth's weren't planning on eating there every day, they just—"

"This is not that kind of issue," snapped RelativeShe. "This is not like that. You're just like those people complaining, mixing politics where it doesn't belong."

"Just like black people don't belong in this company," I said.

"Exactly, because they don't make stuff for black people," said RelativeHe.

"Unless they're rich," I added.

"Forget about rich black people. There aren't enough in this whole country to make a damn difference," said RelativeHe.

"Well no wonder, cause they can't even get jobs in this old clothing company," I said.

"That's not why they're not rich," said RelativeShe. "No one gets rich working these jobs," said RelativeShe.

"So what's the problem?" I asked.

"There is no problem, these trouble-makers are saying they're discriminating against black people," said RelativeShe.

"Well, aren't they?" I asked.

"Well, yeah, but not because they're black for goddsakes. Because they don't make their kind of clothes," said RelativeShe.

"What kind of cloths?"

"Black clothes!"

"You mean like Heavy Metal and Punk stuff?"

"What black people wear!" RelativeShe was getting sort of pissed.

"What do black people wear?"

"Who cares what they wear? They just don't wear this company's clothes," said RelativeHe.

"Unless they're rich," I reminded him.

"Forget about rich!" he snapped.

"But that's discrimination," I said.

"Exactly," said RelativeShe. "It doesn't matter if you discriminate against the rich, and it doesn't matter if you don't hire people who can't sell your clothes. You wouldn't hire a guy to work at Hooters, for god's sake."

"Well, actually, there was a case a few years back—"

"A troublemaker!" barked RelativeHe. "That guy didn't really want to work at hooters any more than I do."

"Then black people don't REALLY want to work at this company—"

"How should I know? It doesn't matter, because they wouldn't be right for the job. Even a black guy said it," said RelativeHe.

"Which black guy said what?" I asked.

"The black guy who was on the news show," said RelativeShe. He used the example of the black entertainment network."

"The what?"

"Totally clueless. See what happens when you don't watch television?" she said, exasperated, to RelativeHe.

"They have only black shows and only hire black actors," RelativeHe explained.

"So you think this is right?" I asked.

"Of Course it's right," said RelativeShe. That's what that whole civil rights thing was about."

"To give everybody the right to be segregated like white people?"

"No, stupid. To give them the power to hire who they want. Anyway, this guy on the news—"

"The black guy," I said.

"Yes, the black guy," said RelativeShe. "It's called fair and balanced reporting. They ask a black guy his opinion and if he says there's nothing wrong with it, there's nothing wrong with it."

"One black guy."

"Yes, that's called individualism," RelativeHe chimed in. "Individual rights and all that."

"For one black guy to speak for all black people on earth," I said.

"He's not speaking for anyone but himself, but if he thinks it's okay, it's okay, because we all have individual liberties and that stuff," said RelativeHe. "So anyway, this black guy's interviewed and he sees nothing wrong with it because there's no way the Black Entertainment Network is gonna hire Dan Rather, even if he's the best reporter in America, because they want a black anchorman. It's their right, just like it's the right of Crumblecake and Fish to sell white people's clothing and hire white people to make them."

"White people make the clothing?" I asked.

"Well no of course not," said RelativeHe. "They're made in Vietnam or Pakistan or somewhere, but white people design them and sell them and all of that and it's their right because they know what white people want."

"They don't know what I want," I said.

"REGULAR white people, not political troublemakers," said RelativeHe.

"Yes, it really does make sense if you think about it," said RelativeShe. "They're not doing anything illegal. In fact, Mr. Smarty Pants, they even hired a black Lawyer."

"They don't hire black people, but suddenly they hire a black lawyer?"

"Yes, because that's the point. A black person doesn't know how white people should dress, but he can definitely understand the law, because under the law We're All Equal. It makes perfect sense."

"So you're saying segregation makes perfect sense?" I said.

"No, that's not what I said at all," said RelativeShe.

"Forget about it, he's impossible to talk to," said RelativeHe.

"Yes, you're right. That's his problem." RelativeShe looked at me and sighed.

"What's my problem?" I asked.

"You don't know anything. We can't discuss serious issues with you because you never watch the news. If you only got off the computer or away from those books to watch TV once in a while, like a NORMAL person, you'd know exactly what we're talking about."

**Adam Engel** wears tuxedos in honor of the Penguin at bartlebysamsa65@gmail.com [illegible] the late Weng [illegible] Square. It makes perfect sense."

"[illegible] makes perfect sense?" I said.

"No, that's not what I said [illegible]."

"Forget about it, he's impossible to talk to," said [illegible].

"It's you [illegible]. That's his problem," [illegible]. He looked at me and smiled.

"What's my problem?" I asked.

"You don't [illegible] because you don't watch the news. If you only got [illegible] [illegible], you'd know what we're talking about."

[illegible]

# DAMNED RIGHT TO BEAR ARMS

"The main reason people must have the right to bear arms is for the balance of power. Once the government even knows the location of all the weapons, the people no longer have the ability to stop despotism. (This, of course, implies that the people would want to stop it, as is clearly not the case in the U.S.) ... As for snipers and mad bombers, they are only the first symptoms of a disintegrating democracy. Americans should expect it to get a lot worse, regardless of any controls placed on weapons." PAPAGORE, *Progressive Review Newsletter*

"Never before has the freedom of U.S. citizens been under more attack from all sides. Even from our President, who swore as his oath of office, to defend the Constitution of the United States . Let the firearm confiscations in England and Australia serve as examples of what can happen and stop that from happening here in the United States ." armed-citizens.com

Let's not beat around the, uh... Bush. The United States Government and its various corporate sponsors (known hereafter as THE MAN), exist for one purpose: to enrich and empower HIMSELF. HE does this in two ways:

1. dominating and debasing all non-Americans and making them miserable
2. sucking the life, liberty, happiness and physical and intellectual resources from Americans to help HIM dominate and debase all non-Americans and make them miserable.

Closed loop. Bad cycle.

Fortunately, there are over 50 million gun owners in the United States. There's still some hope, so long as you don't try to 'interpret' the infamous Second Amendment, but ignore it. Because if you read it carefully, you'll see it has nothing to do with giving anybody but the State the right to bear arms:

> 'The second amendment of the United States Constitution states: 'A well regulated militia, being necessary to the security of a free State , the right of the people to keep and bear Arms, shall not be infringed.' Obviously the need for a state militia has been replaced by the National Guard and Coast Guard whereby trained military personnel are entrusted with the defense of this country against domestic enemies. Their weapons are tightly controlled and safeguarded.' JOE BIALEK, *Progressive Review Newsletter* (italics mine—AE)

Note the Amendment refers to the security of a 'free State,' an oxymoron if there ever was one. Note also that the Constitution is no longer worth the soul of the dead lamb it's printed on.

Did all sorts of research online concerning who's for gun control, who's against gun control, the issues of gun violence in America. Seems the pros and the cons have a few things in common: They all have some sort of insignia on their sites representing the American Flag; they cite the Constitution; they work through lobbying Congress. 'Write a letter to your Representative. We'll show 'em who's Boss, we will!'

Hmn.

They're what we on the left/right/anarchist/libertarian fringe might call The Mainstream. They're the 100 million people who voted for Gush Bore (not including myself, my grandmother and the 15 or so other people who voted Nader just to be spoil-sports). Whether they're for gun control, outright prohibition, tougher registration laws (yeah, registration; why don't I just send my photograph, fingerprints and letter of intent to the FBI?), it all boils down to writing a letter to your congressman or some such nonsense. Now, I don't mind having a lobby group like the NRA to do their bit for the right to bear arms. Just like I'm happy to have the ACLU around to protect my right to speak. The thing is, they're both missing the point. Whether the NRA wrangles lighter gun control legislation from THE MAN is as irrelevant to my ownership of a weapon as the ACLU's lawyers' haggling with THE MAN over my right to speak. THE MAN and his shredded Constitution have nothing to do with my decision to defend myself from HIM or talk trash to HIM. They might, the NRA on the Mainstream right, the ACLU on the Mainstream left, both be doing a disservice by perpetuating the charade that this is some sort of society or democracy, that we do everything all fair and legal around here.

Circumstances change. Governments change. The Law is cold and hard, yet malleable. A tool of self defense is cold and hard, but if properly maintained, won't turn on you, as THE MAN has, as HIS laws have. For verily, they are HIS laws. Always have and always will be subject to HIS red pen.

The Constitution is a blueprint for a State that might have one time existed as a democracy (with black people and women as property and natives open game for genocide) but is now little more than THE MAN's organic cannon-fodder farm. While some Mainstream 'liberals' believe the "right to bear arms" refers to an organized militia (but not a free militia: the police, or worse, the National Guard), and Mainstream 'conservatives' refer to the constitutional right to bear arms as an expression of individuality, both are batty to think THE MAN has anything but contempt for their interpretations of HIS Constitution.

The Mainstream "left," Democrats usually (as opposed to the real left) is essentially asking a State armed with nuclear, biological, and chemical weapons, and using those weapons to pursue aggressive policies worldwide, to "protect" them from civilians who may or may not attack them personally. Is not each individual obligated to protect himself? Is it fair to ask a cop, who is essentially a mercenary for THE MAN, to sacrifice his safety to protect yours? On the other hand, the Mainstream "right," Republicans usually, represented by groups such as the NRA, like good children, seek permission from THE MAN (via laws etc.) which THE MAN, being the ultimate enemy of liberty, has no right to give.

If anyone should be bearing arms it is the Mainstream liberal, not to protect himself from burglars, but from the power of THE MAN. Similarly, the Mainstream right, if it practiced what it preached, would realize that THE MAN has no say in the matter. Self defense is the right of all human beings. The predator the gun owner should be concerned with should not be the "second story man," who, odds are, will not visit his home, but the Police State, which most certainly will, if it has not done so already. Think USA/PATRIOT ACT, TIPS, FBI/ATF, NSA, TIA, CIA, and the new UBER BUREAUCRACY that'll attempt to put 'em all under one roof. Not good.

According to former admiral and ex-convict Poindexter's *Total Information Awareness* (TIA) Office:

> 'The TIA program strategy is to integrate technologies developed by DARPA (and elsewhere as appropriate) into a series of increasingly powerful prototype systems that can be stress-tested in operationally relevant environments, using real-time feedback to refine concepts of operation and performance requirements down to the component level. The TIA program will develop and integrate information technologies into fully functional, leave-behind prototypes that are reliable, easy to install, and

> packaged with documentation and source code (though not necessarily complete in terms of desired features) that will enable the intelligence community to evaluate new technologies through experimentation, and rapidly transition it to operational use, as appropriate. Accordingly, the TIA program will work in close collaboration with one or more U.S. intelligence agencies that will provide operational guidance and technology evaluation, and act as TIA system transition partners. Technically, the TIA program is focusing on the development of: 1) architectures for a large-scale counter-terrorism database, for system elements associated with database population, and for integrating algorithms and mixed-initiative analytical tools; 2) novel methods for populating the database from existing sources, create innovative new sources, and invent new algorithms for mining, combining, and refining information for subsequent inclusion into the database; and, 3) revolutionary new models, algorithms, methods, tools, and techniques for analyzing and correlating information in the database to derive actionable intelligence.' Total Information Awareness (TIA)

That's THE MAN's techno-bureau-speak for YOU ARE BEING WATCHED.

I just hate this terrible feeling of being . . . naked. A boy in his birthday suit defenseless against the mightiest State on Earth. "An Army of One," the commercials say. Well it's a pretty damn big ONE, armed with nukes, ultra-magnetic wave doohickeys, jet fighters, and other toys you and I paid for. Don't I have a right to at least a symbolic trinket of resistance?

Nevertheless, unlike lipstick or a cigarette in a Salinger story, my trinket is a potent symbol. It's like this: I have no illusions that my little weapon will do any major damage to THE MAN; however, if I go down, I'll at least be able to take one of HIS attack dogs with me. Imagine if 100 million people could say that? The MAN spent billions on cruise missiles and stealth bombers so he would avoid the unpleasantness 'and possibility of defeat' involved in house-to-house fighting in Iraq or Serbia or Afghanistan or wherever HE sets in HIS cross-hairs. Think he wants to take on Chicago? And New York? And St. Louis? And all the other major cities of America, not to mention their sprawling suburbs? I suppose HE can bomb the cities and suburbs of the Homeland. But sooner or later someone will realize that if HE does this, there'll be no one left to pay for HIS military or buy HIS crappy consumer goods. Anyway, he couldn't even take a couple of million Viet Cong, or Al Quaeda, much less a hundred million armed denizens of HIS own country.

I'm talking paranoid, you say. Worse case scenario. But this is indeed a bad case, and it's only going to get worse with time.

Can't happen here? Please. Men and women of Arab or east Asian descent are being 'questioned' and detained daily. Yeah, I know:

'Terrorists.' I don't buy it, nor do I believe that I am safe from the accelerating authoritarianism of THE MAN. David Koresh wasn't. What was his crime? Cult leader? I guess they're going to go after Bill Gates, or Steven Jobs, or the guys who run Disney and McDonald's next. Cults with larger followings than Koresh ever dreamed of. And George Lucas, that wicked pied piper, has hypnotized our sacred children into dumbfounded obedience to expensive, intergalactic treacle and numerous product tie-ins.

Every person is obligated to defend himself, his family and friends, and beyond. To fight for liberty wherever it is threatened. Like in America, for instance. Can I forget watching the Feds incinerate children and parents at Waco in order to . . . SAVE the children from their wicked parents?

Ask your Arab or southeast Asian neighbors who, be they citizens, students, or legal aliens, are catching hell from THE MAN and the Idiots Who Love HIM. "But I'm white as a ghost," you say. "And employed, and a nice guy to boot, and I keep my mouth shut." Well, you're lucky, for now, but don't tell me you're off the hook. What happens when THE MAN wants your kids to fight one of his expensive foreign wars? What if one day you do open your mouth? Could happen. Anyway, I'm not talking to you. White, nice guy, fine with me. But keeping your mouth shut? What do you use it for, a repository for THE MAN's chewy chocolaty goodness? Anyway, you're not as safe as you might think:

> 'The evidence is rolling in, and it is unmistakable: the Bush people are assembling purely political lists of individuals and groups to be targeted during some future crisis, real or manufactured. The list makers probably do not yet know what they plan to do to the people on their enemies lists, which are still fragmented among various agencies. However, once such lists are compiled, eventual government action becomes all but inevitable. It is already clear that the list will be a very long one, reaching into broad categories of what the current rulers consider to be dangerous dissenters. In an article titled "Grounded," the mainstream Salon.com related the experience of Center for Constitutional Rights assistant legal director Barbara Olshansky, who was forced to pull down her pants in view of other travelers at Newark International Airport. When the lawyer protested the indignity, a security agent replied, "The computer spit you out. I don't know why, and I don't have time to talk to you about it." Six other employees of the center had been pulled out of an airport boarding line a month earlier. Since all had purchased their tickets separately under their own names, it was plain that the Center for Constitutional Rights staff were on some kind of list. Readers familiar with the workings of bureaucracies will immediately recognize the clanks, squeaks and grinds of cumbersome government machinery getting into gear.' *The Black Commentator*, "Bush's Domestic Enemies List"

Knowing that unlike Nazi Germany, Soviet Russia, Maoist China, HE cannot subjugate an armed populace by force, THE MAN resorts to propaganda. And you've gotta hand it to HIM, between Hollywood, Washington D.C. and Madison Avenue, HE'S developed the most effective propaganda system the world has ever seen. But as WWII, Hungary in 1956, Czechoslovakia in 1968, and Vietnam/Cambodia in 1964-75 proved, even propaganda has its limits. Eventually, when the people recognize how deeply they're being had, and resist, the State resorts to force. Hungarians tried and lost to the Soviets, as did the Czechs, but the North Vietnamese/Viet Cong, with a fraction of the 200 million arms Americans possess, beat the American Superpower, or at least bloodied its nose and sent it home crying like the bully it is. Not with a superior army, but with armed, committed individuals, who would rather die than see their country overtaken by yet another colonial power.

I'll be damned if I'm going to ask THE MAN, who's pursuing death and destruction at home and abroad with a multi-trillion dollar Military/Police apparatus, for permission to defend myself against . . . THE MAN. For permission to speak out against THE MAN.

That's like asking Himmler for a bar of soap and 'permission' to shower.

# DEAR MR. PRESIDENT, WHO ARE YOU?

Dear Mr. President,

Why you send me to be a hero and win medals but I'm poisoned?

Dear Mr. President,

Why I got no groupies? Why I gotta work? I hate my job. You like yours?

Dear Mr. President,

Surely those rumors about your having nothing but paste and pudding in your codpiece are not true. But the Liberal Media is relentless. Heavens, can't we do something?

Dear Mr. President,

Why did they spend my tax money on National Defense when it can't be defense cause defense is when you stand on your porch or lawn with a rifle to protect what you have and I have done no such thing. Would like a refund ASAP.

Dear Mr. President,

The last novel I read was *Finnegan's Wake*. I don't think I'll read another. I don't care for novels anymore. I liked *The Wake* though, and I like poetry. Oh, I also liked *Killing Hope*, by William Blum and *Blowback* by Chalmers Johnson. How about you?

Dear Mr. President,

This sucks. I know "life's a bitch and then you die" and blah blah blah, but really, even my 88-year-old grandmother who was a Commie during the Depression because she had no work (unlike yer granddaddy who sold all sorts of stuff to the Third Reich) and then lost her brother to WWII said it's never been like THIS. Such misery, anxiety, despair world-wide and all you talk about's the war on this; the war on that; the war on this, that and the other thing; all of which, according to one of your leprous courtiers, the U.S. Military can prosecute simultaneously and emerge victorious... Things were a lot better before YOU showed up.

Dear Mr. President,

Why are my toes crusty, cracked, twisted like I'm old? Am I old?

Dear Mr. President,

Did your Mom's dog REALLY write that book, or did she hire a ghost? Rumor has it Millie read little but the sports pages and the comics and didn't have the discipline to complete and submit a publishable manuscript. Hey, I'm just telling you what I've heard...

Dear Mr. President,

My wife is missing some jewelry; I "lost" my favorite shirt; there's only 15 percocet in the medicine cabinet (last count there were twenty) and half that bottle of Single-Malt scotch we'd been saving for company has mysteriously evaporated. Now, we're not ACCUSING you of anything, but...

Dear Mr. President,

Am I really a man of my time? Why does my three-year-old have asthma? What ever happened to Spring? And Autumn? It's always hot or cold but never fair. Once I knew the scent of cherry blossoms and dove head-first into a mogul of brown leaves. Broke my collarbone (there were bricks under the pile), but I had fun.

Dear Mr. President,

May the Lord give you the courage to perform laser surgery and say cool stuff like, "Honey, I forgot to duck," even though you stole the election and you're an imbecile, a shallow boy—it must be embarrassing to have your daddy settle your affairs and get you jobs and stuff and then you mess up every damn time.

Dear Mr. President,

Forget my last letter. I'm drunk and unemployed. I refuse to say "no" to drugs (except for that junk you spray up your nose when it's congested). You think maybe you could get me a job? Have Laptop, will travel.

Dear Mr. President,
Please get the FBI off my back. I'm not dangerous, just bored. Humor me.

Dear Mr. President,
As Jefferson set the table and Washington carved the bird, we went to war. Armed with an egg-launching blunderbuss, I wasted Red coats, Hessian scarves, Sioux buttons... then in the future, on a distant planet, I did jitterbugs and Tangos with my M16, I'm not sure why. Perhaps in the excitement I believed it my duty to smoke them all. Waste 'em without mercy. Have you had similar experiences? If so, please share.

Dear Mr. President,
I wanted to tell of my betrayal, but you being dead for years, it seemed so pointless.

Dear Mr. President,
Do you really need to chew so much gum? Stay away from gassy foods.

Dear Mr. President,
The future holds mud-pies and balls of yellow snow. We know that. But who's gonna eat it, Mr. President? Who's gonna take the hit? We know that too. You promised to protect and serve. Yet it's up to us to defend ourselves from the slings and arrows of a pissed off world with, with what? Fat free potato chips? Chewy chocolaty goodness? Surely your military's not for OUR defense—stirred up hornet's nests and left us naked. Please stop laughing, Mr. President, it's not funny.

Dear Mr. President,
I'm no longer a member of your book club. I hate books. Please do not contact me ever again.

Dear Mr. President,
The manual said "breathe." Can you do that much? Just breathe?

Dear Mr. President,
The undead, snoring in cubicles, arise at night to suck milk-blood of Tofu. What I'm trying to say is: must we have porridge again? The children are starving why won't you feed them?

Dear Mr. President,
What is your problem? WHO ARE YOU?

Dear Mr. President,
Poets are not the 'unacknowledged legislators of the world;' they're merely unacknowledged. Please, talk to me. I know you know I'm out here. Let me know you care.

Dear Mr. President,
C'mon really it's not like you're Lenin or Stalin or Hitler or Mao or even Nixon dark-hearted little men who climbed cursing and spitting to the top of the human pile and did what they wanted to do all along pour gasoline on the haystack burn burn burn—you don't have the brains or the guts though possibly you're just as evil—you're more like Louis XVI a billiard ball without a number a cue ball I think they call it blank white smacking other balls but somebody's holding the stick or you'd be nothing static sit there inert tell me for god's sake who's got the stick who's cueing you all blue with chalk and scared of the planet look at you leader of the "free world" can't even channel surf and chew a pretzel without endangering the security of... of whom?

Dear Mr. President,
We all have our mishegas. To mish is human, to gas, divine. We mish a lot of stuff—zip!—right past our ears while we are doing what we think needs doing. Eventually we tire and go home. Don't push yourself too hard. When you get tired, go home.

Sincerely,
Adam Engel

**Adam Engel** spent the best years of his life feeding the future President, burping him, changing his diapers, teaching him "good from evil," and even cleaning up after the little guy took one pull too many off the bottle of "baby formula." AND THIS IS THE THANKS HE GETS? It's enough to make a man vote Democrat. If you've had similar experiences nursing future presidents/dictators/CEOs contact: bartlebysamsa65@gmail.com

# DEMOCRACY LIVES!

Maybe we've never been lied to at all. It's in the constitution's deceptively democratic language and supporting literature, such as the Federalist papers and "oppositional" writings by Madison and Jefferson and the gang. They all wanted to keep their property, they just couldn't agree on the most subtle, persuasive, game plan.

The country IS and has always been a democracy for Our Masters—rich, propertied, white men. It is a democracy for THEM to this day, regardless of what BuschCo, hired out by the real owners of America, does to the rest of us. Our Masters will vote democratically on corporate boards. Our Masters' "public" servants will vote democratically in Congress, each representative voting in accordance with his/her affiliated corporate interest whose board democratically selected him or her for office.

Our Masters will vote on when and where the next WAR will be, and THEY will vote on when to finally withdraw any semblance of democracy from the masses as surely as they'll vote on how much sugar to pump into your kid's breakfast cereal. The masses never would have known (or cared about) "democracy" in the first place if not for a few do-gooder meddlers in the courts and Congress rewriting the Constitution to include, of all people, the PEOPLE.

Our Masters will be voting long after the 200 some odd year charade of "electoral politics" has been shut down once and for all and "we the people" are put back in our proper places, though mercifully, blacks will merely be imprisoned and economically oppressed, not enslaved (i.e. status quo). And women can pretend that they have "equal rights" as long as no one gets uppity or bitchy. And the Indians or Native Nations or whatever you call them? Well, as now as in the beginning: Fuck 'em.

The Bush legacy at Yale. Skull and Bones:

"Heard his Dad's close to Nixon"

"Whose Dad isn't?"

"Head of the CIA."

"Ooh. Spook me out. My dad OWNS the CIA."

Our Masters laughed at the few hundred grad-students and undergrads studying at Yale due to intellectual predilections, hard work, discipline, vigor, who would end up working for THEM and, of all people, that CLOWN Bush, the cheerleader, "Gofer George" ("Georgie, gofer some beer," "Georgie, gofer some weed," "Georgie, gofer some blow").

As it was then, so it is today.

Our Masters played a huge joke on America's underclass (the other 90 percent of us) by democratically selecting "Gofer George," Class Clown, Buffoon extraordinaire, as "President."

See, their whole plan was to wreck the government as it stood. As militaristic and right-wing as it was, it just wasn't aggressive enough nor did it fulfill its function as The Masters' Corporate Security Agency.

THEY wanted to deal straight with the Military, always the most faithful, straight-talking servants, far more disciplined and effective than those fat, bloviating lawyers hired out as so-called "legislators."

THEY wanted the Government to carry out their financial, foreign and domestic decisions, but because of the whole failure of the Constitution, which makes it necessary to hire politicians, judges, presidents, who depend to some extent on the "people" to "elect" them, so there's all those campaign fees and costly media empires to "persuade" the people when it would be so much easier and CHEAPER to have one servant class, the Military, carry out all these ridiculously time consuming AND EXPENSIVE operations. Including those long, boring, outrageously wasteful "Supreme Court Decisions," which could be handled far more efficiently by a Military Tribunal.

But the Military, coming for the most part, from the people, has to be convinced that it is doing "right." The only way to get direct access is to create such a situation of dire economic, international, ecological, and medical necessity that the military HAS to come in and maintain order under the (giggle) "command" of "President" Bush ("Gofer George").

So, the key to legitimately wrecking the economy, shutting down the government, and causing a dangerous international situation, is to place the most incompetent boob (of the well-born, of course), who has fucked up everything he's ever attempted and in truth is far stupider than his "scholarship" underlings at Yale, in the Oval Office.

The logic is simple, straightforward and impeccably devious: put the sadistic, alcoholic, childish, fanatically uncompromising, anti-intellectual goofball, Gofer George, in the Presidency, and the rest will follow . . .

# DOMICIDE

DOMICIDE
Main Entry: 1 domicile Etymology: Middle English, from Middle French, from Latin domicilium, from domus Date: 15th century 1 : a dwelling place : place of residence : HOME 2 a : a person's fixed, permanent, and principal home for legal purposes b : RESIDENCE 2b
from Webster's Collegiate Dictionary

Being the only Jew at a party is tough-going these days if you're unfortunate enough to believe that whacko theory (still not scientifically proven) that Palestinians are human beings with thoughts and emotions and are therefore deserving of certain rights, among them justice and freedom from oppression. Folks automatically assume you're an anti-Semite.

As if this weren't bummer enough, the screens all over the room displayed half-a-million flag-waving yahoos in Times Square waiting for the bomb to drop, the ball to drop, the shoe to drop; waiting for something to drop. And it was my birthday. Almost my birthday. New Years Eve. I still had a few hours before this year of our wars 2002 became this year of our wars 2003 and my 38th waddled to me in virgin white diapers.

Now everyone knows that many of the most vehement of anti-Semites these days are Jews, especially the ones who refuse to kneel to the dictates of Sharon and his obsequious state-side "supporters" (Perle, Cheney, Rumsfeld, Wolfowitz, Lieberman, Pat Robertson, Jerry Falwell, George Bush etc.). Still, I never should have fallen for the bait laid out by Uncle Dom, so deviously cunning in his ignorance. Eighty-year-old Uncle Dom. Self described Italian Catholic. Mind like a steel trap: cold, hard, empty.

I listened silently as he declared that if Bush wasn't MAN enough to take out Saddam and the Saudis, the REAL culprits behind the WTC massacre, why, Old Uncle Dom would do the job himself. And anyway, why wasn't I supporting Israel, the only democracy in the region? What was I, some kind of Arab-loving anti-Semite?

How stupid I was to ask Uncle Dom what books or articles, he had read on the subject of Palestine!

"None."

"None?"

"Look, I don't have any facts. But what I think is. . . " and he went back to his tirade as the 54 inch television behind us blared the happy flag-waving minions in Times Square. It's one thing to wave the flag on fourth of July if that's your thing, but on New Years Eve? When did this "tradition" begin?

Who can argue with such a brilliant rhetorical craftsman as Uncle Dom? "I don't have any facts. But what I think is. . ." would later have me lying in bed for two days, staring at the wall, as if trying to figure out a Zen Koan. Nevertheless, I had to think of some kind of reply. People had taken interest in our little debate. A good number had even turned their backs to the giant screen and encircled us, perhaps hoping we would come to blows. Tough old buzzard, Uncle Dom was, and I was no kid myself. Still, I wasn't thirty-eight YET, and I bet I could have taken him. But really it would have been so unseemly to pummel my wife's revered uncle in his own home, where my in-laws' annual New Year's Eve gathering took place.

To add insult to injury, Uncle Jay chimed in, "Yeah, what are you, some kind of Jew hater or something?"

Uncle Jay was one of those impossibly fat specimens of Manhood one might see chasing a tiny Philippine "mail order bride" around the set of a daytime talk show, demanding his "conjugal rights." Real wide load. Phone company assigned different area codes to various of his Allegheny-sized flesh ranges so as not to be gypped on out-of-region calls.

"Geez, Uncle Jay. I thought if anyone would understand the complexities of the situation it would be you. You're Irish, for god's sake. Haven't you ever read Ulysses?

"Yes. As a matter of fact I did," said Uncle Jay, proudly. "And I believe he was one of the finest Generals ever to serve this nation. Whatever his faults as a President."

Okay, so I was really out-gunned.

"Look," I reasoned, carefully. "I never, ever said or would say that I didn't support the right of the Israeli people to live peacefully and prosperously behind the 1967 borders, or Israel proper. Same way I support the right of the Chinese to live in China, or the Indonesians to live in Indonesia. But I sure as hell don't support the Chinese annexation of Tibet or all the nightmares and slaughter Indonesia brought to East Timor. Or the Turkish and Iraqi treatment of the Kurds. You can support the right of people to live in peace in their own country without having to condone the violence and criminality of their government. It's like I 'support' the people who live in the U.S., but I sure as hell don't 'support' the policies of that war-mongering bully in the White House. He's not even a real President."

Oops. Now I'd done it.

"Well I don't know what country YOU live in, but George Bush is MY President. He's America's President, voted in by the people of the USA," Uncle Dom declared proudly, truculently.

"Well, no, actually, he wasn't. He was granted the presidency by the Supreme Court. But let's not go there," I said, hastily. "Okay. Try this on for size. You 'support' the people of Italy, right?"

"Hell yeah. I'm an Italian. I must have visited Italy two dozen times. Not including the War."

"What war?"

"What war?" he looked around, grinning, incredulous. "The war to save DEMOCRACY against FASCISM. The Second World War. I did what I had to do in that war. It wasn't pretty, like you kids see in the movies. But I did what I had to. I served my country. And I was young enough to be YOUR son. Twenty years old, I was."

"Okay, then. So you didn't support the Italian people during WWII?"

"What's the Italian people got to do with it? I was fighting' Hitler and Mussolini. I was LIBERATING the Italian people from fascism so they could live free like us, dammit."

"Right. So you admit that you can support the right of a certain people to live in peace and freedom, while not supporting the actions of their government, which, in the case of Italy, was authoritarian, fascist and oppressive."

"What the hell are you talking? You saying Israel is fascist?" asked Uncle Dom, incredulously.

"No, not at all. I'm just saying that a 'people's' will is not the same thing as the will of their government. Even in a democracy, so called."

"Look, I'll tell you what I know, and I know this for a fact," said Uncle Dom. "The United Nations gave the Jews that land in 1948. It was a legal authority, recognized by the world as a legal authority, and they gave Israel to the Jews legally and if the Arabs have a problem with that fuck them. That's why we're gonna kick Saddam's ass. And those Saudis who bombed the WTC. No respect for international authority."

"But it wasn't the United Nations' land to give."

"Well, yeah, England's. But the Jews kicked their asses the hell out of there, and rightfully so."

"It wasn't England's land either. It was Palestinian land, belonging to Palestinians, the majority of whom were Moslems living with, but often fighting against, both Christian and Jewish minorities for at least a thousand years. Where did the UN get the authority to give any land to anyone without consulting the people who lived there?"

"Don't you tell me about the UN. I fought in that damn war to help create it. It's a legal body. A necessary authority created to settle things DEMOCRATICALLY."

"Okay. How about his. Say I want half of your house. . . "

"Fuck you, you want half of my house. I'll kick your—"

"Hypothetically. I want half of your house. This house we're in right now. I go to the local police, a legitimate legal authority, and I say, 'I want Uncle Dom's House.' Now the cops say, 'No, that wouldn't be right.'"

"Damn right it wouldn't," snarled Uncle Dom.

"But what the cops do say is that they'll give me HALF your house. That would be fair, the cops say. Now, since they're a legitimate legal authority, we gotta go along with their judgment. So I move into half your house and you and your family can take the other half."

Uncle Dom got a kick outta this. He turned to our now rather sizeable group of listeners and said, "Getta load of this guy! I invite him to one party and already he's taking half my fucking house."

"Now suppose," I continued, "I start raising a family. Suddenly the half of the house the cops gave me isn't enough. Also, I have relatives coming from all over who want to stay with me. So I start moving into your half of the house and making changes. Add a bed here, do some restructuring there, change the wall-paper. Little by little, your half starts becoming my half. See what I'm saying?"

"No, I don't see. In fact this whole thing about you moving into my house is pissing me off. Let's get back to the real argument. These Palestinians have no right to be fucking with Israel. Ever look at a goddam map? They have these huge countries all over the Arab world they can go to. Why make so much trouble over that little slip of real estate? Crazy. Just crazy is all."

"What do you mean 'Arab world?' Syria? Jordan? Egypt? That's like kicking half the Spaniards out of Spain and saying, 'Hey, no problem. They can just go to France or Germany or, or Italy—"

"It's the countdown! It's the countdown!" someone cried.

"10—9—8—7—6—5—4—3—2—1—HAPPY NEW YEAR!"

Champagne popping, plastic horns tooting, hugs, kisses and another trip around the Sun. I withdrew from Uncle Dom and ushered in 2003 and my thirty-eighth year on this sad planet in the comforting arms of my wife.

"Happy Birthday, baby. Happy New Year," she said.

Behind me I heard Uncle Dom talking to a new group of less adversarial listeners.

"How do you like the nerve of those North Koreans, starting up all this crap with nukes? We're gonna have to start throwing our weight around. Iraq. Saudi Arabia. North Korea. Just take 'em all out, take the oil, and be done with it. You think we can't do it? We can do anything we fucking want."

# DUEL USE FOR THE WEIRD UNCLE SAM SOCIETY

I'm throwing down the gauntlet. I DEMAND satisfaction. I hereby challenge the Usurpers of the United States of America and their Military-Industrial-Corporate-Intelligence-Everything-But-The-Kitchen-Sink Complex to a duel. Yeah that's right, it's me against THEM. Mano a Many-o. I was waiting for some pissed off soul to be MAN enough or WOMAN enough to do it, but since nobody's volunteering for the job as of yet, might as well be chicken-hearted little me.

And don't go comparing me to that freak, McVeigh. Whatever points Gore Vidal made about his motives, he hit a "civilian" building full of workers and children. Another Bin Laden, trained to kill by THE MAN'S army. More Blowback. And we all know that what the wind blows back ain't hitting THE MAN, but WE THE PEOPLE and our kids. Fuck any cracker who thinks he's taking some kind of stand against THE MAN by blowing up our children. That's not what this is about at all. I'm calling for a genuine duel, fair and square. Me versus the Weird Uncle Sam Society (WUSS) and their Military, at ten paces—well, maybe twenty. Gunfight at the OK corral. The five trillion dollar death machine versus yours truly. No innocents involved. This is personal. This is BIG.

After all, except for September 11, 2001, nobody's openly challenged the Usurpers since WWII. And unlike Bin Laden, I'm not some chicken-shit, disgruntled, NIMBY, ex-CIA operative all bent outta shape cause THE MAN inevitably set up shop in my hometown.

He who sleeps with the CIA, gets raped by the CIA, eventually. And unlike Bin Laden, whatever his motives and if he even exists, I am not a fundamentalist terrorist sending rubes to hit a building full of civilians then heading for the hills to set up my own video-cult (let it be duly noted that there are at least one billion humans who practice Islam peacefully on this planet without getting the call to take out over-worked, underpaid office workers in the name of Allah). Why am I talking about Bin Laden? Fuck Bin Laden. Forget about—oh, that's right, they already did.

This ain't so much about BLOW BACK as TAKE BACK. Take back humanity from the WUSS garbed in the flag like gaunt, bleak, old Uncle Sam himself pointing his bony finger at WE THE PEOPLE cause he got his fool ass into another war and needs new crop of blockhead cannon fodder to close the deal.

Now if I remember right from Shakespeare and Nineteenth Century novels and 1950s Westerns, a free man, or a gentleman, could, in fact was obliged to, refuse to duel a slave, an underling, a pauper, a "savage," etc. This was THE MAN'S way of putting folks in their place. The only way to challenge THE MAN was to be one of HIS own. Well, I'm declaring myself, here and now, a free man. I challenge the WUSS and their whole damn army.

True, this might take some doing. For instance, in order for me to duel the entire Military Machine, the WUSS is going to have to call back all their soldiers from all the countries the U.S. has "a presence" in (I think there's about 80 or something, could be more). Well, call 'em home. Nobody's challenging them (the WTC massacre was a criminal act which should have been prosecuted in an international court, not Kabul) anywhere else. You see Saddam throwing down the gauntlet? Or North Korea? Or Chicken-little "bock, bock" Bin Laden himself (assuming he exists)?

I am offering to duel the entire WUSS military machine and every man in it, and I demand my challenge be taken seriously.

Again, this is probably a big deal. Lotta paperwork, troop movements, flight plans, coded messages, leaks to the press and all that. I'm calling out the whole damn crew—Army, Navy, Air force, Marines, CIA, NSA etc.—for this duel and it is my right to face every single one of my opponents. After all, I help pay their salaries. This means, at the set date and time (these things usually happen at dawn, eh? that sucks; really, I'm a night person to the core) the whole mega billion dollar behemoth is gonna have to meet me and my Second (his name's Lebowski; he's a good man; and thorough) to answer my call. This means pulling all those troops out of South Korea, Cuba, Saudi Arabia, Afghanistan and wherever the hell else they don't belong and sending them to do the job they're paid to do, which is defend the

WUSS against ME.

Another thing I noticed about those old duels they had way back when, before we got all civilized and discovered the safety and convenience of DEATH FROM ABOVE, is that those guys faced off over any stupid little thing imaginable. "You hittin' on MY woman? I choose, you, I call you out." "You sayin' my escutcheon's shorter than your escutcheon and has less real creme filling? Pistols at dawn!"

So what am I dueling mad about? Well, whatever it is, I'm sure the Media will twist it into the isolated ravings of a lone madman after the five trillion dollar military smokes my ass, but just for the record, it's no one thing, but a thousand. Let's say THE FUTURE. That's kind of a big thing. Not only has the WUSS failed to recognize the almost irreparable harm being done to the air, land and water of this planet due to fossil fuel consumption, but they're planning to send the military that WE THE PEOPLE paid for to commandeer yet more oil from foreign lands (incurring yet more Blow Back that the WUSS's stealth bombers ain't gonna protect anybody but themselves from) and poison humanity yet further.

More? The WUSS soiled my good name—no small matter for us duelists—for making me complicit in murder across the globe—South East Asia, Africa, South America, Central America, etc. etc.—because after all it's my tax money they're building cruise missiles with instead of schools. And when some pissed off native of another country turns terrorist and blows up innocent people in America, some of those innocent people will inevitably, one day, be my loved ones, and the WUSS could give two shits less about them, and that's enough of an excuse for me to challenge the whole damn Machine and all its evil works to an honest to goodness duel.

Oh, also, Anthony Gankarski ("Come Fly With Me," *Counterpunch*, 1/06/03) got hassled by tiny airport Rent-A-Nazis—as if the air on those flying subways wasn't bad enough! Why bother sniffing glue when you can just crawl into the tube? Then there's that teacher, John Borowski ("PepsiCo Kids," *Counterpunch*, 12/31/02), whose students, and goddamn it even his own daughters, were being poisoned by the PepsiCo empire until some teenage cheerleader said "Generation THIS!" and got her bottled water biz shut down by the "invisible hand," but Borowski spoke out like an ADULT—very inspiring, I thought.

I'm challenging the WUSS, for they usurped the lives, land, livelihoods and rights of WE THE PEOPLE so that we shall die and the artificial, immortal "people" that corporations are legally supposed to be can live.

Sure I'll get smoked in a nano-second, gimpy little me against that monstrous arsenal of nukes, bio weapons, chemical weapons, assorted death rays and tons and tons and tons of conventional ammo, but at least I'll die like a free human and not a yipping yapping dog. I would assume that since I helped pay for their arsenal the Usurpers will have the decency to provide me with a proper dueling pistol, but knowing them it'll be rigged to jam or the powder'll be damp with piss. But hell, I wasn't planning on shooting the damn thing anyway. All I want to do is throw it, just let me throw something at them and I'll die happy.

Yeah, I guess that's about right. I actually have no intention of shooting some poor kid who got gypped out of a decent public education so the WUSS could teach him to cherish his own liberty to be unemployed and illiterate and have nothing to do and no money to do it with but join the military and defend some other kid's liberty to receive a shitty education and eat a vegetarian meal of Ketchup and Pepsi in a dilapidated cafeteria. I just want a chance to face their commanders, that's all. Throw whatever antiquated weapon they'll supply me with—and charge me extra for—at the fat head of one of their West Point COs before they vaporize my sorry ass.

Call the boys home to where the real war is: against ME. No other challenger is calling the Emperor's legions to the field. It's me against the biggest, baddest, most expensive war machine the world has ever known! Bring your camera. It's a FREE MEDIA event. Hell, it should at least be as exciting as the Super bowl, and MUCH shorter. Also, your admission is pre-paid!

True, I'm quaking in my boots. But nothing's ever going to change until WE THE PEOPLE decide to Live Free or Die, and MEAN IT. And really, it's only one life out of billions. Others will come along—maybe. Anyway, I'd rather die now, a free human spitting the fattest, gooiest, throat-clam I can muster at the WUSS than live another minute as an ox-dumb extra in THE MAN's blockbuster war extravaganza against life.

**Adam Engel** might need a Second in case Lebowski backs out—he's a good man, and thorough, but unreliable. Anyone who would like to volunteer to perform the traditional duties of a duelist's Second can contact bartlebysamsa65@gmail.com

# ENOUGH IS TOO MUCH

Dead sheep shuffle. Do the dead sheep shuffle. Get in line. Waste your time.

Get yer gonads groped and your belongings touched by strangers' fingers.

Get shoved, get yelled at.

"No, you ASS, don't go down THAT line, I said THIS ONE HERE."

Reaction of the other sheep not, "Where do you get off telling this guy what to do?"

Reaction of other sheep was, "Where do you get off not following orders like you're supposed to do and getting on the wrong line and making it so much worse for the rest of us?"

Worst of all were the eyes. Not of the tormentors, but of the victims. Spaced out, happy, in a way, happy to have big strong adults 'armed men and women' tell them where to go and what to do, finally some structure in their pathetic lives.

Then again, what did I do? Did I scream "NO"? No. Did I shove my "weapon," a toenail-clipper, in the eye of the rent-a-Nazi who confiscated it? No. I'm as bad as you are. I don't deserve to live, at least not like a free adult.

Fort Lauderdale. Newark. Same thing. Get in line and beg to be let on the airplane you reserved a seat on months ago. The airplane you paid hundreds of dollars so you and your wife could sit in crowded rows with the rest of the cattle. The airplane owned by an airline that laughingly calls you a "valued customer" as their six-dollar-an-hour thugs search you from your stocking feet to your goofy American head.

And me with my hip-replacement! Bad luck. Sets off the beeper every time and it's:

"Step over here sir. Remove everything from your pockets sir. Hip replacement, eh sir? Right hip? Arms to the side and stretched out sir. Yeah, that's it, like you're on a cross, sir. What's this? Antacids, sir? Do you have a prescription for—oh, they're over-the-counter. My mistake, sir. Hmmn. Nothing else on you," re-inserting his wand into its holster. "Must be that hip replacement you was going on about. Okay, you're free to go sir. Yes, that line over there, sir. You're free to go over to that line there."

Yeah, yeah, I know: we don't have it as bad as the Iraqis, or the Palestinians, or the Afghans, or the Chinese.

But just as we pay airlines for the privilege of cattle-hood, we pay THE MAN to make life miserable all over the world. Our only consolation is that we're "free." That is, it's not as bad here as it is in other places THE MAN has devastated. As for China, well, they have their own MAN. But I give them credit for kicking OUR MAN on his fat ass in 1949. At least the woes of Chinese citizens are not our responsibility. Like, say the ridiculous condition of American "citizens" who'll walk straight to the gas chambers grinning self-righteously about how free they are. The Nazis would have loved a crowd like this. Would've saved them a bundle on soap and other "don't worry, it's all good" type props.

Yeah, yeah: It's not as bad here as it is in Columbia or Saudi Arabia or Guatemala, or wherever else THE MAN dips his sticky fingers. But it will be. It will be indeed.

So while the sheep are bahhing about the "dems" and the "repubs," THE MAN who controls both of those groups of bloated, pocket-stuffing windbags, THE MAN who controls most of the world with amazing violence and relentless pursuit of death and fear, is cooking up new ways to beat us down, to mold us into the pathetic model barnyard creatures of HIS psychotic vision.

"Moo," I say. I say, "Moo. Moo. Moo."

I'm disgusted with myself for paying for the privilege of being searched, manhandled, and more or less kidnapped as the plane waited on the runway while some flaccid representative of THE MAN outbid the airline for the flight lane. People have been killed for less. A whole lot less. If fact, THE MAN is killing and killing and killing people for doing little less than not being THE MAN.

Don't you think it's Time to stop whining and deluding ourselves into thinking we're not despicable, weak . . . barnyard animals for not doing what must be done to secure our individual liberty and basic human freedoms?

It was Time ten years ago, 20, 30. We didn't act then, why do we think we'll act now? Especially now, after a quarter a century of brainwashing with depth, breadth and intensity not seen since Stalin was still sleeping in a separate room every night and "The Manchurian Candidate" was a nightmarish "fiction" in the theaters.

We are indeed pathetic. But it's not too late to change. As long as we're clear about what we're talking about. One of us must go. THE MAN, or everyone else.

# THE FAT MAN IN LITTLE BOY

Let's talk about the night The Fat MAN raped you. How old were you, seven, eight, nine? I was eight, I think.

"KABOOM!" the Fat MAN screamed.

"What? What?"

"Only kidding," laughed The Fat MAN, stroking HIS Bomb. "Go back to sleep."

"Jesus Christ. How the Hell'm I suppose to sleep NOW?"

"Relax. If I had really let this sucker go you'd be part of the rug by now. A little Rorschach blot of goo."

"A what?"

"Anyway, I promise to wake you when I come for real."

"Oh. . .well. . . "

"Sissy-pants," clucked The Fat MAN. "You wouldn't want to sleep through our Big Night, would you? Wanna be a little boy all your life?"

"To tell you the truth—"

"Good night, sweet-pea," whispered The Fat MAN. "I love you. Now turn over. That's right. Show your tender side to ME."

Such was my deflowering. I'm sure you have stories of your own. Yeah, it sucks to be buggered by the Fat MAN with his giant, steely Bomb. It hurts real bad. And once you're fucked by the fat man you stay fucked—forever.

But don't be ashamed. It's not an act of sex, but of benevolent violence. Cultural initiation, etc. You won't come to terms with your inner Fat MAN until you admit the truth. Nothing to be ashamed of.

We've all been through it. To deny it would be un-American. We might try something crazy, like exorcize the Fat Man and his bomb from our psyches and make ourselves selves instead of reproductions of HIM. Then we'd REALLY know the meaning of "terror." Nope. HE'S jammed that big old Bomb of His inside us all. The Fat MAN thinks with HIS warhead. HE can't help himself. Deep, deep, way deep inside forever and always, keeping us safe from, you know, The Other.

Of course, innocent that you were, you went to teacher the next morning. How could you have known what unspeakable things the Fat MAN did to HER? You listened, respectfully, as she explained how The Bomb, that hard, cold thing that ruptured what was clean in you the night before, saved millions of lives simply by slaughtering a few hundred thousand.

Too young, too INNOCENT, weren't you, to imagine the enormity of 20,000 some-odd humans vaporized instantly and another hundred thousand or so to die horrible deaths, or worse, live on as ghosts with the Fat MAN'S spunk like acid in their cells? Too young to think about how many people were in the process of being murdered brutally for a few yen that morning of August 6, 1945 (Bomb to the rescue); how many raped; how many making love; stealing; eating breakfast; going to work; or simply taking a crap while reading an old newspaper like good old life-loving Leopold Bloom, when they were abruptly delivered from sinful mortality, the myriad deceptions of the flesh.

Of course, you were further instructed in the ways of the Fat MAN by old photos of the A-Bomb fireball and mushroom cloud in black and white—so passé. The H-Bomb was always in color when you opened your sacred American History text to Eisenhower or later. Its hellish orange sucked all light and color from the room. You and your classmates stared in darkness, the same darkness in which you were all, yes even cute little Jack or Jill or whomever you had such a sweet, child crush on, felt the Bomb between his tight, butt cheeks, her raw, bald vulva. Even they were taken by the Fat MAN, who whispered, "Love me, love me," to them too. Don't feel cheap, used. Nobody's special in HIS eyes. We're all part of a team. One Nation under HIM.

If you were lucky, Rod Serling helped you through your temporary confusion, so confident in his black suit and tie and holding his cigarette, leaving Burgess Meredith alone with broken glasses, a smoldering world, and piles and piles of obviated tomes...

Anyway they, the worthless Jap citizens of Hiroshima and Nagasaki—they were the ENEMY, weren't they? They DID, every single one of them, bomb Pearl Harbor, no?—by accepting the cleansing fire of The Bomb, saved millions of lives, or whatever Harry

Truman and Friends said, so fuck 'em. They're martyrs and they or their surviving friends and family should be proud, damn proud, of all that they sacrificed for peace on earth.

Well, now you have children of your own to offer to The Fat MAN. Don't bother locking their doors or barring their windows—you can't save them from THIS Midnight Rambler. They're HIS, or will be. Why do you think HE let you reproduce?

It's perfectly natural. The way of things. You're not a tax-evader, are you? You paid for HIS salary and benefits, his golden parachute and steely Bomb, didn't you? Might as well let the little tykes enjoy the experience of offering themselves (actually, you offered them) to the Fat MAN.

If you're lucky they'll accept HIM willingly and without unnecessary complications, won't reject him with (yuck, yuck) free-radicals or anti-bodies or some such genetic anomaly. They'll become like unto HIM and conform unto HIS needs, which, of course, serve the greater good.

If all goes well, they'll embrace HIM, eventually, just like you did. Maybe there'll even be schools you can afford and jobs that they can get (not work, jobs; there hasn't been much real work in this country for decades; think about it: what do YOU do?).

If all else fails, there's always this MAN's army...

Give them to the Fat MAN and his... uh... missile... like your parents gave you. Be at peace. Let go. It's inevitable. Really. For all you know, HE'S already deflowered them. Plunged HIS Bomb deep. Real deep. And for all you know, they liked it (kids today aren't nearly as innocent as we were).

HIS seed is inside them now, waiting to bloom.

# FLAG IN THE RAIN

Bored white corpuscles, the wife and I alternately crept and cruised the clogged arteries of Empire on our way to some godforsaken suburb to visit reactionary relatives in the rain.

We passed depressing god awful towns. Same supermarkets, drugstores, fast-food, Starbucks, Gap, Barnes and Noble what-have-you (just like NYC!). Hundreds upon hundreds of flags in every neighborhood, lining every Main Street and pocking every block. You could tell the truly lower and working class neighborhoods cause the flags had yellow ribbons on them, which meant the kids were off from school that day, out fighting for—what else?—The Flag.

On the highway we played "count-the-flag:" Old Glory waved from both domestic and imported cars. Soggy cloth and nylon flapped like rat-tails in the rain.

And of course, the bumper stickers and decals: "Proud To Be American United We Stand Remember 9/11 and The Alamo Valley of Heroes No Smoking Please Sit Down Chew Your Food Forty Times Don't Interrupt Me When I'm Speaking..."

"Why you wanna wear Daddy's clothes?" I screamed out the window at everyone, at no one. "Look at you dressing in THE MAN'S clothes pretending you're Big Daddy!"

We pulled into a Shop-Rite parking lot in one of the wealthier towns—no yellow ribbons on the flags—and parked beside this shiny Jeep-type vehicle, looked like a Brink's truck. But my wife said it was an SUV.

"Americans gotta find some way to blow gas," she said. "Twenty-five years ago it was the Cadillac. Today it's the SUV—hey, look at that, that's illegal!"

"What, the big ugly gas guzzler or the 'United We Stand' bumper sticker on its fender?"

"No, no, the flag in the rain," she said.

"We've seen about two thousand—"

"But look at the shape it's in," she said. "It's a mess."

Soaked and tattered; faded and fringed. I wouldn't wipe my ass with the rag on that SUV.

"Oh yeah. I remember. Something about not letting Old Glory hit the ground or get spit on and stuff."

Years ago, in the Age of the Cadillac, the Cub Scouts taught me the only proper way to dispose of a flag was to fold it neatly and burn it, yet here this guy had this REDWHITEandBLUE shmateh rotting away on his big brassy truck or sports van or whatever the salesmen told him it was supposed to be.

My wife ran in to pick up a cake for our hosts. I wasn't alone more than a few minutes before Flagman walks up to the SUV, keys in hand, and damned if he's not wearing a stars-and-stripes cardigan. Now, why was Abbie Hoffman considered a yippee yappy yahoo radical for wearing a hand-made flag-shirt while this guy's considered. . .uh. . . "normal," in a super-patriotic way, for sporting an off-the-rack Betsy Ross cardigan?

"Hey man, that's illegal," I said.

"Excuse me?" said Flagman, obviously anxious to get outta the rain lest he shrink his sweater.

"You're mistreating that flag. Abusing it, in fact. It's illegal."

"My. . .my flag?"

"Sure," I said. "Can't let Old Glory fade out like an old hippy bandana. I mean, I'm not gonna report you, but. . ."

"Report me? To who?"

"You know. TIPS. The flag codicil of the USA PATRIOT act. Don't tell me you don't know?"

"No, I. . ."

"Anyway, ignorance of the law is no excuse. . ."

"Flag," he said, as if appealing to some star-spangled deity.

"Again, I'm not the type to squeal on a guy who's basically, I mean who appears to be patriotic, but some folks don't take kindly to flag abuse. Also, there's the type who'll do anything for money. . ."

"Money?"

"Yeah. The TIPS people pay about fifty dollars for confirmed reports of abuse. All someone has to do is call the HOTLINE and. . ."

"Whoa. I don't want trouble. Look, man, I'll get rid of it as soon as

I get home."

"What do you mean, 'get rid of it?' You can't just throw away Old Glory like a piece of cloth. You have to burn it."

"Burn it? Ain't that illegal?"

"Yeah. Go figure. But it's also the only legal way to dispose of it. You can look it up if you don't believe me. One of those Catch-22 deals."

"No, it's just that. . .look at it. It's soaked."

"Yeah. That's a problem with keeping a flag in the rain. Well, it's against regulations, probably, though I'm not sure, but you may want to blow dry it first, then fold it neatly and light her up."

"Jesus Christ. Okay, man. Thanks. I gotta go."

And with a chugga chugga zoom and toxic fumes, the flag burner sped off.

**Adam Engel** was thrown out of the Cub Scouts for flag-burning, though he swears he was performing a mercy burning on a tattered remnant of Old Glory and not desecrating a virile, vigorous banner in its patriotic prime. Anyone up for a game of "count-the-flag" can reach him at bartlebysamsa65@gmail.com [illegible] better?"

"What do you mean, 'get rid of it?' You can't just throw it away [illegible] like a piece of cloth. You have to burn it."

"Burn it? Aren't that illegal?"

"Yeah, [illegible]. [illegible] also the only [illegible] way to dispose of it. You can look it up if you don't believe me. One of those Dutch [illegible] [illegible]."

"No, it's [illegible] just [illegible] [illegible]," [illegible] [illegible].

"[illegible]. That's a problem with [illegible]," [illegible]. "Well, it's [illegible] [illegible] [illegible] [illegible] [illegible]."

"[illegible]. Okay, [illegible]. [illegible]."

[illegible]

# FORGETTING BIN LADEN

What cowards! I've never seen anything like it. Send in the Marines to bomb 'em—or what's left of 'em from '91—back to the stone-age. Bomb a city that was erected thousands of years ago and has endured countless Saddams, but only one U.S. of A. Bomb the hospitals where children receive aspirin for cancer—if they're lucky—and old men, who'd be candidates for quadruple by-pass in New York, might have their hearts massaged before they stop. "Dual use" nitro-glycerin pills, balm to hearts in pain, became, under sanction, or perhaps just bad translation, "bombs on the heartland's planes." Blast the widows hanging laundry. Smoke the lanky shepherds' goats.

But of course, we weep like the sky is falling when the sky is falling. When death comes from above—to us; when our towers fall and our thousands die, and centuries-old New York staggers to its feet, bewildered, front teeth shattered, and cries for "Justice," which the President, heretofore branded with a scarlet asterisk (due to his questionable ascent to power), interprets as "Vendetta!"

The asterisk mysteriously fell off Dubya's letter cardigan and he grew bold. He even visited New York for a day and led the cheers for "U-S-A! U-S-A!" As if it were 1980 again and the Russians were still worth beating, or better yet, our alleged ex-boozer and failed CEO was the star of the show this time, first-string Quarterback and not the sideline cheerleader he'd been at Yale. Once it grew dark, of course, he high-tailed it out of town, our Ground Zero Groupie, while his on-camera pals, the workers, went on with the wretched task of cleaning up what remained of the Pylons that once graced greeting-cards from here to Timbuktu. Oh, and pulling fleshy matter from tangles of debris—they did that too.

Well, Bush Inc. certainly showed those Afghans. Those Tally Bans. The nerve of them dressing up women like lampshades and letting Hitler hide out in fortified luxury caves à la Fred Flintstone! The Evildoers must be dead by now, after all those booby-trap snack-packs dropped from heaven like care packages from the Sumerian Sky God himself (Hey, wasn't Iraq in Sumeria or near Sumeria, or thereabouts? Oh, never mind).

But maybe the Evil Doers survived. It's hard to tell with so many body parts scattered about like. . .body parts (shades of Ground Zero, no?) and all those weddings and Bar Mitzvahs and what have you. What did they expect, firing rifles in the air, like Appalachian mountain-folk, like bumpkins? Take somebody's eye out with one of those things. Imagine Brave Pilot Johnson coming home with a glass eye, or no eyes. I've Zero Tolerance for casualties—on our side—though it's embarrassing sometimes, these shooting-fish-in-a-barrel wars. Death from above. Way, way above.

Anyway it won't be like that with our old, nemesis, Saddam, and the Iraqis, fighting for their very lives. Of course we'll have to soften 'em with air mail. True, Baghdad stood for millennia, and they even mentioned it on "I Dream of Genie"—more than once, in fact—it was that famous, but don't you worry, we'll grind it fine as Espresso roast before we dare send in our boys. . .

But again, you never know with these terror types. You don't know where they'll hide or what weasel hole they'll pop out of and BLAM! Like Viet Cong (remember them?) . . .

But that was many men on the moon ago. Things changed. We have the technology. We can make them better than they were. Better, whiter, more democratic. After we blast their brains all over the Gulf and wicked old Saddam screams "Uncle Sam!" in Arabic, just like we did with that other guy, the guy who looked like Charlie Manson. The guy who murdered thousands of innocents, September 11, 2001. . .

Wow, it seems like another life ago, with all that's happened on the News this year. A lot of oil under the bridge, and in and out of Enron. We've been laden with too much info-data and detail, I think. Because, not only don't I remember the giant, bearded Evil-doer, captured and in chains, screaming "Uncle Sam!" in Arabic, I hardly remember him at all.

I don't even recall his name.

**Adam Engel** writes and lives in NYC. His most recent and engaging project was providing editorial consultation for the book, She Comes First: A Grammar of Oral Sex, by Ian Kerner. He supports a war on terror because fear is a bad thing and should be eliminated, so long as nobody gets hurt in the process. He can be reached at bartlebysamsa65@gmail.com

# GALLIPOLI FOR DUMMIES

Hello, Boobus Americanus. It's been almost two years since we last spoke. You've gotten yourself into all sorts of mischief since then. War, environmental meltdown, economic distress. You're a mess. All because you follow THE MAN, even though THE MAN, in HIS current incarnation, is a coterie of fanatics, Chicken Hawks, religious zealots, liars, dual-loyalists and outright traitors.

The first order of business really should be that $400 Billion of YOUR tax money HE and his Congressional YESMEN are spending on a military that exists not to defend your home, but attack HIS enemies. In this case, all those nukes, at least 5,000 stored away complete with missiles to deliver them, might serve you well. For a couple of billion dollars, keep 'em oiled and shiny and ready to launch and I guarantee you no one—except those pesky terrorists—would bother to attack you. If you pulled your $400 Billion military out of all the places in the world it shouldn't be and stopped giving away military "gift packages" to countries like Israel and Colombia, you might even find that even the terrorists wouldn't bother you. Then all you'd need is a coast guard and the organized militias they talk about in the Constitution.

Plenty of guns in America , and plenty of folks who know how to use them. No, I don't think you'd have to worry about enemies at least for a couple of years if you just kept up your mega-death arsenal strictly for security purposes and stayed the hell out of other peoples' business. But that's beyond your comprehension, your development, which stopped at the fifth grade or so. America is GOOD and it needs all that dough to do GOOD DEEDS in the world like blow up foreign citizens to liberate them from their own evil dictators. Of course they'd rather be blown to bits by us than live under repression, as we define it. That goes without saying.

Well, no matter. The fact that $400 billion dollars spent on health care, education, alternative energy sources, environmental cleanup, public transportation, or just GIVEN BACK to the taxpayers Uncle Sam stole it from would go a long way to solving many of our problems at home is irrelevant. We have no say in the matter. THE MAN wants what HE wants and what HE wants is your tax money to build his mighty military. You don't think HE'D pay for it HIMSELF do you? (Though according to Kevin Phillips' Wealth and Democracy, HE might actually have the means.)

Okay, let's pretend that whole "support our troops" mantra is not a cynical ploy to get Boobus Americanus to shut up while THE MAN sends American "boys and girls" to invade and occupy foreign countries. Let's pretend these troops are protecting the East Coast from an imminent attack from the combined forces of Iceland and Greenland , while simultaneously others are sent to defend the West Coast from that Rogue State Aggressor, Tahiti.

Why are veterans losing benefits? Why are troops unfortunate enough to be wounded in action losing combat pay and money sent to their families? Why on earth is the "mightiest military in history" so lacking in "support" for its own troops that families and friends of those troops have to pitch in to buy the proper body armor? Is this 21st Century America or 15th century Poland ? $400 billion dollars and the troops aren't even supplied with the "best gear" to do the job (of defending the "Homeland" from two-pronged invasion from Tahiti on the West and the Greenland-Iceland Axis on the East).

Well, to be honest, I don't know much about military history, other than that Sherman invented the modern slash and burn style of warfare (glamorized in the burning of Atlanta scene from "Gone with the Wind") and that Napoleon had a teeny, tiny little dinky, which might, had psychoanalysis been around in his day, have explained a lot of things.

But I do know that an ill-equipped army is called "rag-tag." Now, some rag-tag armies have done remarkable things, because the soldiers believed in the cause they were fighting for, namely, their home, friends, family and freedom. Washington's men had no shoes at Valley Forge , and the Spartans were massively outnumbered by Persians at Thermopylae. And I'm sure if our troops really were protecting us from a two-front war with Tahiti on the West and the Greenland-Iceland axis on the East, they'd be as motivated as any team, real or imagined, Knute Rockne put on the field for Notre Dame, ready to win one for "The Gipper," whether in flack jackets or pajamas.

But in reality, THE MAN sent "our troops" to invade two foreign countries, Afghanistan and Iraq, for no discernible purpose other than to secure oil, military bases and other corporate/government goodies that have nothing to do with the safety of mom and her frozen apple pie (to be defrosted, nuked, and lathered with canned whip cream when "Johnny and Janey" come marching home again, hurrah).

$400 billion plus extra for the Iraq scam—including no-bid contracts for Halliburton and other BuschCo sponsors—and people must literally support our troops with store-bought equipment? How can THE MAN get away with that without sparking a mass rebellion? Even Hitler and Stalin spared no expense when it came to the sacred cow of the military.

I'll tell you, Boobus, if you don't already know—I know you're kind of slow on the uptake. THEY, THE MAN, the ones who control you and your momma and yer little dog too, know that all they have to do is wave a flag, play a brassy Souza tune, and accuse you of being "unpatriotic" and you'll let them get away with murder. Not merely murdering sub-human foreigners, but your own sons and daughters.

But something happened last week, something extraordinary. An entire platoon said NO. Threatened with imminent extinction because, according to them, the blessed military higher ups were going to send them to battle in old, shoddy vehicles, they refused to be suckers. YOU supported our troops when they bombed Baghdad to bits, and you supported them when they raped prisoners in Abu Ghraib. Will you support these troops who refused to be sent naked to battle? Remember that movie 'Gallipoli,' starring Mel "Jesus and me are Mishbucha" Gibson, when Australian troops were fighting a battle that had nothing to do with protecting Australia but everything to do with protecting British interests during WWI? They were out-manned and out-gunned by the Turks—again, what argument could they have possibly had with Turkey ? Ever look at the proximity of the two countries on a map? But because of the arrogance of their British superiors, who knew the situation but would rather Australians die en masse than allow the Empire to be humiliated by mere Turks, sent them into a wall of machine gun fire, and like obedient little Boobus Australiani, they went (except for Mel, who asked himself, "What would Jesus do?" in such a situation and hence survived to fight more worthwhile battles against drug dealers on the streets of L.A. and British Imperialists in Scotland.

This platoon that said "No" was not composed of lefty academics or pesky "liberal" journalists. Most of them, from what I've read, were "plain folks" from down south where, I'm told, they take the military and their roles in it quite seriously. An entire platoon. Not one "chicken hawk" or a clique of shirkers, but an entire platoon of seventeen soldiers decided to face arrest rather than die needlessly because THE MAN doesn't support our troops.

I'm not sure what this means, Boobus, but I know it's something, something big. How can we the people support our troops if the $400+ Billion army can't—or won't? Well, as I said, my knowledge of military history boils down to Sherman's marauders and the size of Napoleon's pizzle. But this one, this renegade platoon thing, sure is a thinker.

Why don't YOU figure it out.

# THE WORST WRITERS IN THE WORLD, OR THE WORST READERS?

How low are the media prepared to sink in order to perpetuate the fiction that "the War in Iraq" is anything but an unprovoked slaughter and absolute betrayal of "our" troops?

I came across this piece written by a man named David Brooks who pretends to write opinions worth paying for in an overpriced, over-sized "newspaper" whose tacit, if unwritten, motto, "all the news we're not afraid to print" would be the only item worth reading in that rag (besides the outright commercial copy which is at least HONESTLY trying to convince you to buy something), if only they weren't so damn AFRAID to print it.

Thus, dear reader, I present to you what is, IN MY OPINION, the sloppiest, most ham-fisted, graceless piece of propaganda pretending to be journalism that I have ever encountered. The unmitigated arrogance in trying to palm this off as something important enough to be printed as an editorial in "the paper of record" is worth the price of the ad-packed sheaf of staid, white-collar Americana alone.

From what I gathered, between guffaws, this David Brooks was trying to defend the BushCo position in Iraq, so maybe he was just testing out some kind of quantum theory of ballyhoo and mishegas, see if the Heisenberg principle might be squeezed for a 700-word mainstream fluff column.

A lie either glitters like gold or smells like a turd, but it can't both glitter and stink at the same time, and whether it glitters or stinks of course depends upon the position of the observer and the instruments used in the experiment (in this case a word-processor, I assume, running a Microsoft product).

Anyway, get this:

> So an Iraqi-U.S. military offensive took back Samarra, and Rumsfeld said yesterday that Samarra is a model for what is about to happen in other towns in Iraq.
>
> I asked Rumsfeld yesterday how decisions like the one to take back Samarra are made. Are Iraqis like Allawi really deciding when and where Americans fight?
>
> He described a decision-making process that has no formal structure, but involves constant consultations, involving State Department types like Ambassador John Negroponte, military types like Gen. George Casey and Lt. Gen. Thomas Metz, and a raft of Iraqi officials. It also involves the big Washington honchos like Powell, Rumsfeld and Bush.
>
> It was clear from our conversation (and from the way other administration officials talk about decision-making in Iraq) that the charge that Allawi is a puppet is just absurd. Allawi has the best feel for which Iraqi community or faction has to be catered to on any given day, and how best to reach over and get some Sunni support for the government. Moreover, Rumsfeld says the goal is to give Iraqis the room to make their own decisions: 'The worst thing we can do is smother them.'
>
> David Brooks, *NY Times*, "Quickening the Tempo in Iraq" (October 5, 2004)

So, according to this Brooks character, and I assume, the *NY Times*, real investigative reporting is a lot tougher than it looks. There's only one way to get the truth out of an administration under siege: ask them.

"Gee, Mr. President," said young Bob Woodward so many years ago, "I've heard there's been all sorts of immoral goings on over at the Watergate Hotel. Is this true?"

"No. Not at all. If anyone in my administration were to disobey the law, why, I'd take them out to my Father's woodshed and learn 'em to respect the Constitution," said Tricky Dick.

"Gosh, thanks, Mr. President! This would have been an awful mess if you hadn't cleared it all up. I'll go to the office right now and straighten Bradley, Bernstein and the boys out with THE TRUTH!" said a reinvigorated Woodward.

Honestly, I find it unbelievable that even the Times would stoop this low. What's going on? Some kind of collective entropy? Has the mainstream media gone completely over to the forces of darkness? Or do they think we're so punchy by now, what with the relentless flurry of lies, big lies and bigger lies, that we won't know the difference? After all, they told us Bush was "appointed" president; they told us the root of evil lay in Afghanistan, then Iraq, while buttoning their lips to the impossible outrage that there is yet to be a public investigation of the events of 9/11 etc., etc., etc.

Why SHOULD this Brooks guy bother to do anything more than ASK the Wolf if he gobbled up Little Red Riding Hood and her granny? What if the Wolf said, "Yeah, I tore 'em both apart and it was a bloody mess. What are YOU gonna do about it?" What WOULD we do about it? I suppose we should thank "journalists" like David Brooks for sparing us the humiliation of our own desuetude.

# GRAVITY'S ENDZONE: FAN MAIL FROM PYNCHON

I'm bad. Bad to the bone-marrow. B-b-b-bad.

Nevertheless—and how's this for "Un-American" sour grapes?—THE MAN is so deep inside my head I can't even croak-out without melodrama, without conjuring up some fantasy scene outta one of HIS TV shows. True, I haven't watched television regularly since I was about fifteen, but those first fifteen are formative years. While Europeans my age were learning languages and culture, there I was—and I sure wasn't alone—watching "Three's Company" and "Happy Days" so now I can't even check out with dignity. My head's full of sentimental romantic fascist crap. It's an insult to humanity, a fart in the face of life itself. Enough to drive a man mad. For instance, I'm thinking (well, maybe not exactly) wild west shoot 'em-up war movie, I'm the hero saves the day, sleeps with all three Andrews Sisters, rolls mean old Mr. Potter off a cliff, smiles and waves for the camera for viewers of the FUTURE (uh... that's probably you) ...but possibly me and those women from that "Friends" show up all night talking about life and love and sex and death and whatever minor plot twists they typically cram into a twenty-minute episode and I won't have sex with any of them we'll decide we're too vulnerable or some shit like that and it would ruin our friendship or god knows what perversities they indulge in—really, I've seen snatches (heh, heh) of that sit-glum while passing in and out of television blue-lit rooms: their spiel is sicker than de Sade's, who at least wrote about HUMAN stuff or I hit the game-winning HOME RUN match set love (or whatever they do in tennis) forty yard serpentine rush to the end zone TOUCHDOWN but really more like (Zee Plane! Zee Plane!)

Thomas Pynchon reads *Counterpunch.* Why not? If he's gonna read anything, it'd be CP, eh? So Pynchon writes to me:

"Really dig your stuff. Keep cool, but care.

Best,

Tommy Boy"

And for a moment I believe it. It's like when some guy offered the Beatles $50 million to reunite for one concert tour or something like that when I was fourteen, or when I went to visit Keats' house on my first and only trip to England. Only, the Beatles didn't get back together, and Keats' house was "closed for renovation we regret any inconvenience," and that's the way it goes. Then again, there was that one Sunday in the early 70's when Charles M. Schultz accidentally put a real phone number in one of Lucy's cartoon bubbles and millions of readers flooded the lines—"Hello, is Lucy there, what about Linus?"—and the flesh-and-blood people who actually "possessed" that seven digit code had their phones ring-ringing off the walls all day, and when they answered there was a nano-second pause on the other end, a pause of, I don't know, hope maybe? That maybe, maybe, this could be, like, real? But nothing in America is real, is it? Yeah, yeah, I know: Death and Taxes. Fuck 'em both.

So I get this email from <Kenosha.Kid@blicero.gov> and after I get over that cocaine rush of hope and excitement I fall deep into cocaine blues. Dark moon reality cold-cocks me upside the head.

I write back,

"Whoever you are, thanks for the lift. But, as Nancy said, "Say No to Drugs." Too old—really—to deal with this kind of game. I'm sure the real TP would appreciate the humor."

Then he writes back,

"No, really, really. I AM Thomas Pynchon."

And since I happen to know a guy who not only knows TP's wife, but worked on some kind of digital literacy program where TP's kid went to grade school, I write back,

"If you're Tom Pynchon, ask your wife, or your son, who Kevin Kanarek is."

And he write back and tells me. Not only that, he invites me to lunch.

"A-and bring Kevin along too, if you want," he adds.

The fantasy progresses to me and Tom becoming pals. He encourages me to work on a book and gets me an advance and I go into remission just long enough to write the book, and Pynchon and Don Delillo and Ishmael Reed and Robert Coover write rave reviews, and it sells, and I have some money to leave behind for my wife and dog and a legacy for the readers of "The Imperator," the Jericho Senior High School year book, 1983 (why do I still want to impress those people?).

Yeah, well. Back on earth...

I actually was a celebrity a couple of weeks ago, when I went to the National Institutes of Health (NIH), in Bethesda, Maryland, just outside D.C. Not only had I actually lived to the ripe old age of 38 (so far) with Diamond-Blackfan Anemia, but in 1966 or so, the infant Adam Engel was actually one of the first to receive and respond to the Prednisone treatment by THE Dr. Diamond himself. Needless to say, the NIH wants me to undergo some of their test treatments (they call them "Protocols") with nasty drugs—For FREE!—so if one of them does the trick the government can give it away to some drug company that will charge me two billion dollars to use the "treatment" if I'm still alive two years from now. Just call me Slothrop. And don't call the NIH at all.

But why this need for the game-winning home-run? The Super bowl-winning touchdown and spike in the End Zone, all cameras on me? I thought I would have grown out of it by now. No, that's a lie. I thought I would have done something of, for lack of a better word, VALUE, by now, and that thing, a book or something, would have allowed me to grow beyond the tired sports metaphor and die in peace.

But Americans never die in peace. Most of them, at any rate. They're too burdened with all the shit they were told they were supposed to do but never did and probably never could. They're too guilty, too ashamed to die.

Like in that book, A Fan's Notes, by Frederick Exley. Guy can't live his life cause he's not Frank Gifford. Never gonna make that game-winning touch-down for the New York Giants his father so adored. No spike and dance in the End Zone. Just booze, cigarettes, anxiety, depression, roast beef, meaningless labor, death. Like Daddy.

So it was Daddy's fault all along! Then again, who's Daddy, usually, but another incarnation of THE MAN? A mannequin with tapes in his head. DVDs, now. Microchips. Daddy gone digital.

Terrible, but true: most people you meet, particularly in a "professional" capacity, are recorders, digitized to interface in real time, albeit somewhat limited by the unfortunate sloppiness of wet-ware. Meat-puppets fronting for THE MAN. Here's a fun experiment: watch a night of TV News, if you can stand it, then go around asking people, particularly "professionals" in suits, official-looking coats, arm-bands, uniforms, funny hats etc., what they think "about stuff." You'll get minor variations on what you heard and saw the night before. Maybe a harsh opinion or two added courtesy the NY POST or

Rush Limbaugh or Bill O'Reilly or whoever. Like that kid's game, "Telephone."

After all, it was THE MAN, or his white-coated representatives, who condemned me to death. Tell you the truth, I don't feel THAT bad. They tried the same thing with Pynchon's Tyrone Slothrop, but he escaped, sort of. Why not me? Is it not my right as a "free American citizen" to skeedaddle when the Reaper (or THE MAN) comes a knock, knock, knockin on my door? Not by the hair of my chinny chin chin, I say. Go away. Piss off. Die, Death, and yer little MAN too.

Okay. It's settled, then. "I'll die on my own time," as my friend, Paul, said to THE MAN's white-coated toadies when given a similar prognosis almost a decade ago.

Now, it's one thing to cheat Death, but THE MAN is a bit more wily and cruel. How to escape the corny, mawkish scenes THE MAN put in my head, the sentimentality and illusions? Don't think they're harmless fun, those corny greeting cards and clichés. Out of such cerebral dysentery patriots, Liberals and talk-show hosts are made. False feeling. The soap operas and sticky sweet flash-backs (often of experiences you've never actually had) the MAN and his Media slather all over your brain like Aunt Jemima's plastic pancake syrup. Looka dat nice smiling auntie Jemima (a bit updated: thinner, especially the nose and lips; capped teeth; cleaner kerchief; lighter hue) jest so happy to be cooking home style Frankenfood for THE MAN, pouring his sticky brown maple-flavored lab-fresh chemo-spunk all over your frozen waffles.

That's the real sickness anyway... all the rest is just biology.

**Adam Engel** can be reached at bartlebysamsa65@gmail.com. But Death be not SPAM. He has your IP number, Death, so don't try any of those cute aliases like light@tunnel.org or gotcha@butterfly.net It's "Block Sender," all the way, dig? Anything You send gets the bum's rush straight to Engel's "Delete" file.

# THE GREAT AMERICAN WRITING CONTEST

People, especially Bored College Professors and Golf Pros, say Literature is dead, that Americans are too illiterate and hypnotized by mass media to create great poetry and prose. Here is YOUR chance to prove them wrong, and win big $$$, by entering the PEN GREAT AMERICAN WRITING CONTEST. Note: This contest is not sponsored by *Counterpunch* or any other publication. All prize $$$ comes straight from the abysmal coffers of Patriots, Entrepreneurs and Nationalists (PEN).

So, got your pencils sharpened? Your Microsoft WORD updated, licensed and ready to roll?

Let's go Grapho-MANIAC!

**PART ONE: THE BEGINNING OF HISTORY**

CHOOSE ONE OF THE THREE STARTER-PARAGRAPHS BELOW AND COMPLETE. MAXIMUM 3000 WORDS.

A) ALL ABOUT SHERMAN

Sherman's march of flame and slaughter. Sherman's slash and burn. Sherman's big cigar. Sherman ruthless. "War is Hell." Sherman, Grant's right arm. Grant and Sherman and their big glowing cigars. March through cities leave a trail of ashes. Sherman's receding hairline. Scraggly beard. Lean, tough man. Sherman inventing modern warfare. Scorched earth. Prometheus gave man fire and Sherman smeared it all over Atlanta. Lincoln in Washington waited. Stanton waited. They waited for Grant and Sherman. They waited for it all to finish. Lincoln gangly and obscenely tall. Warm hearted storyteller. Stanton squat and cold. Abrupt. Means business. These men had work to do. Grant and Sherman in their muddy uniforms. Lincoln and Stanton in their musty suits. Orchestrating slaughter to preserve the Union. Now we are living in the union they preserved. No such men as Lincoln and Stanton. No such men as Grant and Sherman. Or so we think, as we tell ourselves "We don't need 'em. We don't want 'em." Once, the Yankees beat the Braves in four straight games. The burning of Atlanta. Who must we burn now?

B) FIRST COMPLEX

We dropped nuclear weapons on Hiroshima and Nagasaki and damned if we'll apologize because they started it by bombing our war ships at Pearl Harbor sneaky bastards and anyway something about saving a million lives if we had to invade Japan even though we'd already firebombed Tokyo and fifty other major cities to ash and cinder and only five years after the greatest generation fought the war to end all wars We went into Korea to save the South from the North or both from China or something I mean look at us we were coming apart at the seams communists everywhere thank god for Patriots like Ronald Reagan and Elia Kazan for standing up to HUAC and ratting out their friends, spilling their guts like Jabba the Hut on ipecac for the good of democracy, for us, for WE the people We loved Elvis but were somewhat concerned about his influences and rock n' roll in general because it was bringing elements of black culture into our teenagers' lives and we hadn't told them black people exist yet (except for the maids, bus drivers, dishwashers etc. who made life more convenient). We liked Ike, despite his rather unfortunate relationship with the Dulles brothers and the CIA. Then again, we didn't know exactly what the CIA was doing then, so why would we expect Ike and the CIA not to be protecting OUR interests against communism by offering a square deal to any piss ant country who should have welcomed U.S. Corporate military complex with open arms. After all, better to be exploited by genial US than dour THEM. But the old guy went batty on the way out and mumbled something industrial and corporate and so complex only the military could comprehend...

C) THE BIG FEAR

The big fear. Discussed since we were kids. Peering through the shutter slats. Waiting for the bombs to fall. But it won't be bombs we don't think, now, discussing the big fear for the nth time before the television. What then? Collapse. The Big Collapse. Of the system, the network, the order of things. Retro-Mind. Anti-psychotic Paranoid Narcosis. Death squads. The man at the end of the hallway has a gun. Sudden collapse, or gradually. Words cannot describe what words cannot. The drug just might work. Side effects? Acquiescence. So what? Cows seem relatively happy. Content. Not overly concerned. Until they herd them to the slaughterhouse. Bad scene. Moo moo mooing for their lives. Is that the core of the Big Fear? Not long sleep of Oblivion, but anguished moment of awareness that precedes the blow? Old hat. But really too big to be cliché. There will be a point when time runs out. No mercy then. The pain might be minor, or it might be bigger than all the life you've ever lived, that is, a concentrate of feeling, mostly negative. The fear, the node of all emotions past. Insatiable Future. Irrevocable Now. Crouched before the television, confronting the Big Fear. Death Alive. Pay Per View. After a while even Death becomes redundant. But always manages to horrify. Link to the real and final Home Page. Remember the Old Days? Remember mother? No, we do not. Puff our smokes like graybeard fictions. Patient as Tolstoy for the Word.

## PART TWO: BODY OF WORK

HERE IS A BEGINNING AND END. FILL IN THE MISSING BODY WITH YOUR OWN LIFE STORY. MAXIMUM: 3000 WORDS.

WHAT'S INSIDE (BEGINNING)
Enter. Open. Look inside. Where will the young people go, now that all Homelands have been conquered? They disappear within. Inner space. The final frontier. Let us go then you and I. . . The freedom of an egg. An orb of possibilities. Be a nice Muse. Tell me a story. About the man in his house. Middle-aged, middle-class man. He has a daughter. Sixteen. Real wild child. His wife left two years ago to see where Life is. He goes to work, returns to his suburban home. He tries to be a good father. But he's confused. His daughter goes to the Night Mall to take pictures. To have her picture taken. Or maybe not. Maybe she just goes out at night and. . . . He tries to control her. But he is involved with his work. And his thoughts. Can he protect his child, or is she already corrupt? His son is eighteen. Next year he'll go away to college. Jonathan, the awkward lad. Awkward, but studious. Smart. Nose in the books. This is the beginning of his possibly.

[YOUR BODY OF EXPERIENCE GOES RIGHT HERE, IN THE MIDDLE, BETWEEN BEGINNING AND END; YOU'RE MIDDLE

AMERICA, AREN'T YOU? SEND YOUR BODY (HEH, HEH) MAXIMUM: 3000 WORDS.]

END

Of course the daughter wound up dead in a dark schoolyard. Raped and strangled. Went off to see what she could see, as usual, beyond the safety of the neighborhood. Thing is, she was on her way home and deep into the safety of the neighborhood, not far from home when the creature, the nice boy next door, of course, struck. How many times has that one been done? Sensationalism. Shock value. Where is that good, clean country the Muse promised?

**PART THREE: POETRY LAURA MIGHT DIG**

READ DECADENT POEM BELOW AND ANSWER QUESTIONS IN TERSE, WITTY, ERUDITE HEROIC COUPLETS. MAXIMUM: 100 LINES/50 COUPLETS.

At the Motel
before Now became Then
sudden autumn
drunk, wondering
we were all so
special
Paula alone in the motel room
years like shooting stars
Paul out shopping for booze
and mussels
"We're twice the age we were then.
The time that's passed between
now and then
is equal to the total
of our lives—then."
Paula by the pool
it's not the season yet
just algae scum and leaves
She practiced yoga
and foreclosure law.
He'd kept his figure
and his hair.
Reunion of virgins.
"It wasn't a disastrous marriage
merely a failed one."

Her son is eight years old
and with his grandmother
Mussels, sauce, snacks; wine.
Anti-depressants and Cigars.
Promise me.
See what develops.
"I can try to explain things,
but I'd rather not."

QUESTIONS:
WHY ARE PAUL AND PAULA SO SAD NOW THAT NEITHER IS MARRIED? WILL THEY GET TOGETHER AND BE HAPPY? CAN'T ANYBODY JUST CHILL OUT AND BE HAPPY? WHAT IS PAULA TRYING TO EXPLAIN? FORM FOLLOWS FUNCTION. MIGHT PAUL AND PAULA BE BUMMED BECAUSE THEY ARE BLOWING LIGHT AS FEATHERS IN A DECADENT WIND OF "FREE" VERSE? REWRITE THE EVENTS OF THIS POEM. BIND THIS BLEAK SCENARIO IN STRONG, HEROIC COUPLETS BEFITTING THIS, THE AGE OF HEROES.

**PART FOUR: NEW AGE METAPHYSICAL ESSAY**

HERE, YOU SEE?
Know what you know inside, but not outside. What others know, even if knowing is forgetting what was known before and is no longer known to be true depends on outlook but can be changed since it is not knowing to be known. Eternal focus on in-look not out-look. What is outside will be there always and always change, but in-look is finite and must focus on shaping. Rearranging outlook according to need. Your need to be sure, despite change, of what is true and eternal within your self. Not outside looking in, which will shape you through contortions and con-torture you, but inside looking out. Projecting eternal true you upon the ever-changing there out there. Here, you see?

ESSAY: YOU UNDERSTAND ANY OF THIS? ME NEITHER. I AM OFTEN ASKED, "ARE YOU WILLING TO DIE TO DEFEND YOUR BELIEFS?" WELL, SURE. GIVE ME SOMETHING TO BELIEVE AND I'LL DIE DEFENDING IT. WRITE AN ESSAY EXPRESSING GENUINE BELIEF IN...I DUNNO, IN SOMETHING. MAX, 2000 WORDS

**Adam Engel** ("Peaking: Voyeurism and the CIA," and "Get a Job (for Life): An Unauthorized Biography of Clarence Thomas"), Founder and President of PEN, is hardly qualified to judge his own writing, much less yours. But he's bored and needs something to read, so he figured, "Hell, why not hitch-hike on that famous information turnpike and see what's out there, eh?" Sure, he could have done that "On the Road/Blue Highways/In-Search-Of-America" thing, but really it all looks the same: fast-food chains; motel chains; supermarket chains; retail chains; pharmacy chains. America in chains. Yuck. Anyway, he knows what he thinks—sort of; he wants to know what YOU think. No guarantee he'll actually read your stuff, and if he does and likes it, there's no guarantee he won't steal it and claim it for his own. So enter this contest at your own risk. Good luck. What do you win? Whaddya think you win? Why, fame and immortality, of course. Celebrity. Every writer's dream. Okay, maybe some big $$$ too.

Send submissions to the PEN Pad at bartlebysamsa65@gmail.com

# GREAT EXPECTATIONS: AN IMMODEST PROPOSAL?

Supposedly, despite my vehement protests to the contrary, I have Great Expectations in the land of milk and honey. If I refuse this inheritance, I am guilty, it seems, of anti-Semitism, or worse, being a "self-hating Jew."

Despite years of indoctrination, I never did and never will have any interest in leaving NYC for "the Holy Land." If I were ever in the position of being forced to leave my home, I would not emigrate to Israel, but rather fight to defend my right to live in the "Homeland" to which I was born. Fight, like most people facing eviction from their place of birth, to the bitter end.

I've never even visited Israel, and do not intend to, especially since my wife, beautiful in mind and body but, alas, hopelessly Italian, might not be welcome in "beautiful Israel."

So, why can't we make a deal? I'll take whatever I have coming to me under right of return (return to what? from where?) and cede my property to a single, male Palestinian. I'd give it to a Palestinian couple, but due to my wife's unfortunate genetic situation, it might not be legit. I'm not asking for much: the property equivalent in size to a one-bedroom East Village Manhattan apartment will do.

Now, since this is my property, land that has been "in the family" for 3000 years, I believe it is within my rights to do with it what I please. Hence, I will bequeath this property, once the papers are in my possession, to a single male Palestinian who actually WANTS to live there. If necessary, I will include a rider that this person must be my age—37 years old—so as not to appear to be hustling anyone by say, ceding my land to a 20-year-old and cheating Israel out of 17 years of human life.

A fair deal for all involved, no?

**Adam Engel** recently moved into his neighbor's place because it had a better view. When the guy complained, Engel threw him out the window. Nobody seemed to mind. Anyway, the Landlord said it was okay because Engel's ownership had been written into his neighbor's lease long before anyone in the building had been born.

# HELL OF A TOWN—WHORES OF BABYLON: BLOOMBERG AND THE NEWS

"In a bid to raise some extra cash for the city, Mayor Bloomberg announced plans yesterday to sell New York's good name to companies eager to tap into the city's image as a vibrant, tough-as-nails metropolis. "I don't think you will see a big Coca-Cola or Pepsi-Cola sign across the front of City Hall," joked Bloomberg. "The key is, we want to keep it tasteful." The mayor offered few details, choosing to leave those to the city's new chief marketing officer, Joseph Perello, a branding expert whom Bloomberg also appointed yesterday at an annual salary of $150,000." *New York Daily News*, April 2, 2003

Don't laugh, Des Moines, Kansas City, Butte—you're next. Soon you too will be put to bed by your respective mayor/dictators before eight pm all tucked in with your feetsy pajamas and milk and cookies and you better say your prayers or the boogey man'll jump outta yer closet before you can say, "Hoboken."

"The City never sleeps" because THE MAN is always watching.

Soon all you bar owners, despite your eagle eyes for fake IDs, your hanging the flag in your windows and keeping the televisions tuned to CNN or Fox will be forced outta business because why the hell should a grown up have to pay five dollars for a drink after a hard day's work and not be allowed to light a fucking cigarette on your private property? Might as well buy a six-pack and a box of butts and go home, or find a place out in the woods or the park like you did when you were free and seventeen.

What was that crap Sinatra sang? "I want to be a part of it, New

York, New York?" Yeah, he'd be welcome in NYC with his booze and attitude and filter-less Camels.

And what about you hard working patriots? Doing the early 8 AM to 7 PM "nine to five" thing with the commute and crowds and crappy job—what is it you DO anyway?—and at the end of the day you can have a drink if you want to—ONE, or you'll be 12-stepping your way to rehab-but don't even THINK about lighting up—unless it's pot; I think, at least in NYC, the fine for that is a bit more lenient.

"Either way, aides suggested, the city has enormous marketing potential, possibly in the same league as Nike or Disney. And with the city facing a $3.5billion budget gap, it no longer can afford to pass up those dollars." *New York Daily News*, April 2, 2003

But forget about your selfish little habits. There are important things to think about. Like selling New York City to advertisers and corporations to "raise money for the city." Like turning what was once an international metropolis into a ridiculous, privately owned amusement park "in the same league as Nike or Disney" (don't feel too bad; can't smoke at Disney Land either).

Of course, maybe NYC wouldn't need to raise money if it didn't have the world's largest police force with nothing much to do but bust up protest rallies and hassle black and Hispanic kids (oh, and Arab/southwest Asian kids too; let's not forget about that melting pot). Or what if the Yankees, the world's richest sports team, were to actually pay rent? Or what if the corporations who own the place and rent, sue, poison, medicate, educate, entertain, employ and insure its citizens were to—just a thought—pay taxes?

"Whether it is the [city's] energy and the excitement, or more recently the resiliency and courage, those are attributes that companies want to associate with," Deputy Mayor Dan Doctoroff said. Most independent ad executives yesterday agreed, suggesting that New York could reap tens of millions of dollars." *Daily News*

Yeah, takes a lot of courage and resiliency to turn your common property over to billionaire politicians and ad men.

"Everything the city buys, from tires for the police cars, to paint for buildings, to uniforms for park employees and trash bags for sanitation workers, those are all products that could be put into a relationship with the city," said Douglas Pirnie, a senior vice president at marketing rights giant IMG.' *New York Daily News*, April 2, 2003

So now you can be employed as a Garbage Man and a Billboard at the same time. You won't earn anything extra for advertising whatever corporation will sponsor the NYC Sanitation department, but you'll be courageous and resilient. And a non-smoker, if you know what's good for you.

Oh, it doesn't matter anyway. With every block crammed with

Starbucks, Barnes and Noble, The Gap, McDonalds, and other unique New York establishments, not to mention the monstrous electronic signs and screens of Times Square and all the advertising lights of Broadway and the billboards at every bus stop and on the buses and the wall-to-wall advertisements in the subway cars, who really cares if Bloomberg sells whatever's left of the City of New York to private corporations?

"But there would be limits, others suggested, especially when it comes to the city's most revered landmarks. "It can't be the Statue of Liberty Mutual, or the Statue of Liberty Media," joked Jon Bond of the advertising firm Kirshenbaum & Bond. "That would be inappropriate." But an official soap of New York City? That you could sell, Bond joked. "I mean, who wants the official soap of Columbus, Ohio?" *New York Daily News*, April 2, 2003

I wouldn't want the "official soap" of Atlantis, to be quite honest. But really, what is left of NYC to sell? Insects? Birds? Rodents? I suppose they could stick clever decals on cockroaches, rats and squirrels and advertise URLs on pigeons, but otherwise, not to be a spoil sport, everything's already been lifted.

A few questions though: Were there any people interviewed by the Daily News who weren't involved in government or marketing? Like, maybe, someone who lives here and thinks he or she and the generations that built this City might actually own the place? And what're they gonna do with all those REDWHITEandBLUE flags left over from that "United We Stand" fad? I knew it wouldn't last.

**Adam Engel** is constantly in motion for fear some zealous ad-man might festoon him with corporate logos and garish lights. He can be reached at bartlebysamsa65@gmail.com

# HEROES IN HADES

> In the darker recesses of the world, private contractors go where the Pentagon would prefer not to be seen, carrying out military exercises for the American government, far from Washington's view. In the last few years, they have sent their employees to Bosnia, Nigeria, Macedonia, Colombia and other global hot spots. . . .Motivated as much by profits as politics, these companies—about 35 all told in the United States—need the government's permission to be in business. A few are somewhat familiar names, like Kellogg Brown & Root, a subsidiary of the Halliburton Company that operates for the government in Cuba and Central Asia. Others have more cryptic names, like DynCorp; Vinnell, a subsidiary of TRW; SAIC; ICI of Oregon; and Logicon, a unit of Northrop Grumman. One of the best known, MPRI, boasts of having "more generals per square foot than in the Pentagon."
> —NYT, October 13, 2002

Sing, Goddess, the anger of Peleus' son Achilleus. . .

Yeah, yeah, yadda yadda and all that David Copperfield kinda crap. Cut to the chase: When those Bush Flaks came down to Hades and tried to sucker me into fighting the War on Terror. The only weapon against terror I know of is wine; sometimes opium. But I don't speak for free. I need blood. They knew the rules: no blood, no banter.

I'll be damned if that pin-striped pencil-neck and his boys didn't roll out a cold keg of the finest Panamanian, circa 1989, I ever tasted. Most of the generals, dictators, politicos what have you, ply me with regional blood, Greek, Turkish, Armenian, but these boys knew their stuff; someone at the NSA did his homework and got me exotic.

"My name's Chad. And I represent the President of the United States of America," said the Suit with that ridiculous amalgam of arrogance and innocence those young 'official' Americans have. A kid, maybe twenty-three, twenty-four. Pencil-neck. Ectomorph. Punk.

"'The President of the United States of America,'" I mimicked. "Big Deal."

Chad and his 'colleagues' (thugs; probably CIA) played it cool, but their pale faces turned red as a slave-boy's rectum.

Chad continued, "Oh it is a big deal. A very big deal. Help us take Baghdad and the world is yours."

"What do I want with the world? I'm dead," I said. "And I'd rather be a slave among the dead than the lowliest corporate chieftain in America."

Again, the petty posse blushed en masse.

"You're not supposed to say that. That's not what—"

"—what the poets wrote. Poets lie. You ought to know that. Aren't you a poet?"

"Well. Not exactly. Though I did once publish a clever Sestina in the Yale Review when I was at school. I'm actually an Official Executive PR Intern and Apprentice Speechwriter. For the White House!" he said proudly.

"A speechwriter. And I'm supposed to take you seriously?"

"Well, not me, per se, but the man I represent. The—"

"Yeah, yeah. The 'President of the United States.' Then you are a poet, perhaps the greatest who ever lived, if you can persuade anyone to take that guy seriously. Think I don't watch CNN?"

"You watch CNN?"

"What the hell else am I gonna do? It's the only channel in Hades besides Fox."

"Well then, you're familiar with our situation. We need a hero. Not just any hero. Cops, Firemen, martyred office workers. Boh-ring. They've grown stale. What's more, since we publicly proclaimed them 'heroes,' they've been asking for better benefits, higher pay. We need a genuine military hero to don genuine GI gear for a special high profile mission."

"And what might this be?"

"Terminate—uh, that is, 'take out' Saddam."

"That's it? You came all this way to persuade me to kill one man?"

"Not an easy task. This man is cunning, ruthless, secretive. Evil incarnate."

"Sounds like a job for Odysseus rather than me."

The Bush men looked at each other uncomfortably. Chad the Suit spoke thus: "We'd already hired him for another job: Ossama Bin Laden. Odysseus took ten kegs of vintage Sioux, our oldest finest stock, in advance, then double-crossed us. Must be a double-agent for Terror. Not only didn't kill Bin Laden, he helped him escape.

Some 'hero.'"

"Well what'd you expect?"

"Better than we got. He fit the profile perfectly: family man, entrepreneur, property owner, showed initiative with that 'Trojan Horse' thing..."

"Alright, so you got burned," I said. "Why come to me?"

"Well, because you're—"

"Cheap?"

"Loyal. You're a fighter. The best. Real action hero. Dedicated to his girl, Kryseis, and his best-pal, Patroklos. Put you in U.S. Marine gear, have you do the job right, and Bingo. Media coverage—you'll see yourself glorified on CNN. Best-selling books. Definitely a movie in this. Maybe Spielberg."

"Man, are you people gullible. Not even gullible, stupid. Worse than stupid. Goofy. That's the only word for it. Goofy. Didn't Homer teach you anything?"

"Well, actually, I was quite busy in college," murmured Chad. "I only read the Cliff's Notes."

"Kryseis wasn't my girl. She was my booty. A slave, a kidnap-victim, in your parlance, who I raped at my leisure."

"Please. Keep it down. We have women in our armed forces," Chad peered into the mist and darkness, nervously.

"Women in the army?"

"Worse: Queers." Spat Chad.

"'Queers?"

"You know," he whispered. "Guys who 'do it' with—yuck—other guys."

I laughed heartily at this. Who could believe such a people run an Empire? They won't last long. Believe me.

"What do you think Patroklos was? My tennis partner?" I barked. "I did it better and more often with Patroklos than the likes of your President Bush ever did with his stony wife."

"Good god. Achilleus! You're a hero, for god's sake."

"As is Odysseus. As were all your rapists, murderers, slave-drivers, executives, presidents, kings... the meanest, most cunning, ruthless bastards the poets celebrate as heroes. Where did you Americans find such a childish definition of a hero? Your celebrated 'Hollywood?' In my day, a hero, so called, raped, pillaged, murdered, and generally brought ruination upon the anti-hero—that is, everyone else"

"Well it's different for us," sniffed Chad. "A hero sacrifices, a hero looks out for others, a hero—"

"—is a sucker. Here today, gone tomorrow. No immortality in sacrifice."

"A hero is brave!" whined Chad. I feared he was about to cry.

"You call dropping bombs from five miles in the sky 'brave?' It's boring. Boring, boring, boring. That's the problem with all your wars. No real fun and excitement."

"A war isn't about fun and excitement. It's about business," said Chad with pompous deference, as if he knew the answers.

"Then why you need 'heroes' so called?" I asked.

"For the public. To persuade them to sacrifice, to be brave, to—"

"Be suckers and die for your 'business.'"

"Enough, Sir! You blaspheme!"

"Honestly, you Americans never cease to amuse me. Even your 'players' are like children. Like that damn Prescott Bush always whining about how he should be in heaven at the feet of Jesus singing Kum-bah-yah, instead of down here 'among the heathen' just because he made money off the Nazis during WWII. 'It was just business, is all,' he cries, day in day out. Well, that's my problem with the whole Bush clan. It's all just business. Monopolies. Embezzlement. Fraud. Trading with the enemy. In my day, we would have made short work of such a scoundrel and let the dogs pick what they could off his scrawny carcass. No wonder they don't know how to run a war. Too uptight. Don't know how to have fun. Puny whelps, those Bushes. No real muscle..."

Well, that was enough for Chad and Company to cut off the tap.

"Let's go fellas," Chad said to his boys. "We're wasting our time with this, this degenerate homo!"

I still had enough blood in my gullet to scream, "Tell Dubya, 'the Heroes' of Hades send our regards! We'll be expecting him..."

# I, CLITORUS

Shame on you thinking with your monkey heads these five thousand years. Shame on you all for wasting this planet without at least consulting me.

Your heads above and below incurred this outrageous bill from Mother Earth, but we're out of all the Time we borrowed we have no collateral we cannot pay we're through as a species, finished.

To hell with your priests and philosophers, your Taylor, Ford and Edison, your Bacon, Newton and Descartes.

If only you'd consulted ME, tried thinking with MY head for a change. It only LOOKS small, but that tender button in its little red riding hood is just the peak of a tree of neural networks and interconnected pleasure mechanisms from A to G-spot.

I'm the most complex organ South of the Brain.

What you see is the fruit of what you don't see, the invisible tree of pleasure beyond your Xanadu dreams.

But it's always "size" with you "size, size, size" and can you keep it up for fifteen minutes and the world you've built around this farce is unlivable your sperm ain't so fructifying after all, now that you've poisoned the damned womb.

Look where your two-headed thinking has brought us. Look up from your Popular Mechanics and Time Magazine. Look where we are and quit your "we can fix it" babble cause it's the same narrative, the same failed methods to cure the same pandemic madness.

You should have come to me sooner. Now, I can't help you. Us.

Our children. MY CHILDREN. And of course when it all hits the fan you'll cry for "Mommy" in your agony.

Idiot.

Once, a long time ago, when I was important, before your Totem polls and Sky Gods and Taboos (not that long ago, actually, in Cosmic Time); the Goddess erupted from your awe. No "Holy Men" had to teach you to respect the absolute mystery of ME and the abundance of my Womb, nor could they dominate you from fear, for it wasn't really the "fear of god" with which THE MAN oppresses his workers, it was by taking away LOVE OF LIFE. You thought I was quite important for awhile there, some 200,000 years, the bulk of human evolution.

Yes, it was, once, long ago, evolution. Not this hell on earth most of the six billion folks on this overpopulated, biologically exhausted planet are "living."

And believe me, if you'd been thinking with MY head there'd be no more nor fewer people alive than the earth can sustain. I am, or was, the mistress of ecology. Creatrix of every civilizing invention to satisfy human need and desire (agriculture, medicine, art, the ecstatic song and dance precursors to the "Sex, drugs and Rock 'N' Roll" trip you thought you dreamed up in the sixties) without waste. You name it I figured it out right here between these lithe, muscular thighs.

2,000,000 years of all the food we could gather (though not hoard), clean rivers, sex, love, dancing, equality, share and share alike, then YOU mess up the planet in less than five thousand? Our mothers are rolling in their wombs.

Now nobody but nobody can argue with me when I say you've devastated the planet, you and THE MAN who owns you (while you pretend to be so free). Wrecked it. Trashed like a Frat House after celebration of The Big Game. Goodbye. No saving MOTHER this time.

Soon, very soon: nothing to drink but crude oil and petroleum. The same black goo that got us into this mess cause you wouldn't listen to me when I said leave that slime in the deepest deep, where it belongs, there's plenty of renewable energy up here, where Life is, you don't need that "Little Deuce Coupé" or Maserati or whatever to prove how big your "thing" is, believe me.

THE MAN is, after all, only a man.

But what do I know? Some say all I need is a good licking (I won't argue) and my place is in the kitchen or the bedroom, after all, so what do I know?

I know this: I exist only to bring pleasure. Scientifically proven fact. To make women happy is why I'm here. Ecstasy, my cosmic purpose. Ecstasy, my evolutionary function.

Go ahead, buddy, beat that.

# LES MISERABLE AND THE HACKERS FROM HELL (CYBER MOMMA AND THE OUTLAW COWBOYS)

I had a confirmed reader, once. Hate mailer, of course. Left a message something like, "We know who you are and sooner or later, we'll get you good." Unfortunately he left a phony email address—typical hate-mailer—so I couldn't answer back. So I had my hacker friend, Ryan, brilliant lad, trace the malicious missive from server to server to server all around the world and back again until he landed in the corporate cubicle of one Lester Miserable, my arch nemesis from our days as rival op-ed hacks on the high school paper.

Back in the day, Les had written an in-depth analysis of the high school football team, his thesis being "WE ARE NUMBER ONE." I merely pointed out that neither Les nor I were on the Football team, so we could not possibly be number one. Les Miserable's been my bête noir ever since. Ah well, least he still reads my stuff.

Ryan left a nice little note on the servers of Les's employer, in the mailboxes of IT (it never occurred to me until this writing that that acronym for "Information Technology" is an actual word with meaning: "It"), on the company memo list, etc. Simple message: "You've been hacked. Sorry, but if anyone's to blame it's Lester Miserable. What's he doing surfing the Web on valuable company time?"

After spooking ol' Les, Ryan and I went out for drinks—on me, of course—and talked about the old days when we were gallant digital warriors for a computer security company, Cyber Momma. Actually, I was just a mediocre Systems and Network Administrator. Ryan was the warrior cyber cowboy hacker from hell. Seriously smart dude with serious hacker connections. Real underground anarchist stuff. Kids, really, creating mayhem on the circuit with the goal, stated and unstated, of pursuing knowledge, and liberating information (I assume there's still a difference) from THE MAN.

Ryan was a clean-cut kid from Texas who left Texas because he hated being a clean-cut kid from Texas. Went to an "Eastern University Establishment" on full scholarship to study genetics and molecular biology and what not. Cyber Momma picked him up and settled his ass in NYC before the ink was dry on his diploma.

"How'd you go from molecular biology to computers?" I once asked him.

"Molecular biology is computing," he said and grinned wickedly.

He told me about nano-technology, molecular computing, protein-based software, and other Frankenstein games he and his co-geeks had played at college.

"There's more computing power in a glass of water than in all the processors that exist in the world today," he said and grinned wickedly. "It just has to be tapped. Just has to be tapped."

"Gives new meaning to the word 'tap water,'" I said, a bit spooked.

"Yes. Tap water. Tap. Water. Tap the water," he said and grinned wickedly.

Note: when Ryan grinned wickedly, it didn't mean that he was "up to no good," not always, at any rate. He was just one of those guys who went around grinning wickedly. Affectation? Nervous tick? Whatever. It worked. Especially on a slightly pudgy, very white, neatly dressed young Texan with a shaved head. Note again: Ryan wasn't a "skinhead," he was a hacker prankster, prone to coffee, cigarettes (Nicorette gum around the machines, which were "allergic to smoke," he'd said) malt liquor, Tex-Mex food and—I know this sounds silly and anachronistic—fun.

Then again, fun for Ryan and his network of hackers—that quaint, archaic term for people now referred to as "Cyber Terrorists" in the official documentation; please remember, this was 1997, and "WTC" connoted huge downtown buildings that would stand forever—was getting into places they did not belong. Such people begin with the question, "Why don't we belong there?" move on to "How do we get in?" and conclude with a paper, posted on various websites and news groups, "How You Too Can Get In."

Problem is, hackers often ended up working as consultants for the very corporations that would do anything in their considerable power to forbid their entry—unless they were on the payroll. No, it wasn't a matter of "Hackers have to eat too you know." If it was money they wanted, they could have gotten it with ease—and many did—from YOUR bank account, or mine, or just plucked the random percentage—pennies that drop like so much loose change in cyberspace from multi-million dollar digital transactions. A little here, a little there; these things add up.

No, the hackers were in it for the games and the toys. A company like Cyber Momma had lots of high-tech toys, and even better, lots of enemies whose systems begged for "illegal" entry. That was the raison d' etre of security companies like Cyber Momma. Help client companies hide behind Cyber Momma-controlled firewalls while they in turn attack their rivals, who probably had hired Cyber Momma's competition to protect them.

## The Invasion of Canada

One of the ways Cyber Momma sold their product was to scare the living shit out of potential clients by proving to them that their defense was garbage and their "Firewall" was actually just smoke and mirrors. Often the potential client would be challenged to defend itself and a Cyber Momma hacker like Ryan would burst into their digitally walled city like Virtual Vikings gone berserker on espresso. The biggest such client, as I recall, was Bell Canada—or whatever corporation it was that wired America's Great Northern Lawn (sorry, Canada, I calls 'em as I seez 'em; no offense, eh?).

Cyber Momma's CEO boasted to Bell Canada that "his boy" could crack their defenses and post a message inside the deepest, most secure regions of the Bell Canada Kingdom within 24 hours. This already gave Bell Canada a huge advantage: they know they were going to be attacked, by a specific source, and this heads-up allowed them to "man their stations" in preparation. Of course they agreed.

So one July morning in 1997, armed with a low-end Sun machine running Solaris and Free BSD versions of Unix; a not very powerful Sun server; his trusty, beat-up, taped-together, old Linux laptop (like most of his friends, Ryan harnessed the power of the big toys to a simple, low-end Linux box); all the coffee and Cola he could drink, and a full box of nicotine-spiked gum, Ryan began his quest.

He didn't have much to go on but Bell Canada's public info and IP numbers, etc. But that was enough to get him to the moat. Once he crossed the moat, he picked away at the draw-bridge. Once inside, he snuck past the guards, and so on. It wasn't easy—took a lot of number-crunching, code-cracking, decrypting; a process which would have taken a lot less time had he been using one of Cyber Momma's more powerful machines; but that wasn't part of the deal. Our CEO wanted it raw, real outlaw hacker stuff. Around the twenty-first or twenty-second hour, he got in, did his thing and left. All on digital moccasin feet. The guards hadn't a clue. He left a message on a POP server linked to the machine of Bell Canada's Honcho with the words, "You've been hacked, courtesy Cyber Momma. Have a nice day." The Honcho logged on at the prescribed time, read his email, gasped in shock, probably, and Cyber Momma won the contract.

"You know, once I was in there, behind their firewall, I could have shut down Canada. I mean, I got into the real shit, the control mapping, the whole bag. I was just passing it on my way to that suit's POP server, and even stopping to check that out was wasting valuable time, but, like, you know, if I weren't. . . I mean. . . they're fucking lucky I'm one of the 'good guys.' You know what I mean," said Ryan and grinned wickedly and this time I think the grin was meant to convey something very, very important.

### Something Wicked This Grin Comes

I know what you're thinking: "So what? Some <dot.com> era corporate hack(er) stopped short of shorting out Canada five years ago. Big Deal."

Well, it could have been a very big deal indeed. I suppose Ryan stopped due to a "crisis of conscience"—after all, you blow out the communications system, innocent people will suffer, not just Bell Canada's Board Members and Major Shareholders. He could have been thinking of potential consequences. On the other hand, this game was really being played by Cyber Momma and Bell Canada. Ryan was merely a master player pinch hitting for his boss. He could have claimed he'd made a mistake—though I assume someone like him would rather do jail time than admit to some phony mistake concocted by corporate lawyers—or fallen back on the age-old, "I only followed orders," routine. Maybe what really freaked out Ryan was not a crisis of conscience, but rather, a crisis of consciousness. The rush of power must have been tremendous. Here was this twenty-two-year old pawn in an elaborate corporate chess game who, instead of heading for the "rival king," could have made a (heh, heh) LEFT turn straight off the board and shut out the lights.

### Marx and Frankenstein Get Wired

I read a book recommended to me by my friend, Paul. "*Cyber Marx*," by Nick Dyer-WitheFord.

(I see this coming, Les Miserable, so I'll pre-empt it: No, I'm not a "Marxist" or any other kind of "ist." Too conservative for me, all that pre-planned "scientific" revolution stuff. I want action. I want chaos. I wanna play ball. Why, if I could get into a time machine right now I'd go straight to that old British Museum, grab Karl by his wooly beard, drag him outside, where it's cold and dense with soot and smoke and somber proles, put a rock in his pudgy hand, and say, "Fuck the dialectic and yer little dog, too. It's time to Rock n' Roll, Karl, so cast this first stone through that dainty fucking library window! And I don't have time for the goddamn state to wither away either; you better hurl that sucker NOW!" There. Happy, Les? Thou USA PATRIOT/TIPS hate-mailer cubicle-jockey snitch!).

Interesting reading, that "Cyber Marx." Seems old Karl said some things about technology and the nightmares that would ensue as technology became more and more monopolized by THE MAN (Stalinist, Maoist, Fascist, NixonReaganClintonBushist—same thing; THE MAN'S The MAN; always was and always will be hiding behind that same thin curtain we pay no attention to at our peril).

Now, one doesn't have to have had his head buried in the *New York Times* or mind benumbed by CNN for the past 20 years to know that WE THE PEOPLE have been fucked royally by Capitalism's absolute control over control (high tech means of production, surveillance, warfare, general mayhem, not to mention that little hole in the ozone). WTC. World Bank. Transnational Corporate Globalization. Whatever. What is that figure put out by Kevin Phillips (a Republican, yet!), among others? One percent of the world's population owns 80 percent of the "wealth"—however one measures wealth—while more than half the planet starves? And most of that "wealth" is used to spy on people, blow them up and despoil the air, water and general environment (good god, they're literally choking us to death!)? What kinda New World Order is that? Not even a Brave New World Order. Just plain Blade-Runner-Interzone hell-on-earth type CAUCHEMAR (French word; look it up; also might wanna research the Kevin Phillips' figure; I'm just too confused by all these damn numbers adding to ABSOLUTE ZERO to be a stickler for absolute accuracy; trust me, we're absolutely in deep shit). Capitalism may have triumphed, but the other 99 percent of us went down like Mike Tyson against that big scary guy from England. McWorld has made a big McMess of OUR planet.

But what a lot of these neo-Marxists argue, according to the book, is not only that reports of Marx's death have been greatly exaggerated (by neo-liberal yahoo lackeys of THE MAN —does the name Francis Fukuyama ring a bell? How about Nicholas Negroponte? Or that ubiquitous goofball, Tom Friedman?), but that it's not necessarily technology we should be afraid of, but technology in the WRONG HANDS. Frankenstein wouldn't have been so screwed if only he'd treated his creature with some dignity and respect. But now it's too late for that—no, no, don't apologize, Bill Gates, Al Gore, Paul O'Neil and yer little dog, Bono, too! The damage is done. The creature is becoming a MONSTER, contained only by THE MAN's gadgets.

On the other hand, Frankenstein's creature—in the book, not the movie, in which Karloff plays a grunting thug in a big suit—learns to read and write and speak. If he'd just laid low until the 1860s—well, no. I don't think Marx could have saved him, though he certainly would have helped. If he'd just hung around long enough to figure out how to wrest control of the gadgets and whirligigs from THE MAN, well, he might have become a contender. So what if he was ugly? Dick Cheney sure ain't no prize, and he's made out of lightening-zapped dead tissue too!

What the writers cited in "Cyber-Marx" seem to be arguing, from various angles, is that Marx made some major points, but he wasn't the damn Bible. If fact, that was the trouble all along, treating Das Kapital like the damn Bible. Look what happens to folks who treat the Bible like the Bible! No, what the author of "Cyber Marx" seems to be getting at is that Marx's analysis of Capitalism in general, and Capitalist controlled technology in particular, is quite relevant to our current situation. Quite relevant indeed.

Been having fun working more hours for less money at your meaningless job enriching TechnoCorp Inc. lately? Or are you one of those who really enriched your corporate lords by getting downsized? Or did you hit the jackpot and spread the wealth to numerous conglomerates by getting into serious debt, or going to prison? Or perhaps all of the above? Well, you can always help out even more corporations by taking out huge loans and going back to school. As THE MAN says, the road to success is through Institutionalized Education (as opposed to staying home and reading on your own and maybe talking to friends; but I'm not sure, I think gathering in groups to discuss ideas might be illegal now; again, who has time to do all this research?).

**Nota Bene:**

(whatever that means; I know, I know, I should look it up on Latin Dicionary.com or something; I'll leave that to you; and while you're at it, why don't you go shopping, not to support your President—you don't really have one—but to help the economy, such as it is, and buy *Cyber Marx.*[1])

While Ryan was hacking systems, I got shipped off to defend the integrity of the network at one of world's largest law firms. Major Cyber Momma client. I sat among the machines in the basement of a tremendous skyscraper on Lexington Avenue. Manning the Fire

[1] http://www.amazon.com/exec/obidos/ASIN/0252067959/counterpunchmaga#noop

Wall to prevent hackers or rival law firms from accessing "private data." Checking out the incoming and outgoing messages. Spying on the Lawyers high above, making sure they weren't surfing the web for illicit purposes. That is, visiting porno sites.

Turns out these fine, six-figure income lawyers were indeed scoping out virtual beaver, big time. Males mostly, which is why The Firm moved to take action. A female employee complained when she passed the computer of a male colleague around which several other male colleagues were congregated with obvious hard-ons stretching the limits of their Barney's slacks. The Senior Partners smelled sex (in the form of a discrimination lawsuit).

So, the ingenious CEO of Cyber Momma sold the not-so-ingenious Senior Partners of The Firm the latest in snoop scoop software, which it was my duty to install and demonstrate to a cabal of Senior Partner Poo Pahs.

"Howdy, Partners," I said to the Firm's Elders.

None were amused. So I proceeded to demonstrate the inadequacy of censorship, even censorship of the high tech sort.

"Type in 'Playboy,'" one of the Elders said, excitedly.

I typed in "<paleyboy.com>" instead. The gaping vagina that burst onto the screen—one of the Partners claimed to have seen teeth; I didn't see any—was so steamy and wet I thought it might melt the monitor.

"But, but... how can this be?" stammered the Seniorest Partner.

"It's like this," I tried to explain, slowly, using simple words, just to be sure they understood. "The manufacturers of this software guarantee that they've tracked 200,000 porn sites and add patches with up to 20,000 new sites, which we are licensed to download from their site, each month. Right?"

"Right!" yessed the men who were not used to getting KNOW! for an answer.

"Well, there's about 20 million sites on the Web with millions, not thousands, being added each week by users all over the world. Right?"

"Well, if you say so, you're the expert."

Actually, I wasn't. I pulled those numbers outta my head. But they seemed accurate enough.

"Now, considering that porn is the most lucrative, in fact the only lucrative business on the Web, what percentage of these already existing sites, not to mention new sites, are porn sites?"

"Oh. Oh... OH!"

"Precisely."

Then there was Juliette, the Firm's in-house trouble shooter, a sixty-something-year old grandmother, born black in Jamaica—and still black when I knew her—who had the unenviable job of fielding calls from panicked Partners, Paralegals, Extra-legals, Sub-legals, and various other Legals 40 floors above.

"What's that, you say?" Juliette would ask politely. "You broke the Internet? That could be a problem. But maybe you didn't break the entire Internet. Maybe you just crashed you browser. You know, your browser. The window where the web sites appear. What do you mean, you're not on the web? Your screen is blank and it won't go on. Hmn. Did you try plugging in your machine? Right. Now reboot. That means turn your system on again. Oh, it's working now? That's good. Oh, no need to thank me, that's what I'm here for."

She'd slam down the phone, mutter "assholes," and wait for the next high tech emergency.

One lovely autumn morning as I approached Lexington and 53rd to start the day, I saw a COMMOTION. Hundreds of the firm's employees hanging around outside the building.

"What's going on?" I asked some guy in a suit.

"Fire downstairs. In IT. The Firm's afraid it might have lost billions of dollars in data."

"Heavens," I said

I walked a few blocks to Barkley Rex Cigars, bought a double-corona Dominican, and puffed away in the smoking room, watching the Asian Economy collapse on CNN. By the time I got back, the commotion was over and I went down to the basement to check the damage.

What happened was, some guys were using a soldering iron on the air-conditioning unit and it set off the fire alarm. Now, this wasn't just any fire alarm system—after all, they had to protect billions of dollars worth of data—this was a Halon alarm system. That means that once the alarm goes off, they turn on the Halon release doohickey and anyone at IT has about sixty seconds to get the hell outta the basement before the Halon gas is released to suck all the oxygen out of the air and stop the fire before it laps nary a lick of data. For some reason, the system didn't work, and no Halon was released. This reason was obvious: the Halon release mechanism had not been turned on.

Juliette caught hell for not taking one for the team and defending the integrity of the Firm's data. You see, there were about twenty people down there before I arrived, and Juliette—no spring chicken, she—was the last one out. As everybody at IT knows, the last one out must turn on the release mechanism.

"Are they crazy? Are they insane?" I can still hear Juliette fuming. "They expect me to turn that switch and get my ass out of IT in sixty seconds before the Halon kills me? So they can save the data on their damn machines? Then what? They'll send my family a condolence card and a basket of fruit? Bullshit."

I left IT, Cyber Momma, and the whole game not long after that. There has to be a better use for computers, networks, data systems, software, and I'm sure we'll find one. Once we take back every damn one of them from THE MAN.

That's when I began to read about Richard Stallman, and the GNU/Linux/Free Software movement, and the concept of Copy Left distribution of data and software. It was pretty big for a while, and I think it all still exists. It might indeed be growing a bit too powerful for The MAN not to take notice. Ever wonder why corporations like IMB and Hewlett-Packard are starting to brag that their hardware runs Linux, a free, unlicensed operating system? But don't take my word for it. Look it up.

(By the way, Les Miserable, you DON'T know who I am; I ditched that guy a million years ago and I ain't never goin' back; have a nice day!)

# LIZARD BRAIN ON LINE FOR THE LOG FLUME

Pyrning in a widening gyre, invoking my ire, began at 42nd street and 3rd and three hours later wound up on 72nd and 1st, finally. First avenue was our destination all along. Every few blocks or so the cops would say "just a few more blocks then you can turn on to 1st," until the whole parade of us "silly authorities: by prohibiting a march they created one" wound up on 72nd street, where I had the privilege of listening to Angela Davis speak on the radio.

"Where is she? Where are the speakers?" I asked.

"Fifty-first street," said an angry woman. "Welcome to the new technology of crowd control."

Magic Mountain at Disneyland. Log Flume at Great Adventure. Not so new, I thought. I'd waited on many such lines as a kid. At least this one was free. And unlike the teenagers working at Disney and Great Adventure, the NYPD representatives were very polite unless you misbehaved. Unless you were a naughty "protester." An unruly child. Then you got what was coming to you.

Like the couple who tried to push their baby carriage, complete with baby, across 49th or 50th street. I forget. Silly me. I was too dumfounded, awestruck, outraged, mad to the bone, to write all the details in my notepad. True, it was a stupid thing to do, confronting the thugs with your baby as a battering ram, but the four sturdy male cops and two equally buff females could have easily prevented the couple from going down the "illegal" street by, well, blocking them from going down the street. Instead, the Sergeant grabbed the father and tossed him to three alpha-males who pounded the guy into the pavement while another cop grabbed the baby carriage and the two female cops tried to restrain the woman who cried, "Give me my baby! That's my baby!"

A crowd of about a hundred dropped from the march toward nowhere for a while to bear witness and plead with these baby-bashing, family-wrecking brutes who live off our tax money but not in our neighborhoods (dial area code 516 for Long Island, 201 for New Jersey) to do the right thing, the decent thing, and let the couple and their baby go.

Question: Why did such a large crowd allow half a dozen ruffians to get away with such an outrage? Easy. Because the men and women in blue, our "heroes," were armed. You think we stood there like hushed puppies before the attack dogs because we respected their "authority?" Authority to do what, beat up a family for trying to do what everyone assumed we all had the right to do anyway (especially since this was not a "march" but a "rally" meeting around 50th and 1st), just cross over from 3rd to 1st down any damn street instead of marching 30 blocks with our little signs and banners? If they were merely rent-a-cops with guns we would have done the same thing. On the other hand, if they were "New York's Finest" without guns, we would have rescued the couple and their baby, grabbed the thugs and brought them to the, well, the POLICE!

Which brings up an interesting point. This whole affair seemed to me to be less about citizens asserting their right of free speech in a democracy than pleading with a police state to be allowed to show themselves and their families in public and listen to some keynote speakers, even if it meant walking through a maze of police barricades to do so. The only authority the cops had came from the pistols in their holsters. How else would half a dozen "officers of the law" on each street hold back thousands of marchers? And we're not talking crazed "radical elements," but students, elderly women, families and assorted peace-loving others. Never again will I nod my head in assent when someone brings up that old, "how can only three guards with machine guns hold back three thousand prisoners in Auschwitz?" Same way five or six cops with Glock 9mms on each street kept away thousands of protesters in NYC, Saturday, February 15, 2003.

"I don't blame people for wanting to walk their own streets," a man said.

"It's just one long line," a cop answered.

"To where?" I asked.

The cop, smirking, shrugged.

Every street from 42nd to 72nd connecting 3rd to 1st was closed by five or six cops with guns. "We own the streets" all the nice people cried. No you don't, THEY do, I said, to myself. If you owned the streets, you'd be on them.

But it was a nice march, a nice family affair.

Why would anyone bring a kid to a march unless they were sure that the cops would keep everything safe? Of course, they could have believed the march would be safe because this is America the Democracy and NYC the cultural hub of what-have-you. It was safe because this is America , the most heavily armed Empire in history, and this is NYC, the most policed city in the Empire.

Maybe I'm alone in the opinion that, to paraphrase Malcolm X about the march on Washington, "they wanted all of those people outta town by sundown, and sure enough all of those people were out of town by sundown." Or maybe the cerebral subtleties of the protest went right over my lizard brain. 'Cause lizard brain was what I was "thinking" with as I walked past all these armed cops. Fear. Rage. Desire for what? Freedom? Power? Revenge? "No blood for oil," the placards said. I couldn't agree more. But no blood for freedom? Impossible.

Silly me. Still under the romantic delusion I'd been under since I first started marching in these staged events at 20, thinking of the movements of the 1960s and 1930s, that protest meant taking the streets, not borrowing them from THE MAN and agreeing to all terms of the temporary license or face nullity and void. Saturday I realized, finally, that this isn't about peace at all, but power. THE MAN has the power to bomb, humiliate, control. We The People are more or less powerless to stop him. Occasionally HE throws us a bone or a rally to make us think we're doing the democratic thing. As long as we're "outta town by sundown."

The most prevalent figures on the marchers' placards, besides the ridiculous, odious George Bush, were heroes of the 1960s: Malcolm X, Martin Luther King, and John Lennon. Photos of Malcolm X and MLK, and quotations from Lennon, plus that "Who Would Jesus Bomb" thing. Now, what did these men have in common? They got killed for opening their mouths. True, Lennon, though a great artist/entertainer, was not a religious figure like Jesus, or a moral/political leader of Malcolm X or MLK's stature, but he did open his mouth to say "Give Peace a chance" as well as a bunch of other stuff that got him on Nixon's shit list, and he did project himself as a rebel against THE MAN. After all, nobody ever took a shot at Paul or Ringo. What all of these men had in common was that they meant business, and people who mean business are never safe.

Angela Davis said something to the effect that Saturday's march was the greatest outpouring of public protest since a million people marched to express their displeasure with America's obscenely huge nuclear arms stash in 1982. A million people marching up and down with signs and chanting slogans is an impressive number. More impressive however, is the amount of time, money, energy and evil cunning that went into improving and increasing the U.S. nuclear arsenal over the next 21 years. I don't know how many people were at the rally Saturday. A lot. Thousands, perhaps many, many thousands. I'm sure that it was empowering for people, which is nice.

But I never felt so powerless and humiliated. Like every thug from Bush down to officer Buttcheeks of the NYPD was laughing at me, at us, at the whole show. And they're gonna have their damn war anyway.

I suppose it's good for people to march like this so they can let themselves be heard. Express themselves. But it seems to me like we're in an emergency situation. Something that calls for more than taking the family out for a day of waving signs and chanting rhymes ("One two three four, we don't want your oily war," etc., along with many old '60s standbys), then back to The Life on Monday.

No matter how many people turned out, the entire event was merely that, an event, choreographed by THE MAN to frustrate, exhaust, and humiliate the majority of participants. Rallies are great to get people out together, show them that they're not alone, create a sense of spirit and energy, like the old pep rallies in high school.

But real change is probably going to mean changing the way we live. And real protest is going to be dangerous and frightening. Rated X or R at least. Not something for the kiddies.

Maybe it's just me. I'm not really into crowds or marching or shouting pre-fab sing-songy slogans. If I want to express myself I'll write a poem, or a letter to Dear Abby. I used to go to "events" like these because I thought they were necessary, something that had to be done. Maybe they're not. Unless we, the alleged protesters, mean business. If giving peace a chance means not killing people who've never done me any harm, I'm all for it. But if it means knuckling under to irresponsible, merciless, armed authority, we might want to consider other chances.

I went to the rally thinking of the horrible fate of the Iraqi people and wondering if anything could be done to change it. I came away thinking of the horrible fate of the American people, and wondering if anything can be done to change it.

# MANNAHATTA!
# (A TALE OF TWO CITIES)

And Eastward bound was I. Away, away from Riverside and crossing Central Park to Xanadu did Donald Trump a stately pleasure dome decree. Away, away from mongrel hordes. Away from the Museum of Dead Things and Hayden's belly full of stars. Ghosts of Indians bleat in the wind, chanting, pleading for renewal...

Eh. Fuck 'em.

**[Scrivener's Note:**

Look away from the New Yorker magazine, where old prose goes to die (the heady days of Cheever, Salinger, William Maxwell as gone as DiMaggio and the Dodgers. Updike remains to sleep, perchance to dream of getting laid writing the same old white line)! Why does this "journal" still exist? Could not someone flush it from our misery? It's an institution, friend, and institutions stand, relics that they are, to remind us we're mortal, thank god, this won't go on forever, and anyway, we're not as boring as we thought we were, just look at that there institution swaying in the wind, begging, albeit with patient dignity, for oblivion...]

Mannahatta! Wondrous city of flags! Not only real Yankee-doodle flapping in the wind flags, but flag pins, flag mugs, flag shot glasses and condoms and REDWHITEandBLUE Christmas lights on every tree caught in the great tree Diaspora outside Holy Central Park where tourists skate in the seventy-degree November air. Don't whine to me about Global Warming—my environment was always self-contained, a Greenhouse under strips of cobalt sky (and airplanes, lots of airplanes overhead, this being the hub of Modern Civ).

**[Scrivener's Note:**

This week-end, for our anniversary, my wife, and I went for a "home vacation" on the UPPER EAST SIDE. True, we were treated like white trash, because they could easily tell we didn't really belong there, but at least we were admitted entry and saw something interesting, or rather didn't see it.

There are no black people there. I used to think Woody Allen was a racist for creating an all white New York, but he was right, at least about the Upper East Side: A black person in anything but a servant's role would be as ridiculous in one of his movies as an Alabama truck-driver would be in one of William Trevor's Irish or English burgs.

Maybe black people just don't want to hang out with white people anymore; maybe they're bored with them. Could be. But there were many people of color in Central Park. People of all races in the park, but not in the Museums or Theaters or on the Streets, except to clean up or collect tickets or—literally—"operate" the elevator in the Metropolitan Museum of art. One man, in a uniform, spending his day pushing either "One, Mezzanine, Two, or Three." No wonder he freaked out when I got on the elevator and pushed "M."

"Hey. That's my job. I do that. You just ride the elevator, you don't work it."

"Sorry, I didn't know."

"Well make it your business to know. I push the buttons. Don't push my buttons."

I mean, this ain't Iowa, this is New York City. There are easily as many black people as white people. I'm not talking about some liberal affirmative action friendship nonsense where I seek out genuine African-Americans, drag them out for drinks and dinner, and brag that some of my best friends are black. I'm talking about natural social interaction.

This is unnatural. Apartheid-like. Weird. To walk for blocks and blocks and stay at a hotel and go to restaurants and not see a single black person who was not in some servant's capacity, outside of Central Park?

Mannahatta! greatest City on Earth I just paid $80 for Stromboli and a pickle it was worth every penny and espresso too and chocolate on my pillow left by the maid in my hotel room Mannahatta afoot and light hearted I take to Fifth avenue and amble to the Met where tourists shell out twelve dollars a piece for a "suggested" donation though they've no idea it's optional they worry will they have enough to get grandpa through the GATES OF ART he's a senior citizen but where's his ID celebrity is in the air and celebration Richard Avedon Exhibiting exhibitionists: Marilyn Monroe looks sad; Andy Warhol looks sad and full of scars and holes; Abbie Hoffman, eyes closed, is sad; Sam Beckett is sad—so what else is new?—and across from the Chicago Seven are the men in suits and uniform who ran the War oh glorious, glorious dramas for the ages and everyone is sad!

**[Scrivener's Note:**

Any artistic/political/literary/social whatever movement of any importance began with lower class whites and blacks and immigrant Irish, Italian, Jews, Russian, and more recently Latino, Arabic, Indian, Asian etc. Let's not forget that the Beatnik movement fed on the forbidden fruits of the Harlem Renaissance and Jazz culture. . . and the last mass movement to have any affect on "Fashion and the Arts" were Punk and Rap in all their permutations from style of dress to poetry. . .

Art never comes to the Upper East Side or the Museums until at least a quarter century after it's happened. . . but even so, now that everyone's becoming a REDWHITEandBLUE American, where's all this art and music gonna come from? Not rich white folks, or even "honorary" whites made up of "success stories" of the aforementioned groups.

Who can afford to live in the "dignified poverty" necessary to (I'm not gonna say "make art" that's so corny), do stuff? Not that you have to be poor. It's always better if you have money to do stuff, and lots of people who do stuff do it best once they're free of financial burdens and can focus on other things. . . Knut Hamsun notwithstanding, that hungry artist crap is crap. . . you don't have to be hungry, just alive. . . but most people don't have money. . . once, you could devote a minimum of time to making money and the rest to doing whatever it is you do. . . then, if folks liked what you did, you could make some money selling it, or teach or get a sponsor or win an award or something, whatever. . . you were choosing to live in poverty in the Lower East side, Chelsea and other areas (except Harlem, where you had no choice) and do that whole waiter/artist thing "immortalized" in RENT.

Well, I took a look at some East Village one-bedrooms and studios, where not even seven years ago, my wife and I were paying $650/month. . . same studio now for $1800. . . same one-bedrooms "renovated"—they put in a dishwasher or something—now starting at $2100. . . that means, in order to live in a shit-hole, you need a full-time job, and a well-paying one too. You're not choosing to live in a shit-hole because you'd rather devote yourself to playing the kazoo or writing the great Sanskrit comic book; it's literally the cheapest place you can afford to come "home" to after your ten plus hour day of working/commuting being insane. . . that, my friends, is fucked. Gated communities for the upper-middle class—you have to be "up there" in order to afford to live in a shit-hole and pay first and last month's rent and get your security cleared...

Mannahatta! Heed not the provocateur, the conscience, imprisoned in brackets now and forever, a footnote fussbudget, but revel in my dream Art and Fashion Capital of the World the glossy 'zines proclaim so buy a piece of New York and take it back to the farm or wherever the hell you're from show them thar cynics in Town Square what yer made of... Oh yes we've Statue of Liberty statuettes and WTC souvenir autographed photos of the dead and pricey stuff too you have to pay our experts to appraise—well, you have your objets d'art, go forth fulfilled... go, go. Shoo.

**[Scrivener's Note:**

This place is gone. The Big Guys have taken it all. You have no life if you work all day in an office cubicle for "big bucks" to live on Avenue D—no mind at any rate... and what about the people who work all day in less glamorous pursuits, cleaning the cubicles, say, who don't make big bucks, like... the working class people who used to be my neighbors around Tenth street and Avenue C? Some of them were even students of mine when I ran the Writing Center at Touro College on 23rd street and taught freshman composition for a grand total of: $25,000 per year before taxes—and I was the rich "professor"; what about those folks? Where did they go? Westchester? Great Neck? I mean, they can't just vanish, but how do you make room for whoever's making the 50-100K needed to live in their fine neighborhoods (refurbished, of course)? I smell a rat. I smell many big fat corporate/real estate/political rats...

Mannahatta spires rise above your hip hop happy cuchifrito no tickee no shirtee Kim chi teriyaki why you always Russian Jew York Yankee sauerkraut in turban and sub turban hashish hookah herbal tea pink—oh, oh, oh and violet pussy belly-button girl drumbeat Madonna in the park with Cardinal Sin the real McCoy Ciao fun 24 dollars and 43 pesos fer yer pot melting to boiling point perverse show bum open to all players from Hellish kitchens and the lockstep faces of diversity...

**[Scrivener's Note:**

Gotta take off for a while. Travel. Kinda cowardly to jump ship, agreed: But the Apple is rotting to the core. Big world out there. Lotta languages to learn. People to meet (and not kill, or want to kill just cause the *New York Times* etc. tells us to). Not everyone bleeds REDWHITEandBLUE—do they?]

Oh Mannahatta, rise above your ancient ethnic dark, dark-minded, outrageous self-centered self and become America at last!]]]]]

# MAN TALK

> "Walter: Nothing changes. Goddamn Nazis.
> The Dude: They didn't say they were Nazis. They said they were nihilists.
> Walter: Nihilitsts? Fuck me. Say what you will about the tenets of National Socialism, at least it was an ethos."
> —From *The Big Lebowsky*, by the Coen Brothers

So I went to THE MAN and I said, straight to HIS face, "Who's fooling who, MAN? I mean, what kinda hustle you trying to pull? That's two countries destroyed in two years and Iran and god-knows-who else on the way. What happened to Al Quaeda and Bin Laden and all the other excuses for Police State laws and rhetoric and all that killing?"

THE MAN said, "Freedom, democracy, eternity. We the people united stand Superpower bless us God. This land your land my land Daniel Boone."

I said, "Yeah, yeah. Flags for the children and a Chicken Hawk in every pot. Come clean, MAN. We're catching on. Lotta folks are wondering what really did happen on September 11, 2001. Facts, rumors and suppositions jam the Web, yet YOU closed down the investigation of the single most deadly attack—aside from YOUR own nuclear testing—ever on U.S. Soil. What gives?

THE MAN said, "Brave, brave Fireman. Postage stamp. Statue. Hero, hero. Ham on rye."

I said, "Yeah, we've heard the 'hero' thing, it's old. Today's hero could be tomorrow's homeless 'loser' (ask your Vietnam and Gulf I Veterans, or Tom Paine) You lied about Weapons of Mass Destruction. You lied about respecting States Rights (or you wouldn't be in power). You lied about so many things related to 9/11 that one can only suspect you're hiding something. Else why not a full investigation to 'get' the terrorists? Unless there is an investigation by someone impartial—if that's possible—other than the Gallery of Graft we used to call 'Congress,' why don't I just believe everything that's out there until I know the truth? After all, as someone said, the most unbelievable conspiracy regarding 9/11 is the story foisted upon the world by your Mainstream Media."

THE MAN said, "Truth in truth lies gravid with The Beast. Protect you. I. Will defend. Us. All of us. In this. Together. Spawn of Saddam's poison seed neutralized, deleted. Get a job. Buy stuff. The markets are free and safe."

I said, "Yah! You're not protecting anyone but Big Oil and the Old Gory Glory Flag Factory and whatever other private companies you hired out to 'fix' Afghanistan and Iraq. A hundred billion dollars already and more on the way? While the U.S. is in economic meltdown. Crisis. And you cut taxes for the super-rich but not the other 99 percent of the country except the super-poor? And you cut overtime pay (to increase the ranks of the super-poor?). And you talk about needing us to buy more troops to deploy and 'support.' What are you thinking?"

THE MAN said, "Rebuild this vale of tears. Better than it was. Better, stronger, faster."

I said, "How, by smoking civilians with high tech weapons? By ignoring the worldwide economic nightmare, and the approach of an environmental seizure? Don't you ever think of your own grandchildren? What, are you gonna lock them in a giant, climate-controlled dome while the rest of us have our faces pressed against the glass?"

THE MAN said, "Close the door on your forever forgotten bleeding heart junk science not worth my dime-time. Rasta la vita, mother-fucker. Adipose."

I said, "Fine, fine. I'm sure you'd be happy to steer me toward extinction, as I would you. But a lot of people are getting sick. Food is poison. Water is poison. Air is poison. Your own Flag-waving sheep are in for unexpected tumors. Who's gonna deal with all this sickness? You? How are even your 'supporters' going to live in the wasteland you're creating?"

THE MAN said, "Apple a day no smoke. Work out. Oat Bran, Broccoli, Marmite. Don't eat pretzels. Meat is good. Beef the red in RedWhiteandBlue. Freedom Fries. Prairie Oysters. Viagra. You are who you eat suggest don't go down on Laura."

I said, "Forget about it. I might as well be talking to Stalin, in Russian, for all the sense I'll get outta you. But let me say, there's something uniquely wrong with you. All your paved highways lead to Death.

"Imagine the worst. If the Nazis got their way: Hitler's little theme park. Wouldn't be good for the non-German majority, but I guess if you landed in a space ship from Planet X, you'd see a bunch of Germans in clean cities, green fields and not much else. Slavic slaves. A Jew or two in a museum or zoo. Nightmare, from the non-German point of view, and probably the German too, but a form of life. A mad vision. Same with the Zionists. They got their way you'd have a bunch of settlements in "Greater Judea," clean cities, green fields, Slavic slaves, and a Palestinian or two in a museum or zoo. Bleak vision, again, but still a form of life. Something the tourist from Planet X might have seen elsewhere, in other totalitarian pockets of the galaxy.

"But you , Corporate MAN, your vision, if fulfilled, would be grimmest of all, for it yields no survivors. Nothing. Dead air, dead animals, dead oceans. Ghost cities. Brown, rotting flora under gray-black sky. Green money in your vaults useless. Who you gonna pay? All the money sucked from the consumers of the world can't buy you an apple from dead trees. The Tourists from Planet X would think they stopped at a Ghost planet. Trashed and abandoned. Nothing, not even totalitarian ant colony life, in this wasteland. This sooty rock"

THE MAN said, "Bright shining burning screaming not my problem Sodom and Gomorrah. Door-to-door chariot my House to Heaven's Gate. Crush the people cleanse the people love the people bread and butter."

I said, "I hate you. Hate you. You're destroying just about everything that made it tolerable to be human. Six billion people will curse the day you appeared out of the Cosmic dust. But it will be too late. You'll have long since returned to dust, oblivion, while screams of terror, outrage, will reverberate throughout the globe. I wish your vicious Deity were real and not merely a grotesque delusion in your Depleted Cranium. I'm sure the billions of folks you're helping to whack would appreciate front row seats when your freak fantasy god kicks your ass from Hell to Eternity, AMEN."

# MIDNIGHT'S INNER CHILDREN (LOST IN *THE TIMES* WARP)

> "Many describe a nearly frantic compulsion to remain playful, flexible and fun in the face of realities like fixed-rate mortgages or lawn care. Mitch Anthony, president of a branding and design firm in Northampton, Mass., is a full-fledged adult: he has children, a closet full of suits and a picket fence that cost $10,000."
> —*The New York Times*, August 31, 2003

> "What ever happened to 'plain old crazy?'"
> —Chris Rock

I don't know how I became immortal. Never thought much about it. Can't remember Lenny, the owner of this increasingly heavy burden of flesh we share, saying to me on any particular day, "You're going to be twelve years old forever." It just happened.

I was Lenny's little secret. Never knew how many of us there were until I read this story, "I Don't Want to Grow Up!" in the venerable—to grown-ups—*New York Times*.

"From childless fans of kiddie music to the grown-up readers of "Harry Potter," inner children are having fun all over. Whether they are buying cars marketed to consumers half their age, dressing in baby-doll fashions or bonding over games like Twister and kickball, a new breed of quasi adult is co-opting the culture of children as never before. Most have busy lives with adult responsibilities, respectable jobs and children of their own. Call them rejuveniles."

—*The New York Times*, August 31, 2003

"Rejuveniles," my asshole. Those freaks are freaks. Super freaks. I mean, me and Lenny, we know we're "out there." Way out there. We keep a low profile. We REMAIN HIDDEN. Nobody's hurt by our little micro-Cosmic Order. It's a secret, entre nous, totally irrelevant to YOUR business, so just turn around and keep walking. Know what I mean?

Lenny lives his part of his life, I live my part of his life. Works for both of us. He gets the wife, Gloria, and I get the kids, Jackson and Jillian (though usually I'd rather play alone). He goes to work, I play computer games while he's there. Anyway, I'm not into the whole "adult responsibilities" scam, but since I never had one before, maybe one of you grown-ups can enlighten me: What does The Times mean by a "respectable" job, and what's a "not-respectable" job? You can't be all THAT "respectable" if you refer to one of the most important, influential people in your life as "Boss" and get all wobbly kneed when you see he's in a bad mood.

"They are not stunted adolescents. They are something else: grown-ups who cultivate juvenile tastes in products and entertainment."

—*The New York Times*, August 31, 2003

You remember that old joke about the two alcoholic brothers, one rich, one poor. The poor one is a crud boozer bum with rotten teeth. The brother with deep pockets and Country Club membership "enjoys a fine wine with a nutty bouquet" blah, blah, blah. Same principle as "grown-ups who cultivate juvenile tastes" as opposed to "stunted, infantile American."

Admit it. You laughed at Linus's blanket because you empathized. You too were scared shitless of the world, but too young for booze, drugs, cigarettes or fire arms and you didn't have the guts or desperation to carry around a fetish object to calm your rapid-fire nerves. Linus was too old for that damn thing, he should have kicked the habit like a man—which addressed another issue tackled in another of Schulz's week-long "Snoopy Soaps." It was funny because Linus was supposed to be a precociously neurotic seven or eight-year-old, not the humiliated owner of a fifty-something-year old bundle of head, limbs and torso that's seen much, much better years.

Such is the tragedy for so many like Lenny, the urchin-abled—some call them maturity-challenged—but you know, who wants to be defined in the negative? I might even encourage Lenny to do a study on it: "Drama of the Gifted Inner Child in Midlife Crisis."

I know all about this subject, having been twelve years old for, oh, about 35 years. The guy with whom I share this gargantuan mortal coil, Lenny, is 46 and works some corporate job where they lock him up every day for ten or twelve hours and make him read and write stuff and someone usually brings him lunch, steamed veggies or something like that. Poor son-of-a-bitch. Makes six figures at least but... how could he live without me? Surely he'd crack up.

I know I don't really "exist" the way Lenny does. Though to be fair, I'm certainly not imaginary. My experiences DO reside in Lenny's memory, I DID happen, but only up to a point, an age—eleven or twelve, thereabouts. Maybe thirteen. Some days I feel almost fifteen.

I'm Lenny's little boy lost, his hide-a-way. He goes to his little cubicle at the office and when the boss ain't looking I play with the games on his desk top; weekends and play-time with the kids are my time. Makes him look like a terrific dad. As for Gloria, his (our?) wife—I let him have her too. I mean, I could stay up all night just gaping at those big, round titties or that hairy wet between her legs (looks like the mouth of a fly, to me, or some strange "exotic" fruit one might discover at the Specialty Mart), but that wouldn't be enough for Lenny. Adults need to release tension, I understand that. We've worked it out well between us. But it's not like we don't KNOW we're (Lenny, to be precise; after all, I'm just a kid; not even that: a grown man's memory/fantasy of a kid) completely insane! Those rejuveniles, like. . . only in America. Who wants to hang out with such a posse of Disco-era atavisms, anyway? I wanna play, I wanna play with kids my age.

There's the rub, though. Kids "my age" reached my age around 1976. Different world back then, Different toys, games, movies, television. Even a coffee maker of those days would be almost unrecognizable in the modern, plug-n-play kitchen. Not that I haven't adapted to the new-fangled techno-gadgets they foist on Lenny's kids during play-time, but really I'm a creature of my time. The music, games, fads, sports heroes, and general entertainment of 1976. I'm no child psychiatrist (pun), but you don't need Freud to figure out that Lenny's inner life peaked around thirty years ago. I mean, I don't know. Who am I? I'm an anthology of days, a collection: The Best Of Lenny.

Same with these rejuveniles, only they're too delusional, like the rest of the country (I may have stopped developing at twelve, but I read the news), to recognize their own withering faces in the mirror. This whole "society" is "in denial" of reality, or whatever the Best Sellers and Talk Shows call "freaking out" these days.

"Celebrated by market researchers and fretted over by social scientists, rejuveniles come in all ages but are mostly a product of the urban upper classes (free time and disposable income being essential in their lifestyle). Evidence of their presence is widespread. According to Nielsen Media research, more adults 18 to 49 watch the Cartoon Network than watch CNN. More than 35 million people have caught up with long-lost school pals on the Web site Classmates.com. ('There's something about signing on to Classmates.com that makes you feel 16 again,' the '60 Minutes II' correspondent Vicki Mabrey reported.) Fuzzy pajamas with attached feet come in adult sizes at Target, along with Scoobie Doo underpants. The average age of video game players is now 29, up from 18 in 1990, according to the Entertainment Software Association. Hello Kitty's cartoon face graces toasters. Sea Monkeys come in an executive set."

—*The New York Times*, August 31, 2003

Gone, gone, these people are. Long gone. I worry about Lenny's kids growing up in a "culture" where lunatics are "celebrated by market researchers" and "fretted over by social scientists" rather than "soothed and sedated by professional healers." And where do market researchers fit into all this (as they do several times throughout the Times article)? Is that the new thing? Trying to squeeze insurance or better yet, cash, outta the batty, the bonkers and the emotionally distressed by fixing the charts and pathology manuals to read "normal?"

"A 2001 market research study by American Greetings, the creator of Strawberry Shortcake and Care Bears, showed that 'purchase interest' was identical among women who wanted to buy a doll for their child and those who simply wanted to rekindle a love affair of their own. 'This consumer wants Care Bears in their life,' Ms. Joester said. 'And not just to share with their children.'"

—*The New York Times*, August 31, 2003

They never mention the fact that nearly all the tchotchkes these rejuveniles cream over date back to their own youth. No shit. They're not into kids' toys, fads and clothes per se (I've never seen a rejuvenile with a game-boy; then again, I've never seen a rejuvenile at all, have you?), but the crap they remember from their own days in The Garden. So it's not just wanting to have fun like a kid, it's wanting to have fun while being a kid. Again. Reaching for seconds before their own kids experience their first taste. I always thought parents who drink and smoke pot with their teenagers were a bit "off," but these people, these rejuveniles, are stealing youth and childhood artifacts from their own beleaguered tots. Poor Santa Claus can't make sense of all this. Just sits around the lodge, Thanksgiving, with a bottle of potato vodka, listening to "Alice's Restaurant," cursing corporate media, post-modernism, the wretched Calvinism of his elves...

"While some marketers court rejuveniles directly—'Who knew you and your daughter would have the same best friend?' asked an advertisement for a revived line of Strawberry Shortcake dolls—others speak to the rejuvenile soul by simply selling to kids. The Honda Element, the Tonkalike mini-truck introduced by the company as a 'combination dorm room/base camp for active young buyers,' has been marketed mostly at extreme sports and surfing events, said Andy Boyd, a spokesman for the American Honda Motor Company. But the average age of Element drivers, Mr. Boyd said, is 40. 'That's exactly what we anticipated,' he said. 'It's a new definition of the family buyer—someone who doesn't want to give up their individual character even though they're getting older.'"

—*The New York Times*, August 31, 2003

The Greeks had Philosophers to tackle the "big issues;" we have Marketers.

What's with this so-called "newspaper" anyway? Why do they send reporters out to scoop "hot" fads for advertisers to exploit? I suppose "someone who doesn't want to give up their individual character even though they're getting older" is a good description, in this context, if your "family buyer" happens to be Snow White's Evil Stepmother or Dorian Grey. Or Michael Jackson.

But most people have to change as life proceeds and they accumulate knowledge and experience (which include, though it's not profitable to say so, pain). Those who can't evolve, dissolve, like Lenny. They can go out into the grown-up world and get things done, but they forever remain lonely children in their parents' backyards. Eight, ten, twelve years old, talking to themselves, or an abstraction of a recollection of self, an alias, on the swing-set. They live with ghosts of themselves, shadows of the Past.

Like me and Lenny.

But the thing about me and Lenny is we've been friends since the fourth grade. He needed me then, like he does now, but in a different way, and he liked me so much he decided to keep me, just as I was. Which is why he grew up and I remain just as I was, as we were. I have a feeling some or most of these rejuveniles are merely hyping and Romanticizing the past. Mainlining nostalgia.

What makes the past seem "better" than today is simply this: you survived. You lived. So if you go back to the past, you know that whatever happens, you're gonna come out okay. Like the hero of a TV Cop show. The present and the future hold no such certainties. You can spin the propeller on your beanie all you want; death and tragedy can leap outta the evergreen suburban hedgerows before you can say

See what I mean?

"While there is nothing new about adults reveling in kiddie culture—Shirley Temple, Roald Dahl and Pee Wee Herman all had plenty of adult fans—market researchers say an especially strong wave of childishness began about two years ago."

—*The New York Times*, August 31, 2003

So according to the "Paper of Record," this Gamin Guerrilla movement started about two years ago. Now what, pray tell, happened two years ago that turned almost all Americans into frightened flag-waving children running to the school bully for "protection?" Please. These people are about as deep and complex as a "Li'l Lulu" comic book. Though somewhat less compelling.

Most people might say the rejuveniles are no sicker than Lenny. But

I never thought of Lenny as "sick." He has this thing—me, I guess—that he knows is a bit strange, a vice even, but it lets him get through his sorry ass existence, so he keeps it—me—in his own skull. Doesn't let it interfere with what's important to him. Like Gloria and the kids. He even integrated me, to the best of his ability, into his work and social life, such as they are. But he never pretended we were "plain old folks." I'm sure he'd rather be rid of me, and he knows this, only he doesn't have the will to let me go. He lives with himself (and me) as best as he can, tries to "do life" as best as he can.

But not the rejuveniles. Oh, no. They have to make over the world. Turn their "alternative lifestyle" into a kind of party in the Hamptons, a hep-cat statement about the unspeakable. It's not enough to accept your addiction to a certain pleasure, though it brings you pain, and either you deal with it or not. You have to keep the pleasure and get rid of the pain—as if the relationship weren't symbiotic; you have to have it all.

I think this whole rejuvenile thing is about greed. Can't have just one over-indulged childhood, you need two. I wonder how many adults who were abused as kids are rejuveniles? Or something worse—in America—than a childhood of parental abuse: How many of these rejuveniles grew up dark-skinned and/or poor?

The U.S. power elite has nothing to worry about. Nothing. They can pull off any military/economic/legal scam they want and get away with it. Who's going to stand up for people, Alfalfa? Bart Simpson? Buckwheat? Of course Californians drafted Gary Coleman for Governor. The Mainstream Media think he's a harmless, grinning, slap-happy "boy." And don't forget about Arnold to bring in the under-eighteen crowd. The under-eighteens can't vote? Lame excuse. Any decent Republican worth his ill-gotten capital gains can win California or any other state, with or without votes. Who do you think dropped Dubya like a duffel bag of stinky diapers on our heads, the Stork?

Well, Americans are not my problem. Just like the *New York Times* is not my problem. And me and Lenny try not to be anyone else's problem: we live our life and shut up about it. I went to the Times Web Site to check the weather forecast, that's all. The headline sucked me in.

I won't grow up, I'll buy stuff. All the stuff my parents bought me 30 years ago I'll buy again, not for my kids, but for myself, at seven times the price. The Peter Pavlov Complex.

Life is okay for me. Really. I provide Lenny with great memories, living memories. I am memory, living. Every time I pick up a baseball or quote a passage from "The Hardy Boys" a thrill zaps Lenny's aging spine. His kids bring him joy. But the feeling of raising a kid just can't compare to the—I'll admit, adulterated—memory of being one.

Most people accept their kids as a substitute for what is lost. The rare but creative lunatic, like Lenny, will find a way to have his kids and be one too.

I may have frozen in time when Chevy Chase was in the White House, but I read the news and other things (with Lenny's extensive vocabulary—smart guy, Lenny, did real well in school ever since I showed up to occupy his diversions and save him from what could have been a killer Ritalin regimen). I don't know whether the "culture" is crumbling to pieces before my eyes; the new media tactic for steering people away from real issues like the environment, economy and Empire is to focus on the whims of a few crazed, wealthy white people; or the *New York Times* periodically makes up this kinda shit to drive Lenny and like-minded individuals to a level of lunacy beyond the capabilities of Bellevue Hospital, to the only place where they could possibly find honest help: Sesame Street.

Just say "NO" to Time. Visit Adam Engel's Rejuvenile Revivalist Patchouli Palace Head Shop and Emporium at bartlebysamsa65@gmail.com

# A GOOD MAN IS HARD TO MISFIT

Used to call me the Misfit cause I couldn't do nothin' right—least not in this world. Now they call me "Mr. President," jest like Paw said they would. My brother Jeb, he said, "Daddy got you a job is all. It jest happens to be a real big 'un."

Yeah, I reckon so. But hell. Ain't like I weren't civilized and socialized as a young 'un. I got my schoolin' done and then my higher learnin'—Yale, Harvard—and you can be sure I raised holy hell a-ruttin' and a-hollerin' and a-drinkin' so hard it's a wonder I learned me anything a'tall.

But I growed up, some—the hard way. I flied me a plane clear 'cross Texas durin' the War 'gainst the Indian Chinese. Tore into the cold earth for liquid gold—lucre is all; the black blood of Mammon that lubricationizes this sorry vale of tears. Even run me a baseball team. Quit drinkin' too. A-yup. No thanks to them alchee-holic 2-steppers and their K-Mart religion: Meetin' secretly in dank basements every blessed afternoon a-whinin' and a-cryin and a-kickin' and a-screamin' up every damn one of them god awful 12 steps. No sir. Not me. I answer to a much Higher Power...

I been saved—twicet. I been reborn. I remember the good Rev. Jimmy Swaggert—before he becomed a blubberin' whoremonger—I remember him preachin'—on nation'l TV he preached—about them atheists and communists at the Harvard Divinity school, or mighta been the Harvard school of Guvment, same thing I reckon, he preached, "When we die, you can go to Harvard. Me, I wanna go to

Heaven." And it damn near brought the house down. Not a house of God directly, more a stadium like. But I felt the good word touch me even through the color TV box.

I got the callin.' Look in my eyes, you'll see. I got the callin.' I see it, I see it all: Fire and Redemption, even for the Jews. Oh yes. Oh yes siree. Why, I got me a whole kitchen full-a Jews. Wolfowitz, aptly named I might say, and Perle, a man even the meanest, low-downest, orneriest killers at the Pentagon calls "the Prince-a Darkness" (and they ain't far off the mark). Even got me that Ari Fishbaum speakin' in tongues to the liberal communist Media. Think that was a accident?

Some folks, usually furriners and leftist intersexuals and A-rab terrorists and such, they think I take "orders" from fat ol' Ariel Sharon. Huh. No more'n he takes "orders" from Pat Robertson, or gives 'em to Jerry Falwell. We're all in this together. Yer with us or agin' us, like I been sayin' all along. Well, least since them World Train Towers got blowed up in New York City—and it weren't me what called it "Hymie Town," neither. Ask yer fancy-talkin' adulterizin' colored feller 'bout that 'un.

When the Evil among us is destroyed, when the Rapture comes, them Jew-boys—gathered in Israel every last one of 'em by then; least that's what's written in The Book, and I ain't talkin' 'bout no egghead scholar book or the Baseball Encyclopedia neither; I'm talking bout the one true only book that matters—anyways, them Jew-boys'll see the wickedness of their ways and fall a-weepin' to the feet of Our Savior and beg His forgiveness and rise to Heaven with the rest of us Believers. And they won't be 'restricted' when they get there. No. They'll be treated jest as fine as if they was reglar baptized Christians.

There're good Jews, I tell you. From Ari to Ariel, I only keep company with good Jews, the ones what'll see the light when it shines upon them. It will—once we gather all the Jews, both good and bad, in the Holy Land, which might take some work, specially flushin' 'em from cosmiccomican areas like Los Angelees and NYC, but Ariel Sharon and them AIPAC fellers,' they're studyin' on it. They'll find the way...

Ronnie Reagan, he knew what was comin.' He saw the Apocalypse and prepared for it with the correct military hardware to put the communists and other evil ones to flame; trouble was, the folks around him, Georgie Schultz, Jeanne Kirkpatrick, James Baker III, Bill Casey, even my own Paw, they was more innerested in hedge-a-money in this life than heaven in the next. Now, I'm sure Ronnie had nothing 'gainst hedge-a-money if it was gonna help bring on the reign of Heaven, but hedge-a-money for its own sake, for love a nuthin' more'n Riches n' Power in this wicked world... that just don't figure.

Not to Ronnie, not to me.

My Pappy's a good man, and when The Lord comes, I know Pappy'll jump like a lamb into His arms; but he saw that hedge-a-money as a good thing in itself, not as a step toward Heaven, and that kinda thinking don't make no sense to me, no sense a'tall.

Well, that don't matter no how. There's work to be done, and we're a-goin' do it. We got the firepower and we got the faith. Light all them heathens up like Roman candles, smoke 'em outta their holes, burn 'em, burn 'em all, like The Book says. My Paw told me it was Our Destiny, America's Destiny, to do the work of the Lord. Well, that's directly what we're goin' do.

Yeah. I know what yer thinkin.' I don't like it any more than you do. I got nuthin agin' the Iraqi people, personally. But it's gotta be done—

"What Fun!"

"Shut up, Donald. Ain't no enjoyment in this life."

You'll have to excuse the impermanence of my assistant, interjectifying like that in the middle of my. . . obsequy. "Rummy" didn't mean no harm by it, I reckon. Rudeness is all. Rudeness and ign'rance. You see, Rummy don't unnerstand that Saddam, like most fellers, Ossama too, would be a GOOD MAN if, if only he had. . . if only he had someone there to shoot him every day of his life.

# MIS-PERCEPTIONS OF PALESTINE: IT'S ALL ABOUT OLIVE OIL

## The Root of the Problem

Alright. I've gone a little nuts, but I'm armed, so it's okay. A cold cartridge laid upon a damp palm—a talisman of sorts—or snapped into the cylinder, like a slap to the kisser, promotes alertness and clear thinking. Keeps you awake, at least, and it's better for the bowels than coffee.

So obvious the cause of this whole mess. Here in bed with me night after night. No, I'm not talking about my rifle, but my wife. Italian. Her ancestors were Roman. Roman. So? So read the Bible, shit head. See the root, the Latin root, of all this evil. Judas mighta sold out Jesus, but it was the Romans who strung him up, lynched him, and if you look at what Jesus was doing, among other things—busy guy—it was inventing a means to defeat an unbeatable Empire: non-violence. Scared the crap outta everybody, and not only that, it worked. Render that which is Caesar's unto Caesar, indeed.

But that's just a Testament, after all, penned by Greek Platonists and disgruntled Rabbis. I'm talking about History: Diaspora. The Roman conquest of Palestine. Exile. The whole kit n' caboodle. The Beginning.

My wife's fault, of course. Her whole family posing as these kindly, hard-working American types who merely know how to cook better than anybody else when all along they had the guilt, the GUILT for this whole mess perched like mute parrots on their strong, bronze ROMAN shoulders.

Next door, my in-laws were throwing their annual Christmas party. And what were they celebrating anyway, under all that Santa Claus mishegas, but the lynching by their ancestors of yet another loud mouth Jew? A Jew who spoke out once too often and too candidly. A Jew who didn't know his place. Started to make more sense then. Their kindly "tolerance" toward me, the Jew in the family. Worse: the loud mouth lefty atheist non-aligned Jew, who wouldn't know the meaning of family if he were a piglet at the teat. Hell I didn't have a decent conversation with my own mother until at least three years after she was dead.

Started to make sense that it is all THEIR fault, not only that Middle East nightmare half a world away, but the harsh here-and-now reality that I, who want only to be left the fuck alone, am drafted into Judaism due to anti-Semitism bred of 2000 years of squatting from one hostile country to the next, culminating in the Slaughter Of All Slaughters (well, there were the Armenians, and the Native Americans, and the Africans who died en route to "democracy" and the Cambodians and—but hell, you know what I mean) by the Germans. And if you read Tacitus or any of those Imperial Roman courtier scribes, or even saw the movie, "Gladiator," you know what the Romans did to those blond-haired, blue-eyed tree folk (no wonder they went all starry-eyed and metaphysical and loony; Kant and Beethoven were only the beginning).

Good god, the Romans fucked up EVERYBODY. And when they weren't crucifying folks or shuffling populations hither thither and yon they were inspiring others—yes, even in DEATH—to do the same (hint, hint Britain; hint, hint, US of A). We won't even mention the Catholic Church, which took the bag Paul swiped from Jesus and buried it under a mountain of neat Roman hierarchy. And where is the Pope located anyway, Mahwah, New Jersey? Bullshit. It's all the Italians' fault. No wonder these people overflow with gusto and joie de vivre and the wine and the food and the whole Fellini Life's-A-Sexy-Freak-Fest thing. You'd be happy too if you'd spent 20 centuries getting away with murder and nobody—well, maybe the Greeks—blamed you for anything except "Rocky IV!"

### Nobody's Innocent

So I loaded my rifle with those hollow-point, banana sized cartridges and went next door and damn if I didn't mean business.

"Adam. Where were you? Put that thing down. The macaroni and gravy are ready."

Think they can get out of it with ingenuous ethnic banter, eh? Calling spaghetti and tomato sauce "macaroni and gravy" when everybody in the world, from Martha Stewart to Chef Boy Ardee, knows it's spaghetti and goddam tomato sauce!

"It's your fault!" I raged. "It's always all everything entirely and to infinity been your fault. And now you're gonna pay!"

"What are you talking? Put that thing down, you're frightening the kids."

Oh, right. Yeah. I'd forgotten. My nieces and nephews, ages one to fourteen years. Innocents. But are they REALLY? Can we honestly say that a five-year-old Palestinian is "innocent" of terrorism? Or a six year old Israeli is "innocent" of racist imperialism (not to mention killing Jesus—but it was the Italians who did that; the Pope even admitted it was an inside job)?

"Nobody's innocent," I said, righteously. "And nobody's getting outta here alive!"

I looked around at all the tschotchkes these benevolent folk had collected from various cultures on their way to World Conquest: Christmas trees, wreathes and other doo-dads filched from the Celts or Gauls or whatever pagan tree-huggers were into all that forest-and-pine-cone crap; turkey and yams from Native Americans; pasta from the Chinese; Frank Sinatra lifted, bourbon, tux and all, from the Mississippi Delta. I wouldn't be surprised to find on my mother-in-law's bookshelf, secreted behind the all art and poetry, The Protocols of the Elders of Milan.

Old—too old, in my opinion; so old she's barely human, more of a metaphysical argument, a lingering dream—Aunt Delia leaned over and whispered to her slightly younger and more vigorous brother, Vincent, "Isn't that the nice Jewish boy who married Maria? Does he have a job yet?"

"Shut up. The nice Jewish boy's deer rifle is fixed upon the Family Jewels. In case you didn't notice."

"Adam, you've been drinking again!" said my wife. "What is this about?"

"What is this about? What is this ABOUT? About TWO THOUSAND YEARS is what it's about. World conquest! Empire! The Middle East is burning my brain and it's all your goddamn fault! Uh... ethnically speaking, honey. Nothing personal."

"Oh, Christ. Is he going on about one of those commie things he read on the internet again?" said my brother-in-law. "Why don't you just take that damn laptop away from the poor guy—it's making him nuts."

"Oh, I get it. I know what all this is about," said old Uncle Vincent.

"You do?" asked the fifteen other Conspirators Against Universal Peace And World Stability.

"Yeah, yeah," he sighed, wearily. "Let me tell you, if I knew it was gonna come to this, I wouldn't have lived so long. Damn olive oil."

"Red wine too," his sister piped in. "And Garlic. The Italian diet is—"

"Shut up!" barked Vincent. Then he turned to me. "Okay. So you put two and two together. Congratulations, Einstein. You talk about two thousand years of suffering? Try two thousand years of listening to grievances and heart-ache. The fruits of Empire are sweet but they rot quick. Straight to the core. Did we know the wine would turn to vinegar? Does anyone? We thought we were heeding the Destiny's call and all that Caesar crap."

"Two thousand years? Vinny, I didn't know you were that old! If you're my younger brother, that must make me—"

"Shut up, Delia!" the chorus screamed.

"So you admit it!" I crowed triumphantly. "At last! I've hacked these centuries of wilderness down to their Latin roots! Why don't YOU deal with the fundamentalists of Abraham and all his batty sons, for a change? Moses said this and Jesus said that and Mohammed said this other thing. Do I need to hear this? It's your problem, old man, not mine."

"Look, it was a long time ago," said Vincent, lighting a Di Nobili. "So many battles, 'police actions,' cities put to siege. I can barely even remember conquering the Jews. All I do remember, and it's very vague, is marching drunkenly and chanting "Hierusalem est perdita" or something like that, in Latin. Marching. Marching. Always marching. Then a lot of hacking and chopping and blood and women screaming and children crying and badda-bing-badda-boom—we had Palestine. We posed for a frieze with one of those, whaddya-call, candelabra things and some newly minted slaves. I'm not completely sure what happened next. A lot of bureaucracy, paper work, that kind of thing. Again, it was a long time ago. I'm not the robust Centurion I used to be."

"That's it?" I asked.

"Well, it was a heck of a battle. You people put up a damn good fight. But we were the Empire. Nobody fucks with the Empire."

"That's not what I mean. That is. I don't know. I expected HISTORY, I expected—"

"Lights! Cameras! Action! Kaboom! Like CNN. And all you got was the fuzzy war-story of an old man. Welcome to the world. I know how it is. Think I wasn't young too, once?"

My righteous outrage caved in upon itself like a black hole.

"It's like this," said Uncle Vincent calmly. "Kind of like what that nice Italian fellow, the chemist, Levi, said, 'the Palestinians are the Jews' Jews.' Well, what were the Jews but Rome's Palestinians? Always making trouble, always clamoring about your 'right' to the land you'd lived on for generations. Same old stuff about your god as all the other outposts of the Empire. So, like with everybody else, we let you have your god or gods or whatever your tribal customs demanded. Just render your money, loyalty, and when necessary, your bodies, to Caesar when he needed them, and you were okay. The others behaved themselves. Why not the Jews? It's not like we didn't warn you. But you were threatening the stability of the Empire. What with the suicides at Massada and your guerilla networks. We were like the Americans in Vietnam. Or the Israelis in Beirut. Finally, we had to close down the whole show. Break up the group and disperse you. Nothing personal, just politics. Good politics, in my opinion. After all, it did, temporarily at least, for Rome, solve that pain-in-the-ass Palestine problem. . ."

Cold bummer. Empty reality blues. I loosened my sweaty grip on the rifle.

"Mommy, why is Uncle Adam holding that big gun? And why is he sad?" asked my six-year-old, nephew, Donny.

"He's just playing, Donny. He's pretending."

"Pretending to be what?"

"I don't know. Some kind of terrorist or something. Like on TV."

"He doesn't LOOK like the terrorists on TV."

"Enough talk, Donny. Eat. It's Christmas."

She filled his plate with macaroni.

"More gravy?"

**Adam Engel** has lost his mind. Anyone in possession of his mind is kindly requested to send it as text—no attachments, please—to bartlebysamsa65@gmail.com

# U.S. TROOPS OUTTA TIMES SQUARE (LIFE IN OCCUPIED NEW YORK)

Camouflage. Boots. Automatic weapons. Real Vietnam stuff: Spooky fetid atmosphere; scared, bored troops who don't really know why they're there in that hellish jungle. Fat commanding officers, confident of overwhelming victory, hitting on female troops. A stressed-out populace, hoping to get where they're going with as little hassle as an occupied people can get away with.

But this ain't Vietnam, it's Times Square Station.

Yeah, yeah: support "our" troops. Support 'em in Afghanistan, Iraq, Saudi Arabia, South Korea, Japan, Europe, Greenland, Timbuktu, Atlantis, Mars. Support 'em anywhere you want except New York City.

If you think I'm gonna smile like a just-pissed-my-pants Democrat and welcome an invading army, you're as dumb as Dubya thinks you are. As dumb as he thought Afghans and Iraqis were—boy is he learning different. Bring the boys and girls back home; let them enjoy healthy, happy, peaceful lives—far away from me. Troops who are originally from NYC should be sent somewhere else... I dunno... Fort Munchaussen or the next pip-squeak axis of evil Terrorist-State-of-the-Month they can conquer without too much risk of personal injury. I don't care. Just get 'em out of Port Authority and Times Square Station and god knows where else in the Big Rotting Apple they're squirreled away.

What happened to Posse Comitatus or Habeas Corpus (more on that later) or all those other Latinate terms no one seems to care about anymore (with the possible exception of those with bank vaults full of E. Pluribus Unum?).

This is no joke. Kids not old enough to shave or buy a drink or a pack of smokes (the legal kind), toting M16s in the subways and bus terminals, hobnobbing with middle-aged cops. Young Black and Hispanic and lower class White kids defending rich old White men's rights to conduct business as usual and scaring the daylights outta everyone else. Makes you want to go to a bar and smoke a cigarette and talk to a fellow New Yorker in low tones, exchange furtive glances, flash secret signs of rebellion. But you can't smoke a cigarette in a bar cause this is New York, the City that won't wake up.

That whole "nothing phases New Yorkers" thing has been perverted by THE MAN to HIS advantage. If you're not phased by a dozen young men and women with automatic rifles hanging out in the places you travel through every day, have been traveling through since childhood, you're not a "hip, jaded New Yorker," you're a brain-dead Zombie.

I don't know what YOUR situation is, YOU out there, in America. Maybe this kind of stuff turns you on. I checked out some awfully sexy female troopers with deliciously phallic M16s between their thighs. The guys are good-looking too, if that's your preference.

Now, I like to think of myself as being as goofy and degenerate as any other American. When "my" President says to go shopping while the hyper-armed U.S. Military wipes out some poor, bedraggled, hopelessly out-gunned "nation," why, I go shopping. Or, to paraphrase that great Patriot, Oliver North, if my President tells me to stand on my head in the corner and have myself an inverted wank while the Bush twins explore each others' sexuality, Hell, I'll do it. But I'll be damned if I'll tolerate soldiers in Times Square.

And I have nothing against the soldiers themselves. They look scared outta their minds down there in the subway, the old cops proud to be able to distribute donuts and wisdom to fellow uniformed protectors of the peace. Blacks, Hispanics, corn-fed Caucasian country kids. All the cannon fodder who would be in school or employed, in a real country, or in jail or guarding the jails, in ours. Fortunately, we have a big old military and lots and lots of enemies to give these kids something to do. But not in New York City.

I would think that any "terrorist" worth his salt would come up with something a bit more creative than trying to hit a place swarming with cops and armed soldiers, so if one place is "safe" god knows how many others are potential targets. Do we need a commando in every household, and a chicken in every pot to feed him?

On the other hand, with all the noise and confusion down there boggling the minds of our brave boys and girls in uniform, I doubt it would be too hard for a guy with a suitcase full of god-knows-what to set it off right where the soldiers stood.

Regardless, if there really are terrorists plotting to mess up NYC and this is not simply a device for the Bush Administration to introduce yet more authority into our lives, I guess I'd rather take my chances with a pistol and my own paranoid eyes and ears than be terrorized daily by "our" troops. It's bad enough to have a standing army of 40,000 of New York's Finest handing out tickets for cigarette smoking, sitting on milk crates without a license, or having too many words or letters in a deli sign advertising lunch specials. Now we gotta deal with the fucking army?

Well, my priorities have sure changed. You don't see many Palestinians in Occupied West Bank and Gaza marching to get China outta Tibet. They have immediate, pressing issues at home. So too does occupied New York.

Sure, we gotta stop the U.S. military machine from taking over foreign countries; we have to find out why there are so many, mostly dark-skinned, inmates of U.S. prisons and what, if anything, most of them actually did (smoke a joint? think about smoking a joint?). There are nearly a thousand prisoners in Guantanamo Bay being held without trial or even that war-prisoner Geneva Convention protocol. When they were Germans and Italians and Japanese, way back when, they were called POWs. Them being Afghans and all, we tag them "terrorists" and strip them of what were once known as Human Rights.

We have to face the fact that Muslim—again dark skinned—Americans and foreign visitors have been taken away and held indefinitely, without habeas corpus, and demand from the "authorities" what they are charged with, not to mention the several thousand more Muslims who were forced to register with the government in the greatest Federal outrage against civil liberties since the Japanese internment camps.

We have to find out what really happened on 9/11 and why the government refuses to hold an open trial and get to the bottom of this monstrous event (could it be that, like with OJ, the feds are too busy looking for the "real" killers to answer key questions?). We have to feed, cloth and educate our children, heal our sick, provide for our elderly and—oh, that's right. We're in AMERICA. Whatta my talking that socialist crap? Well, forget about the children and other vulnerable members of society—let's stick to the foreign invasion of New York City. The Occupation of Manhattan.

Reality begins at home. Before we attack these other issues we must get the U.S. Military out of NYC, and whatever other cities in which troops are stationed. Disney and Warner Brothers in Times Square was bad enough.

Yanqui go home!

Regardless, if they really are [illegible] plotting to mess up NY[illegible] and this is not simply a device for the future administration to [illegible] for some [illegible] I guess I'd rather take my chances with a pistol and my own personal [illegible] and [illegible] than standard daily by [illegible] "brains" [illegible] had brought in [illegible] calculating a fine of $250 for [illegible] New York [illegible] handing out tickets for [illegible] smoking, sitting on milk crates without a license, or having too many words or letters in a cell sign advertising menu specials. Now [illegible]

[illegible] have [illegible] changed. [illegible] machine [illegible] They have [illegible] as [illegible]

# PISS OFF, NSA
# (AND OTHER RADICAL HIJINX)

Don't be too surprised to meet a violent death within the next few decades. Just because the concentration camps in America aren't "active" yet doesn't mean "we" aren't Nazis. Take Iraq, for instance. If we forget about the dubious ideas of "Nations" and "Clashing Idea Sets" we might see the Iraqis as... uh... HUMAN BEINGS. In which case Iraq has been one giant concentration camp since 1991. Think of it as a "test run" for Homeland Security. After all, THEY know when you are sleeping, THEY know when you're awake...

For instance, some folks say the NSA has a SUPER-MAGIC MOJO VACUUM that can suck all the data outta all the software of the world, suck the rhythm from our loins, suck the oldest, dampest long-forgottenest, memories of Mommy from our numb cerebrums.

All together now, in unison: PISS OFF, NSA!

What are we supposed to do? Beg, plead, humiliate ourselves yet further?

"Kiss the flag, kiss it, tastes good that REDWHITEandBLUE, don't it?"

"Yessir, Sir/Ma'am/Sir, sir. Oh, yessir!"

"Well, it better. If you know what's good for ya. It damn well better..."

Are WE really as whipped and cowardly as they think we are, or as they think we think we are? Are THEY as super almighty powerful (and benevolent, as long as we behaves ourselves) as they tell us they are? When is enough finally enough?

Check this out:

Tried to start a discussion group with a couple of like-minded radical trouble-makers: i.e. fellow pissed off, outraged, citizens, K. and P. (names compacted to initials to protect the guilty). I 'bcc'd' a whole lotta folks, just about everyone on my mailing list.

Wrote something like, "Yo, we're starting a living debate on the web we're just gonna talk about stuff talk till we're blue in the face or red in the face or white in the face about how sick and fucking tired we are about being REDWHITEandBLUE in the face and no more bullshit about the Democratic Party come down from Heaven and save our souls. No moderator, no group identity, name or philosophy other than, 'Say yer thing but be prepared to back it up.' Welcome Greens, Reds, Pinks, libertarians fascists anarchists leftists rightists and everything in-between-ists (even Democrats and Republicans, or their lobbyists, a pox upon their proxy Houses!) for debate. I mean, say whatever you want, who's gonna stop you?"

We thought maybe the thing might grow, you know, like the commercial says, "And they told two friends and they told two friends and so on and so on." A networking phenomenon. A "free roving argument" that would metastasize and engulf the planet in ideas. A "virus" if you will, albeit a benevolent one (or maybe not so benevolent).

Of course, my prematurely (and immaturely) imagined Borgesian labyrinth of networks and inquiry fell flat on its face and ended up being just me and a couple of other guys talking about a paper one of us wrote about anarchism and jawing about French neo-Marxist post modern philosophers like Virilio and Massumi and Foucault—you know, the kind of stuff that makes Powell and Rumsfeld sweat. With each new insight by Derrida, George Bush Jr. is quaking in his boots.

Only two people of the four dozen I bcc'd wrote back. The first person asked to be removed from the list immediately. And I thought, "Rightfully so." I mean, people are bothered and harassed enough by evil Mainstream Media rays, why do they want to hear a bunch of radical yahoos yammering about god knows what. I realized I was perhaps overzealous and intrusive by bcc'ing everyone in my address book, so I wrote to my two compatriots, bcc'ing the rest, a sort of apology:

"In my growing conviction that the State is forcing us to either submit, or resort to extreme measures, I jumped the gun and tried to "jump start" this "living debate," "language virus" or whatever it is by drafting dozens of people into it, rather than explaining the nature of what we're doing—that is, nothing much, yet, just talking—and waiting for them to voluntarily jump on the bandwagon was precipitous, naive and somewhat arrogant.

"By bcc'ing everyone whose email I had in my address book, I may have slipped from anarchism to totalitarianism in one great leap of the 'Send' command. People are already overloaded with information, and in general don't like to be bothered. I think the three of us have some interesting things to say from varying points of view. That's a start. Maybe if we keep up the dialogue among ourselves, gradually inviting friends—flesh and blood or "virtual"—into the discussion and encourage them to invite others etc. this 'spontaneous network' will actually be spontaneous and grow organically. So, "talk" to you guys tomorrow. As for the rest of you kind folks out there—colleagues, friends, virtual and otherwise, fellow travelers on the information super turnpike to the stars or whatever it's supposed to be—I apologize for drafting you into this 'open' dialogue or intruding on your privacy in any way. If you would like to be part of this discussion of course, feel free to respond to this final or any of the previous 'bcc's.'"

But it occurred to me that the guy who asked to be taken off the list was one of those "work-with-the-system-and-Media-that-we-have-to-prevent-it-from-doing-even-more-damage" types. I have no interest in the Mainstream Media and their hokum; surely there must be other alternatives for genuine discourse and action.

Now I respect this guy very much for his gradualist approach (if we dig the pit slow enough, maybe they'll reconsider shooting us today, cause they'll never get our mass grave covered up before sundown, not at this rate) , but the problem with working within the Mainstream media is that the Mainstream Media has been working WITHIN ME for over 30 years, and man did it do a job on my poor little noggin!

I hate the Media, the Corporations that own it and the pushers who peddle it. They tried to kill me; they drove me insane!!

They turned me into a goddamn consumer goods buyin,' slogan-spoutin,' prescription-pill poppin' zombie! Fuck them, man. They're the one's that drove me to try to debate real stuff outside of their prepared script in the first place. I mean, I was a good boy once. I was ready, willing and able to devote myself to working in the service of society. But it turned out that there was no society to serve. It was all a hoax, a mirage, a fig of my imagination—that tiny oasis where one can actually eat the coconuts and drink the milk. I'm tryin' to get away from them "Mainstream" freaks. I'm trying to LEARN me some stuff!

But then I got another, more instructive email, warning me, with good reason, that the NSA/NSC has been monitoring phone calls and faxes for years; hence, how easy it must be for them to use their SUPER MONSTER MOJO DATA VACUUM to suck up everything on every network—the backbone of which was DARPA's invention in the first place—and run a search and find everything they might ever want or need, whenever the hell they might need or want it.

Well, as the paranoid pot-smoker in Naked Lunch said, "I GOT THE FEAR!"

Here I thought I was doing something positive and constructive and enjoyable—reading books and articles and discussing them—and now I'd intimidated the entire U.S. Government Military Intelligence Complex. Damn!

Surely they were out to get me and my compeers. Maybe that's why nobody emailed us back. It wasn't that they didn't give a fuck about our stupid debate, like I at first erroneously believed; in fact, they yearned to get online and chew the fat about Proudhon and Bakunin and what not, it's just that... they were afraid! And rightfully so. It made me think. What did they know that I didn't (besides what the hell Derrida might possibly be talking about)? Could it be that even K. and P., the only people who were actually willing to join my little debating club were... SPOOKS?

I never felt so... POWERFUL in my irrelevant, sorry-assed, pimple of a life!

Imagine that! The NSA/NSC would take the trouble to monitor and perhaps, who knows, the sky's the limit (literally), prosecute an erstwhile insignificant toe-nail clipping of a man like ME. I mean, nobody but friends and family has ever paid any attention to ME before, and here the entire NSA (or some pathetic cubicle jockey on a PC—I can't picture the Feds using Macs for some reason; I don't know why) is going through all the trouble to open up Windows Office XXX or whatever and create a file and take up space on one of their giga-mega-terra-bit-byte drives just to keep track of ME for—what did I do again?—oh yeah, for sending out an email to various extreme-right-extreme-left-extreme-burger whacko hot-mailin' yahoo-searchin' cable modem-usin' netizens, calling for—gasp!—some kind of debate and maybe plan something radical, like steal the patina panties off the Statue Of Liberty or unleashing Hegel's dialectic at a crowded intersection! Goddamn Me I'm bad-ass! Wonder what mischief I'll be up to next?

Then I thought of all the kind, innocent folks that the likes of ME were, well, corrupting.

Poor *Counterpunch*! Poor well-intentioned but hopelessly naive Cockburn and St. Claire! They had a nice, safe, mainstream 'zine going until I came along and fired up Lucille (my laptop) and, what with my international reputation as a radical dissident who can and will profoundly influence the course of American politics with everything I say, put them and all the innocents they publish (Chomsky,

Said, Nader, Bill Blum etc.) at unspeakable risk!

Surely, now the word's out, all America's gonna be creating free and open discussion groups and maybe linking them like small communities, and the NSA's gonna have to shut down the whole operation, all these cells, "discussion groups," so called, inspired by ME.

Well, I feel bad about all that, but really, the ALL POWERFUL GOVERNMENT will take care of ME soon enough, so no more editors or writers or anyone else will have to worry.

That is, except YOU. Why are you reading this? Why are your eyes here, where they surely don't belong—why, in fact, do you have *Counterpunch* book-marked? Shouldn't you be clicking your mouse elsewhere, like the USA Today site maybe, or Christmas shopping on <BuyStuff.com>? You think the NSA doesn't know you're reading this sentence right now, this very moment? Who do you think's writing this? Do you really think we'd let such a dangerous, infamous, radical jokester like Adam Engel exist for longer than a nanosecond after pulling such a stunt? Please. Give us more credit. That's why they call us "Intelligence," fool! Cause we're intelligent.

Ha. Ha. Ha ha ha ha ha ha ha—watch yourself! Carefully. We are, and we don't like what we see. Or rather, don't see. Why aren't you smiling? Why the HELL aren't you smiling?

**Adam Engel**, aka **Adam Engel**, occasionally writes under the pseudonym of **Adam Engel**. Maybe you can reach him at bartlebysamsa65@gmail.com. And maybe not. Careful. Remember the Turing Test: you never know who's really at the other end of that line . . .

# PSYCHO TERRORISTS FROM OUTER SPACE

IMAGINE, if you will, a Power even greater than the U.S. Military:

"Aliens! Terrorists! They're jealous of our Freedoms and our stock options!" cries Dubya, crouched in a fetal position under the Presidential desk.

It's true. Psycho Terrorists from the Galaxy of Pissed Off Aliens have begun amassing squadrons of flying saucers over Planet Earth, and they mean business. They want us to catalog and submit all our WEAPONS OF MASS DESTRUCTION (WMD) in three weeks or there'll be hell to pay.

Gadzooks! We wouldn't be able to hand over the WMD on one military base, let alone the hundreds we keep throughout the world, not to mention various loose cannons, literally planes, nuclear subs, secret laboratories, in Universities mostly. Fuhgetaboudit. We'd need years, decades perhaps. But THREE WEEKS is the Psycho Terrorist Aliens' ultimatum or else.

Furthermore, they want to bring democracy and freedom to America. Seems like Earth is not the only planet that deems us a bunch of dithering serfs. Word gets around.

But we Americans are non-violent. We can't even stand up to a gaggle of donut-bloated cops with pistols, let alone the AWESOME MIGHT of the U.S. Military. How could we possibly bring freedom to America? Impossible.

"Tough noogies," the Pissed Off Aliens say. "Bring back freedom of speech and the Bill of Rights or WE will."

Now, it would be fine if the Psycho Terrorists From Outer Space went through the appropriate political channels, so to speak, to free Americans from tyranny, but that's not the game plan. Seems the only way to free us is by pummeling us with e-bombs that'll darken our cities and Shocking and Awing us with the relentless bombardment of weapons terrible to behold, all delivered conveniently from outer space, so there's no way for us to retaliate.

Holy Moly! What're we gonna DO?

Well, we can hope for COMPASSION. Maybe these Pissed Off Aliens also have lives, work, love, friends, family, homes, hobbies, pets, toys, cherished tchotchkes, etc., just like us. They probably do. But maybe they just don't give a good goddamn. Appeals for compassion and understanding will go nowhere. They do not and never will consider us "just like them." We're Americans.

Perhaps we can hope for COURAGE and DIGNITY among the alien generals? Surely they know we are no match for them, that it'll be like shooting fish in a barrel, that we'd be no challenge to their much vaunted skill and bravery at all.

But they make it perfectly clear that they don't want a fight. They want to snap the spine of America, break the people's will, destroy everything we know and love as quickly and easily as possible with zero casualties on their side. Oh, also, they want to check out the effectiveness of their latest weapons.

Last-ditch effort to reason with them: "It's impossible to satisfy your ultimatum, especially within the given time frame. We know our leaders are cruel assholes but it's our problem, not yours. We pose no threat to you or your galaxy, leave us the f**k alone!"

But the Psycho Terrorists from Outer Space have no mercy. In fact, they kinda get off on our helplessness and terror.

Finally, we appeal to Earth's other nations (strange, but of all the Nations with WMD and ruthless governments, the Aliens chose only to go after us).

"Americans," our Co-Terrestrials at the UN spit. "Wicked, spoiled children. May you rot in Hell!"

And so we bid farewell to our friends and loved ones and the homes we love, and wait for the Terrorist Aliens to zap us to dust and ashes. Of course, we know they're not really after our WMD, which are merely toys to the likes of them, but our cherished, universally envied CONSUMER GOODS.

We also know that while most of us "plain folk" and our progeny will die, our asshole leaders, the ones the Psycho Terrorist Aliens claim to be after, will come out of this without a scratch. There may even be room for some of them in the New Regime.

# QUEER AS GRASS (PARANOIA AND THE MAN)

It just occurred to me, I mean really occurred to me, that pot is illegal. For the first time since I was sixteen, when EVERYTHING was illegal, I smoked two puffs ("hits," they called them in 1982, or "tokes," I think) and it helped me get to sleep. This is a good thing. I stopped smoking pot at sixteen because it made me paranoid. I'm still paranoid. But at least now I can trace the source of my paranoia to THE MAN and fight back. With THE MAN outta my head, the pot actually mellows me out and helps me sleep.

I have a particular problem, though. I was born with a rare blood disease called Diamond Blackfan Anemia, of which there are about 600 known "cases" in the world, most of whom die at around age thirty-one. So far, I've been able to beat the curve with Prednisone, which destroys your bones, gives you diabetes and other maladies, and makes you crazier than a shit-house rat. Also, I've been tanking up with about half a dozen transfusions a year. Thing is, the Prednisone isn't working as well as it used to. After that's done—a year, two years, maybe three—I have to do "transfusion therapy," which you can only do for a year or so because iron accumulates and messes up your heart, and finally the end of the road: Bone Marrow Transplant. Twenty-five-percent mortality rate. When I had my hip replaced at age thirty-two because of complications caused by Prednisone, the mortality rate for that was less than one-percent. A failed Bone Marrow Transplant entails a rather yucky, painful death. Murderous leukocytes run wild. Savage anti-bodies loot lymph nodes, smash platelets and generally fight off the bio-matter of your donor as if it were a virus. The operation itself seems awfully unpleasant, complete with chemo-therapy to kill what's inside of you. I have a friend who went through chemo. They prescribed him narcotics, which really spaced him out but did nothing for the horrible nausea except make it worse. So he had to go out and hustle pot so he wouldn't puke or get so spaced out he couldn't work. Hmm.

This rediscovery of pot after twenty-two years is a good thing because I'm on a very large dosage of Prednisone, which makes you feel like you've just mixed bourbon and amphetamines, mean and sleepless, and traditional valium-like sedatives don't work for me. Tranquilizers mess me up bad all next day. So I've been taking two or three shots of alcohol to help me sleep. This is not a good thing. Alcohol is the worst drug possible for someone suffering from any kind of anemia. Bad for the bone marrow, among other things. Well, thought I, I'll just do what some of my doctors have been telling me to do and switch to pot. But wait a minute, thought I again. This is illegal. I can't just go down to the corner store and buy a joint, which is all I'd need for the week. I have to find some kind of "connection." Someone to set me up with a "supply."

This turned out to be easy enough—was I the only person in America NOT smoking pot?—albeit costly and inconvenient.

Now, in my twenty years of adult life I've been prescribed tranquilizers, sedatives, amphetamines, barbiturates, narcotics, and of course steroids by honest, legitimate doctors, the same doctors who encouraged me to smoke pot but could not prescribe it, because it's illegal. A plant. That grows in the ground. Or in one of those incubator things people keep in their closets or backyards. Sure, I can easily go out and buy a bottle of bourbon which will damage me physically, and, combined with the steroids, turn me into a truculent, possibly dangerous person. But I can't take a hit of pot to help me sleep.

Look, Boobus Americanus (mind if I call you Boob, for short? You seem overly enamored with those things anyway, though any sex therapist, or woman, will tell you you'd be more of a "man" with your woman if you paid more attention to her clitoris), do you think I'm some kind of moron? Do you think I'm gonna take addictive sedatives/tranquilizers, whatever, which happen to be expensive and artificially manufactured by Big Pharma, or kill myself with alcohol, when all I have to do is take a few hits off a more or less "unprocessed" weed? C'mon, Boob. We've been mortal enemies for some time, now. I thought you gave me more credit than that.

If your employer, THE MAN, thinks I'm gonna risk a bone-marrow transplant before my time because of his outrageous, irrational, useless—except for putting young black men in prison—law," he's as dumb as YOU are. And surely HE'S not THAT dumb.

Something else occurred to me, after talking to a friend from Canada, where pot and gay marriages seem to on the way toward becoming legal.

In addition to participating in "proper" sex (you know: genital intercourse which may result in the procreation of life THE MAN can use as labor or cannon fodder), I've also indulged in cunnilingus and fellatio with willing (often quite willing) women over age eighteen, and occasionally even anal sex with women (again, quite willing) over the age of eighteen. Some of these practices are supposedly illegal in various parts of YOUR America, but really, that was always just a joke to me.

But it's not a joke to my gay friends and relatives. In fact, for doing with a member of their own sex the same things I've done with members of the opposite sex, they can find themselves in grave trouble indeed. I haven't really been all that politically active on this issue. Maybe it was a "well, I'm not gay (although one never knows, does one?), why worry?" type thing. And anyway, if you don't want hassles, just clam up and lock the bedroom door.

Well, it goes somewhat beyond that. Besides the fact that "free speech" (hah!) should entail being able to demonstrate public affection for any person you feel affection for, "privacy" (double-triple hah!) means you don't have to lock the door if you don't want to (unless there's kids or pets in the house) cause you're not afraid of anyone barging in (figuratively or literally).

Anyway, suppose I fell in love with a male over the age of 18 and allowed him to perform fellatio on me and I performed anal sex on him. Maybe I wasn't "really" in love. I was all "high" on pot, it was dark, he wore a dress, I thought he was a woman, etc. That kinda thing. It's not my mind-set in the morning that counts, but that I used my genitals against the will of THE MAN.

Now I'm open to all sorts of trouble: job discrimination, gay-bashing, snide remarks in conversation and on the airwaves courtesy imbecile talk-radio hosts.

And what if I did fall in love with this member of my own sex? What if we moved in together and had a long happy relationship? Can't share Family Plan health insurance. Can't go out in public like a real couple unless we're in Greenwich Village or San Francisco or similar environs. Can't do a lotta stuff. Why? Because we used our own dicks as if they belonged to us and not THE MAN.

Now everybody knows that alcohol makes many people violent, crazy, and physically ill, and cigarettes, sooner or later, make many people sick or dead. But I never heard of anyone smoking a joint, then beating up or even killing a friend or family member in a violent rage.

Nor have I ever heard of many people—except Nelson Rockefeller—being harmed by safe sex among consenting adults. What not everybody knows—or what many pretend not to know—is that, though it couldn't be more obvious, THE MAN doesn't care if you develop cancer, or blow out your liver, or get drunk and rob a convenience store—he's got a whole prison industrial complex just waiting to serve you. What really bothers THE MAN is that YOU—this goes for YOU as well as me, Boob—might harbor illusions that you own your lungs, brain, genitals or any other part of your soul or person, when really it all belongs to HIM.

Well, forget about that. I reserve the right, the "freedom," to smoke pot every night before bed and to follow my Johnson wherever it's welcome. Well, maybe not everywhere. Though HE came on to me awfully strong before the "war" with Iraq, THE MAN stopped returning my calls weeks ago. As I said, I'm for freedom among consenting adults. I don't have time for that "playing hard to get" shit.

Though I will say one thing. Ossama Bin Laden (whoever he really is and whatever he really did) and Saddam Hussein (whoever he really was and whatever he really did) sent chills down many an American spine, but they got theirs. They sure won't be taking away our cherished freedoms now. THE MAN did that for us years ago.

The movie's getting weirder. Jump-cut from *The Graduate* to *American Beauty*. Nevertheless, Adam Engel remains in the theater, where he can be reached at bartlebysamsa65@gmail.com

# RADICAL LANGUAGE

Language has been so debased by media that even in so-called "high art" (poetry, drama) sentences that one might easily hear spoken on Oprah or some other "real people" show, or sit-coms, have been "current" for the past 20 years.

Take William Carlos Williams, who wanted poetry to represent "natural" speech. His work became more complicated later in life when he realized there is no "natural" speech. There are as many different dialects of English as there are boroughs in every English-speaking city.

Politically, poems and novels written in "regular" language are using the language that injected racism, sexism, capitalism and nearly everything we know into our brains, where language either is thought or influences thought.

Gertrude Stein and Louis Zukofsky, who remain unreadable to many, though it is not difficult to learn to read them (the idea that art and literature be "demanding" of close scrutiny, as opposed to the "throwaway culture" of mainstream media, is consistent throughout the avant garde in the 20th century) began to challenge the language of the dominant society by repeating words and sentences, re-ordering syntax (grammar rules either form spontaneously or are dictated from ON HIGH) etc. They were followed by the New York School of poets and painters, which included John Ashbery, Frank O'Hara, Larry Rivers, De Kooning and other radical artists.

Since the early seventies, a new group of artists, loosely referred to as the LANGUAGE school, took the breaking off of "allegedly reality-based natural language" as a serious political issue. First of all, they began, taking off from Stein, to view words as signifiers first and foremost, rather than as "pointers" to the signified. This means that, rather than describing an object "realistically," which is a form of artifice in itself, they would use words as singular units of both meaning and ambiguity. For instance, the famous Gertrude Stein sentence, "A rose is a rose is a rose," refers to the fact that the word, "rose," means nothing but itself. Also, Stein, and later the LANGUAGE poets, described objects often with nouns and syntax that evoked the thing without using dead, clichéd description.

More recently, LANGUAGE poets such as Lyn Hejinian, Charles Bernstein, and Ron Silliman (also an inveterate blogger) have conducted poetry and prose "experiments" in which, for instance, in the case of Silliman's *Ketjak*, each sentence is viewed as an individual unit, often unrelated to the ones that come before and immediately after. In the same work, Silliman repeats various sentences throughout, in order to show that the same sentence can have numerous meanings, depending on context.

In addition to creating what Silliman called "The New Sentence" these writers have written brilliant literary criticism on how to read their work, why they write against, rather than for, the language of Newscasters and politicians and even many respected writers. Marjorie Perloff's *Radical Artifice*, is an excellent introduction to avant garde poets and painters who, like Jackson Pollock and Andy Warhol and others, create "unorthodox" works influencing both poetry and painting (the two have had an incredibly creative relationship with each other since the turn of the century, when Stein began to try to write the way Cezanne, Matisse, Picasso and others painted, creating "landscapes" with words). Her *Tender Buttons*, which you can download for free on line, and *The Autobiography of Alice B. Tolklas* are also primary introductions to this radical theory of art.

I am writing a series on Stein, Zukofsky, the New York School and the LANGUAGE school not to enhance people's appreciation for poetry, but rather because I believe the Left, in order to create a new world, must toss the racism, sexism, egotism, etc., that is inherent in "regular" language, the language we were born to, receiving daily doses of images and words by the thousands each day. What one learns immediately is that nearly all the sentences created by copywriters, who often write better poetry for advertisements than many Establishment poets publishing in the New Yorker, are in accordance with the alleged "plain speech" and grammar approved by the corporate culture that commissioned them.

This is directly applicable to the clichés, tropes, "pre-fab" sentences (e.g., "Have a nice day!") of corporate, mainstream media and advertising, print and image, that leftists rightly complain about. Yet, though the average article found in most "alternative" zines/sites is better written and reported than anything one might find in the mechanistic "journalese" of the *Post* or *Times* or reinforced, along with carefully selected sound bytes and video clips of TV, most of the progressives are using the language of the Master to tear down HIS house.

Thus far, only a small group of avant garde artists have found the means to combat this language. Rather than complain that Americans are duped by the Media into wars, corporatism, environmental neglect etc. etc., we should present an alternative method of reading as well as writing. William Blum's *Killing Hope*, was researched by Blum using the radical technique of relegating his sources to mainstream reports available to anyone. For him, it is not so much a matter of reinvigorating the language with real (original) sentences and syntax, but teaching people to "read between the lines."

In addition to teaching a different way of reading, many writers are creating texts, such as Lyn Hejinian's wonderful, short (115 pp.) *My Life*, an autobiography in which places, times, dates, are deliberately ambiguous, and proper nouns are never used. The author shifts continually between "her" and "she" and the present and past tenses, and reaches an element of "strangeness" which I'll talk more about in a later essay, of a kind that one will almost never encounter in mainstream TV, advertising, or literature. Reading LANGUAGE poetry requires thought and concentration, as contrasted to "mind candy" of Media.

Linear narratives, a phenomenon of 19th-century Industrial culture, are no more "real" than non-linear. Does the story really end on the last page? Does "realism" actually describe reality? Perhaps in the surface world created by corporatism, but it is no more absolute than Newtonian physics, which was taken to be "reality" until Relativity and Quantum Mechanics went deeper into the "unseen" in the 20th century. Just as painters became more abstract when "realism" was supplanted by photography and film, language must reflect the subjectivity of the author, not the accumulation of artificial detail and dialog that creates the "heroes" and "characters" of mainstream fiction. In LANGUAGE writing, the main event is the language itself, in which the smallest unit of signification is not the paragraph, as with the novel and many poems and plays, but the sentence.

Thousands if not millions of brilliant essays have appeared on the web, but how can we expect people whose minds were deliberately closed by the age of 12 or so by media and "education" to refute corporate media or even understand alternative ways of thinking if their deepest thoughts were not come upon by research or experience but "injected" by media? People say we are a nation of children, and they are right, but that is because the language of capitalism/corporatism/militarism, the language we were born to, is supplemented daily by the very sources that are allegedly "informing" us, i.e. mainstream "news," political speech, corporate advertising, and even corporate approved Pulitzer prize winners who appear on Oprah. Does anyone even know who Pulitzer was and what he was about? It sure wasn't excellence in what we might call reporting or literature, but tabloid, "yellow journalism," like that of William Randolph Hearst's empire, pointers to the status quo and compliance to corporate/government authority.

I will try to present various "alternative" writers not to study literature or writing, but to explore how various techniques of reading, writing and the creative use of grammar, idiom, and words, once learned, can literally radicalize readers by pointing to new ways of thinking and deflecting the explosion of propaganda that fills our days, whether we're looking at magazine ads, billboards, TV, listening to radio, or even reading mainstream newspapers without seeing what the words, in their "correct" (economically and politically authorized) grammar are really saying.

## Stumbling Upon Ideology

In the spirit of LANGUAGE writing, I tried an experiment of my own. Using a program called *Stumble*, which "spins" the web like a roulette wheel, stopping randomly at a site culled from the millions of English language pages in existence, I "lifted" a sentence from each site, then randomly stumbled on to the next. Of course, there is an element of subjectivity, for I chose the sentence from each website; nevertheless, my options were limited to the sentences available on each site. A few times I linked some sentences with connectives or added a word or two of my own—in brackets—but ultimately, this is a sampling of the language of the web (I did deliberately skip the occasional "lefty" site). My "theory" was that, outside the small number of left/progressive sites, a more-or-less random sampling of sentences pulled from mainstream websites would create a "collage narrative" of our culture. Additionally, though I chose sentences from numerous sites arbitrarily, one sentence per site, the "voice" of the piece would sound as if it were written by one author, for in the general discourse of our "society," there really is one AUTHOR, and that is the language itself, an "official" language reflecting our obsessions with money, technology, violence. Again, my purpose is not literary so much as political. To explore the possibility of subverting the language of Media, suffused as it is with the predatory, authoritarian propaganda that, regardless of the text or who actually "wrote" it, is ultimately the language of Power in the form of technology/corporatism/militarism.

"The page is only the documentation," wrote the poet/blogger Silliman, "or the page is more, the field, resistance."

Below is the result of my experiment of creating a "prose-poem" using a sentence from each page I randomly "stumbled upon:"

## MEDIA FRANCA
## by
## THE INTERNET

At about the same time University College London published a number of establishment legal positions, the US declared itself Libya. "The one duty we owe to history is to rewrite it," said Oscar Wilde (or maybe he wrote it). Archery goes back thousands of years, yet today's equipment has made improper advances. Anyway, there are various ways to exploit and use the Internet profitably.

Where did that end and this begin? 'This' is everything to everyone, regardless, so why not let our mortgage experts help you determine "how much house" you can afford. Or perhaps refer the matter to Mr. Johnson Wang, Managing Director of Sinosteel Corporation. We deal on the following Products listed: [product product product, uhn; product product product, uhn!] One of our backers is an American soldier about to eat the spilled brains of a dead Iraqi man with his brown plastic Army-issue spoon.

"You want to catch them off guard," he whispered. "You want to catch them in their sleep," he winked.

A kitchen then they have a storage shed-type deal. Each tool is described by one or more attributes: natural cleaning formulas, concoctions and witches brews. MOST are non-poisonous.

As any geek can tell you, Fascist regimes tend to make constant use of patriotic mottoes, slogans, symbols, songs, and of course, flags everywhere, not to mention the C++ and AWK programming languages.

Arrogance, ignorance, and principal errors of judgment created the anarchy and warfare that engulfs Iraq today. And lest we forget, "seven" is the smallest number of faces of a regular polygon that is not constructible by straightedge and compass. [On the lighter side], hundreds of well-known on line stores like Barnes and Noble, Staples, and Amazon.com have a place within their shopping cart that gives a percent or dollar amount off your purchase. You might even know someone who has had it removed.

As Sun Tzu said, "All war is based on deception." This is only the beginning of proof we were all lied to. For instance, according to the

Constitution, Congress cannot suspend habeas corpus except in times of rebellion or when public safety requires it.

George Bush originally displayed neither a love for nor disdain for religion, but the feeling that the New World Order should not involve itself in matters of religion. He had fallen into a classic trap—he forgot why he went into politics in the first place. But, he reasoned, fundamentalist skills make you look great in the kitchen. Final Signs are everywhere. APOCALIPSA is coming Soon. Your picture will be shown.

Whether you work for a business or want to start your own, check out our articles on marketing, hiring and more. String theory is radically changing our ideas about the nature of space, opening up the possibility that extra dimensions, rips in the fabric of space, and parallel universes actually exist, leading to focuses on top management and those aspiring to positions of corporate leadership in business. Don't keep it to yourself.

Want to melt those years away? Travel to an outer planet! Stop wasting time folding shirts the normal way!

Here come the odious excuses. If you have set yourself on fire, do not run. A lighthearted measurement of which famous artists have the greatest "mindshare" in our collective culture. Manage your server infrastructure efficiently.

A little known naturally-occurring gemstone called [moishenite] is superior to diamonds in every essential way: cut, color, clarity, durability, fire, brilliance, and cost. The house was designed for young professionals who need minimal space while they focus on career... For everyone's easy reference, let's discuss plunder. If you need help, start here.

A South African monkey was once awarded a medal and promoted to the rank of corporal during World War I. With this in mind I started to ponder making my own book: Building from natural materials does away with producers profits and the cocktail of carcinogenic poisons that fill most modern buildings.

Throughout 2005 and 2006, a large underground debate raged regarding the future of the Internet. Do not feign respect for technical incompetence. We are not claiming to be experts on anything, we are merely doing what we can to gather knowledge and share the acquired information with the public.

We are conducting a survey about your usage of media. It describes the laws of motion for atomic particles and describes the spin of electrons that had previously been predicted.

Where did that end and this begin? 'This' is everything to everyone, regardless.

# ROTTEN TO THE CORPS

That woman's impish white face and the rattish mug of her assistant, using hooded brown bodies like giant dildos: striking, humiliating, creepy, but not abnormal in a place where "striking" means airstrikes; "humiliating" means demolishing of homes and livelihoods, not to mention rape and plunder; and "creepy" is blood, blood, blood everywhere, and not a drop to drink.

Usually, during the bleak hours in which I force myself, nightly, to face the news on websites, such as this one, I read the text and just glance at the photographs, but this gnome-like white woman and her pudgy white male counterpart molding naked brown bodies like clay into various obscene positions was grotesque enough to hypnotize. Something you don't want to see but can't help looking at. A corpse in the road or a fight in a family restaurant.

And of course, over the next few days this obscenity was spun by Mainstream Media into the old "bad apple" theme. The "truth angle" of this particular narrative, using the plot standards of freedom and democracy versus totalitarian oppression, and the 'made-for-TV' characters of an evil dictator and his terrorist minions: liberating Iraqis from their political sovereignty, oil, and earthly incarnations. Yawn.

But first the minds of the heroes and patriots who, by joining the military, unwittingly 'volunteered' to carry out this dirty-work had to be flooded with flotsam—"mad dictators and evil-doers; Weapons of Mass Destruction; undercurrents of racism, ethnocentrism, and religious zealotry"—in order for the "crusade" to begin.

And of course a fake set of "morals, ethics and standards" had to be put in place so the "few bad apples" who inevitably went too far in their eagerness to please THE MAN with gung-ho hatred of HIS enemy could be distanced from the rank and file and used, depending on the situation, as "heroes" or "fall guys."

So after a year of bombing, shooting, beating, humiliating and terrorizing 20 million Iraqis, suddenly photos of this creepy woman and her goofy cohort pop up, showing how different the BAD APPLES are from the rank-and-file killers. So it's okay to follow the incineration of 100,000 Iraqis in 1991 with UN-supported sanctions that by 1996 killed 600,000 people, most of them children, according to Madeleine "It was Worth It" Albright. The day Hans von Sponeck[2] resigned, the counting stopped, and so the only tally of those who died in the years leading up to March, 2003, is one compiled by Iraqis, and who's gonna trust THEM? It was okay to further terrorize these people with a FULL INVASION—complete with depleted uranium, cruise missiles, and cluster bombs for full Shock and Awe/Razzle-Dazzle effect—that's been going on for a year and shows no sign of ending soon (and of course the effects of the uranium 238 will be greater as years pass and yet more DU nuggets are pumped into bodies, buildings, and vehicles).

BUT, while it's okay to turn an entire country into rubble, killing many hundreds (thousands?) of civilians, in the process of taking out the evil Saddam (what ever happened to him?[3] Must be sitting in the same Paris café with Bin Laden, reading Camus and writing his memoirs), collateral damage, and all that, and the inevitable accidental shootings of civilians at "checkpoints" blah, blah, blah—it's bad, VERY BAD, to play S&M Twister with POWs, molding their masked brown bodies into scenes out of de Sade or some porn-flick interpretation of The Master's sadistically boring prose.

Study the faces of the torturers and it's evident they think they're doing a good thing. That they're providing fun photos for the troops to send home to Mom and Dad. That they're avenging the families who lost loved ones on 9/11/2001 (though the WTC incidents are unrelated in fact, they are one and the same in the MEDIAted lives of many, many Americans, as scribblings on bombs ("It's Payback time." "This one's for 9/11," etc.) attest. The fact that Mr. and Mrs. War Crimes filmed their fun and games supports the supposition that

---

[2] As U.N. Humanitarian Coordinator in Iraq. Resigned in 2000 in protest against Iraq sanctions policy.

[3] Too bad we now know. Another murder. AE

these folks thought they would receive the approval of the folks back home, the troops in the field, even (if unofficially) their superiors.

Why should they NOT have thought this? After all, unlike the censored photographs of G.I. coffins, these photos only displayed one dead body. Their fun and games humiliated the POWs, but did not, as far as I know, kill them. The U.S. has been treating these brown Iraqi bodies like clay to be molded at will since 1991, to far more deadly effect. Perhaps it was the sex angle, the juxtaposition of absolute power and sex that so offended their fellow troops and superiors. After all, it's one thing to murder Iraqis by the thousands, like decent, patriotic soldiers, but to simulate homosexual sex, why, that's DISGUSTING. But then, as it is always said of rape, it's not about sex, it's about violence. Power.

For days we heard the official outcry of military personnel: "They let down their fellow soldiers, they let down their country"; "They abused their position"; "We would want American POWs to be treated with respect, so likewise we must respect enemy POWs," etc., etc. Right on up to Bush's "outrage and abhorrence" that the process of death and destruction his father unleashed in 1991, in which Iraqi bodies were abused and destroyed in every conceivable way, should culminate in the acting out of concupiscent fantasies by HIS G.I.s, sexing up HIS holy war. As if he'd caught Rumsfeld and Powell getting all gay and perverty with each other during HIS inaugural ball.

If only the photographs weren't so damn symbolic: smiling white faces ordering faceless brown bodies into 'unnatural' sexual positions; or if only the abuse hadn't been sexual at all, Mr. and Mrs. War Criminal might not have earned the "Bad Apple" epithet.

After all, the majority of "our boys and girls" are good soldiers. They adhere to the rules of war and merely bomb, shoot, beat, (and if previous wars are any indication, we must assume rape) Iraqis and destroy their property, homes and livelihoods. For heaven's sake, we support our troops precisely because they're clean, honest, efficient killers. They don't get all gross and perverty and film the enemy having simulated homosexual sex!

It would be a good war, really it would. If not for a few Bad Apples.

these folks thought they would never. (Case point: I'm the folks that [illegible] spoke, the moment we [illegible] each other, [illegible] automatically) their humanity.

Why should they be? I have thought that [illegible] up, with the centuries of [illegible] computational [illegible] Decaturing [illegible] characters only displayed and read nobly. Then, they and gazed [illegible] at the [illegible] but not, as far as I know, with them. The tool has been reading these brown huge bodies like clay to be molded as well since 1981, or [illegible] [illegible] was the sex appeal [illegible] of [illegible] and [illegible] [illegible] [illegible] [illegible] [illegible] [illegible] [illegible] [illegible]

# SAMSON AGONISTES
# (CONFESSION OF A TERRORIST/MARTYR)

> "But what more oft in Nations grown corrupt, And by their vices brought to servitude, Than to love Bondage more than Liberty; Bondage with ease than strenuous liberty. . . "
> —John Milton, *Samson Agonistes*
>
> —"She's so cool, wanna see her tonight... She's so cool, wanna see her tonight..."

The Damned, Damned, Damned, Damned

Mother visited me in my cell not long after the Philistines, having nabbed me, The Warrior, sacked my town.

"Of all the shiksas in Hebron, you have to shtup a narc with "government agent" scratched all over her painted face?"

"But I knew that ma! I was using her, to, to get to the 'inside.'"

"Hah! Inside of who?"

"Mom!"

"I died the day you married a Goy!" Mothers can be so cruel and unforgiving. Also, right. I had no idea Delilah was working for THE MAN. Not like my first Philistine bride, who I married for the Wedding Banquet. Big Bash. Wasted the guests and servants, then ambled into town to finish their kin. And finally, my betrothed, after I "consummated" the marriage.

What was THE MAN gonna do, kill me? Him and whose army? I'd already destroyed so damn many.

"Tell me a secret," whispered Delilah one night when I could see her (though not through her, an ability which would have helped my cause immensely).

"I don't wanna."

"You don't love me."

"Lemme sleep on it. I'll tell you in the morning."

"Get out! Get out and don't come back until you're ready to talk."

She was hot, sizzling, like oil upon an altar. Sure there were maidens "as fair" from my own people. But you read *Genesis*: forbidden fruit, etc. So one night I whispered in her ear while we were fucking. She hadn't even asked me that evening—cause for suspicion. Perhaps that was her plan.

I woke up next morning bald as an egg. Not even strength enough to break the cords they bound me with much less kill the goons who proceeded to hang me upside down and scorch my eyes with molten bronze. No excuses. She didn't even get me drunk—I don't drink wine. All brawn and no brains? Stupid? Or just tired and in love? Really in love. Even warrior/saviors go soft and human and squishy inside, on occasion. That's when THE MAN gets you.

Delilah light of my life, before you cut my hair off and your goons put out my eyes, I was your Hercules, your dreadful circumcised...

Back in the day I crushed their legions with a bone. Back in the day. Had I a sword upon me I'd have skinned them like the lion I tore apart with my infant fingers—how old was I when I smote that rough beast, five, six? On a level field I was unbeatable. On a level field. I wasn't born for this, to be led before them by a slave-boy for their thrills; to be worked like a slave and beaten like a slave and laughed at like a clown and then dismissed to sleep on stones like an old blind beggar fool!

I can't on. I must go on. THE MAN is not all seeing and all powerful: his henchmen miss the obvious things. The little things such as: The almost imperceptible growth of my hair. In by inch day by day, in every way, I grow stronger.

"Oh Lord, what long-haired Nazarite will next You call to sacrifice himself upon the alter of The Man of Play Doh and his Silly Putty gods 'in defense' of the folks back home?"

DON'T BOTHER ME. I'M BUSY.

"Honestly. Who's next? Your own first born?"

THOU SPEAKEST VAIN WORDS UNTO THE LORD. BUT, IT'S AN IDEA...

She visited me in my cell. Before the festival of Dagon and the games—had I but eyes to see I could have beaten their best youths. .. Olfactory rush of perfume and her natural scent a burst of pheromones they knocked me for a loop...

"Dare you come to me in my misery, oh whore?"

"Just business, Sammy. You know I always loved you," her voice was like a hand caressing me. Then indeed, she caressed me with her hand.

"Business. What did they pay you for my ruin?"

"Not money. Blood. These are my people."
"Your people who make servants of mine."
"And when you were on top? Who were the servants then?"
She reached under my tunic—
"I... why do you..."
—and ran her fingers through my hair—"It grows..."
"What—the hair..."
"That too—"
She squeezed—
"Why do you come to me?"
Harder.
"To 'level the playing field.'"
"The—
"Tomorrow they will parade you, a trophy, before the games—"
"Uh—"
"Blind, tired under the burning sun... you will beg to rest against the pillars of the Great Statue of Dagon..."
"Buh—"
"Yes. I will be there too. No more business. You and I. Together."
"Together."
"The end."
I came in her hand. She rubbed my gray Jewish spunk on her bronze Philistine breast. Nothing more was spoken when she left.

They came for me in the morning. The slave boy whose lot in life it was to lead me, reluctant dog that he was, took my hand, wiped snot on my shoulder. Drums, trumpets, roar of the drunken crowd. Happy to have tamed the Hebrew beast. Fat and drunk with wine and music. Powerful. Safe. What right have the philistines to drink and eat and celebrate their games while Israel starves, the men of Judea bent under fat masters? Our women abused by worshippers of Dagon serpent fish-god or whatever reeking of sex he's so damned ugly at least Yahweh has the decency to keep himself unseen...
"Boy! Lead me to the pillars of Dagon. I would like to rest..."
He sighed and spat upon my feet. Apparently, I'd wakened him, this brat born to serve as I was born to... kill? defend? I pressed a palm against each cold stone pillar and prayed.
"C'mon, Yahweh. After all I've done for you and our 'People.'"
WHAT HAST THOU DONE FOR ME LATELY?
"Well, look at me. I'm all messed up. Blind."
I GAVEST THOU TWO HEADS. IS IT MY FAULT THOU THINKEST WITH THE ONE BENEATH THY TUNIC?
"Just one more job. For old times' sake."
WHOSE "OLD TIMES?" MINE, OR THAT STRUMPET'S IN THE STANDS?

"She's your creation, Almighty, All-seeing, All-knowing Lord. If You created such a whore, was it not for a reason? To tempt me? To get me here, now, in a stadium packed with idol-worshippers, that I might smite them?"

AND THE WOMAN.

And myself.

ABOVE THE PILLARS IS THE STATUE OF DAGON.

"So I'm told."

I AM A JEALOUS GOD. I HATETH DAGON'S FISHY GUTS. TAKEST OUT DAGON AND THE REST WILL FOLLOW...

"Read you, Lord. Roger and out."

Flaccid Philistines and glitter wives. Roar of faces. Trumpets. Drums. You're out there Delilah I can smell you though my eyes are black holes my living senses burn like 10,000 Samson-blinding suns. . .

So, I leaned against the pillars that supported the Great Statue of Dagon (as well as the rest of the stadium) and with a shake of my suddenly very long, very thick and very curly black hair, I huffed and I puffed and I pushed the house down.

# SCHLOCK AND GAWK

Again I saw that goofy puss on enormous screens around Times Square and glossy magazines and color photo Gab-loids galore peddled alongside *Hustler* and *Chic* and other clean, honest, American porn at corner kiosks, and despite myself I laughed and gave Dubya some degree of credit for his courage. Imagine not merely owning a mug like that, but exposing it daily to worldwide scrutiny and certain ridicule! On the other hand, it is a beastly face, both goofy and menacing, the face of an angry mutt, a punim I'm sure had been pummeled much by the sons of other oilmen, spooks and politicos during its formative years. Might be the reason behind all that inarticulate rage.

We Americans must be a craven, sinister lot to "rally round" such a kisser and follow its hollow eyes to only god knows what circle of hell. Or maybe we're just a nation of children. Somebody must lead the children, since they are obviously not responsible for themselves. Someone must save us from ourselves.

True, we're bombarded on all sides with propaganda, but who isn't? People the world over pay lip-service to their government's bullshit, but they don't take it SERIOUSLY. Can you imagine showing someone in that Axis-Of-Evil-To-Be, France/Germany/Russia, *USA Today* or the *NY Post* or *TIME*? The ridiculous prose, the blazing graphics—all for about three pages—then ZAP! right to the celebrities and how rich and playful they are. Oh, and beautiful and lovelorn and tormented by TIME and Fame.

I watched the Americans around 42nd Street and Broadway-Times Square—with their heads down like dogs who crapped Mom's Persian rug—close; Iran's next—or better yet: Raskolnikov. They knew they'd done something horribly, horribly wrong, something that no one, not their lawyers, shrinks, Yoga masters, dieticians, would help them get away with. But all they could talk about was the perceived payback, not the crime itself:

"We're on high alert."

"Do you think they'll hit New York again? My Uncle Dom has a place in the Pocanos."

"Just stay away from crowds..."

"Oh, what about the children?"

Yeah, what about us, stained as we are with other children's blood?

Think about that scene in Kubrick's *A Clockwork Orange*, when our long-suffering narrator, Alex, takes his ultra-violence kick a step too far and kills a woman. His erstwhile youth probation officer, Mr. Deltoid, comes to visit him at the station house and explain some hard facts. Like for instance, Alex is in a different league now. No longer under Mr. Deltoid's cruel, yet familiar, quasi-avuncular jurisdiction.

"You're a murderer, Alex. A MURDERER!"

Those damned and damning Gab-loids like flashbulbs in our faces. True, the "Grey Lady" or "Iron Maiden" or whatever the hell they call the *New York Times* peddles as much poop per paragraph as any other paper, but at least the NYT attempts to make it look real. They go on at some length, 20 inches and more in those articles, to mimic objectivity and in-depth analysis, even though they're going over the same lurid, Pentagon-approved twaddle and could probably insert "dummy" sentences, like naughty kids writing "punishment essays" after school ("This sucks!" in the middle of a two page essay on "How to Behave Patriotically in Class," etc.). Really, who would notice?

But do we children believe everything the fourth estate (heavily mortgaged to what Blanche Dubois delicately dubbed "epic fornications") tells us? Hell, even a child—uh that's us, I think—can look at all the keen graphics they're hawking and see a bunch of U.S. soldiers bogged down in the sand, fighting an angry native populous (last time it was mud, not sand; it was mud in Vietnam, was it not?) or giant mushrooms of fire erupting from a city that from far away looks very much like LA.

What, are they gonna tell us that no civilians are gonna get hurt, maimed, killed, obliterated, that perhaps thousands of human beings aren't being wiped off the planet by blast waves and fire? Are we stupid? Are we insane? Have we no grasp of the reality of the situation, or are we so sensitive to our powerlessness that we lay awake at night plagued by syndicated Kafkaesque nightmares in rerun (the rights to

Franz's nightmares are owned by Fox, I think, but I'm not sure)?

It sucks being a kid.

Imagine if, in this nation of 280 some-odd million decorticated zombies looking for the optimal personal solution and feel-good formula for weight loss, self-esteem, pine-scented genitals, whatever we're supposed to be lacking, whatever essential trait we were somehow born without, there were ten million committed ADULTS. That's not even five percent of the population. Imagine if we were part of this cabal of Grown-ups. Ten million of us to stop paying taxes, march en masse to OUR capital to demand an immediate end to this illegal, immoral, insane war. Ten million MATURE HUMANS who might threaten to really screw things up by standing up for Truth, Justice and the... the American (??!!) way. Or even just sit down and do nothing—in the middle of our respective town plazas or main streets or whatever. Traffic jams. Resistance. Rebellion, dispassionate yet absolute. Bartleby the Scrivener: "I would prefer not to." How would they clean us up? Kill us? Throw us ALL in jail?

Possibly.

For instance, what's with those brilliant colored blast photos on the cover of every journal, website and magazine? Intended to titillate or intimidate? I mean, We The People, minors that we are in every sense, are still SOMEWHAT important, aren't we? Should we be worried? They wouldn't try to shock and awe US, would they? They're not trying to scare US with all this high tech military might we paid for with our hard-earned dollars. Right? Uh... RIGHT?

Oh, fuck it. Who wants to grow up here anyway? Maybe it's time for a bunch of us kids to just up and leave. Skeedaddle. Become bona fide RUNAWAYS. Find a way out of this interminable childhood in some foreign land. We'll grace the sides of ten million milk cartons, we'll be famous.

Just don't look back, or you'll turn into a pillar of salt.

The minute he stops vomiting, **Adam Engel**'s gonna pick his ass up off the bathroom floor and high-tail it to the Island of Lost Boys or Misfit Toys or someplace where "the Main Stream" is wide and full of fish, plants and clear water.

brain mechanism [illegible] I [illegible] Fox, I think, but I'm not afraid.

[illegible]

Imagine it: a whole nation of 280-some-odd million dumbfucked zombies looking for the optimal personality so that we feel good for [illegible] lose self-esteem, [illegible] were supposed to be [illegible] we're expected that we were [illegible] now live without. There were ten million committed ACOA'S ([illegible] percent of the population), that's as if we were part of the cabal of [illegible] million of us [illegible] taxes, [illegible]

[illegible]

# SOMETHING KILLER

After decades of Killing Hope all over the world, you would think the American people would have watched the last helicopters lifting reporters and refugees out of Saigon and stopped to think long and hard. Then again, time is relative. About fifteen minutes, half hour tops, of hard thinking is way more than Boobus Americanus can handle before lunging for the remote.

Bullshit $87 Billion to "rebuild" a country we had no right to destroy in the first place!

Rebuild what for whom? (don't hold your breath for museum exhibits featuring first edition cuneiform tablets of the Enuma Elish or Code of Hammurabi). Oil of course—"everybody" knows that. But who else? Everybody else, as long as they're incorporated (it's not hard; I once incorporated myself to make some extra cash on insider trading; also, it's the only way to get The Law to recognize you as a person). If Halliburton and Brown and Root build it, Disney, McDonalds, Starbucks, the Gap and all the rest are sure to come. It's called "gentrification." Used to be "urban renewal." Played the same game on the Lower East Side of Manhattan. Wouldn't be surprised if Baghdad becomes THE hot night-spot in 2013, despite the "criminal element," which in this case wouldn't mean muggers or what have you—though there'll be lots of drugs—but "terrorists" and other unruly natives ready to spill their own blood (and lots of ours) to get back their land. Their land, their country, their history. That we seized by force. We beat them up and stole their lunch money. Now we're gonna build a whole new cafeteria that maybe some of them can work in, if they're qualified. One day, after much struggle, boycotts, lunch-counter sit-ins, they might even be allowed to eat in the cafeteria as well.

But why get all bent out of shape? It's only "another thing." There are so many things. I'm sure sweatshop workers in Vietnam, or Coffee Serfs in Central America, or all those pain-in-the-ass poor people ruining the quality of life all over this planet aren't giving much thought to Iraq. Americans might, since everything from Healthcare and Education to Veterans benefits (!!!) and Transportation is being taken away from them and given to their "enemies" in Iraq. But who cares what Americans think? Congress?

Bush: I need unlimited war powers.

Congress: Okay.

Bush: I need at least $87 Billion to clean up the mess I made with my unlimited war powers.

Congress: Okay.

Bush: Get naked. Touch yourselves. Tell me who you love.

Congress: Okay. Okay. Okay.

But while we can and should blame Republicans and Democrats alike (very alike) for being either raging, blood-thirsty Chicken Hawks or spineless, poll-sniffing lap-dogs, all our "elected representatives," though they seldom represent us, sure do care about what the folks at home think when decisions must be made or elections won (stolen). They want to be liked. They have to be liked; it's their job. It stands to reason that if the greatest danger they face is being disliked, they sure aren't going to risk taking a position that will make them unpopular with their constituency. Hence, the Patriot Act, the annihilation of Iraq and Afghanistan (remember them?), pledging allegiance on the steps of the Capitol, and all the unspeakable depredations they allow Bush Inc. to pull off on behalf of cronies and business associates are the result of their fear of being disliked, either directly, by people who actually follow what they say and do, or indirectly, via the Media, which can poison an ambitious Senator's persona before you can say "sound bite." The PACS and Lobbyists may rule business-as-usual, but come election time, allegedly, it's the voters these craven tax-suckers fear most.

If this is the case, then the responsibility for the nightmare America has become might possibly lie with the "American People," or a large percentage of them. Our "democracy" is a laughingstock, true, but only once the bums are in office and wrecking stuff at the behest of corporate sponsors, PACS, the parents they can never impress, etc. It's quite possible that the much ridiculed American people are more powerful than they appear. If a Senator is afraid of looking like he's "soft on terrorism" or "unpatriotic" because he or she would rather not follow an unelected thug and his band of gloomy sociopaths into the abyss, whose fault is that? Could it be that they're afraid of the American people? That all those flag-waving yahoos, whether they vote or not, put the fear of god in them (which they passed like a hot potato onto unsuspecting school children)?

True, less than half the people vote, but you don't have to be a registered voter to scare a Congressman. Waving a flag, draping your car or house in flags, talking shit about cherished freedoms you no longer have or can say good-bye to soon... these things make an impression. They infect the mood of the country. Voters too don't want to appear "soft on terrorism" or "unpatriotic," if only in their own befuddled heads. Thus, in order to get elected by the half of the population that votes, you have to appease not only them, but the flag-wavers who help create a climate of fear, hatred, jingoism, and overall dismay.

Again, who gets blamed for this? The voters and non-voters, who form a kind of symbiosis of willful ignorance, or the Representatives who serve them, on election day, then bow before more sophisticated, moneyed masters?

We can scold The Media, but really, that's like blaming a used-car salesman for selling you a lemon. You knew the guy was a hustler, a liar, a fake, but you bought the car anyway. Why? Only dealer in town? Go to another town, or get together with other potential buyers, boycott the bastard, and run him out of business. Nobody has to watch TV or read Corporate Monopoly-owned newspapers. There are literally thousands of news outlets on the internet, domestic and foreign, of all political persuasions and points of view. So being an ignoramus is no excuse. Unless you're a willful ignoramus, in which case you'll follow whatever instructions are barked by the telly so long as you don't have to think. But willful ignorance can be a crime itself. Like willfully ignoring Auschwitz or Guantanamo Bay.

Of course, there's another possibility, horrifying to contemplate: Maybe millions, perhaps tens of millions of Americans are just plain mean, selfish, frustrated, blood-thirsty clowns. You can joke all you want about our "un-elected President," for Gore did win the popular vote. But it was hardly a landslide. Fifty-million people voted for George Bush. Fifty million people who knew about his record as a criminal, a thug, a dim-bulb who flickered but never shined at any time during the 2000 campaign; they knew about the shady business connections, the fact that this man failed in everything he ever attempted in life except his stunning success at vacating Texas's Death Row.

The Terror began and ended on the morning of September 11, 2001. However, the Reign of Terror began later that evening and continues. The litany of self-inflicted domestic wounds, from budget cuts in favor of increased "defense" spending, to reactionary attacks on all things "un-American," particularly the Bill of Rights, to a seemingly deliberate neglect of education, the environment, healthcare, workers' rights (for those who have work) is breathtaking. How can a people allow itself to be so abused? Is this some kind of nationwide S&M game, or has Uncle Sam exchanged his tri-color tuxedo for a hair shirt?

We are indeed vicious, war-like savages, morally bankrupt, cowardly, corrupt. But you see, that was part of Saddam's plan. First, in 1991, he provoked the U.S. into a massive slaughter of his people (he is/was a ruthless monster, no doubt about that). Boy did we have fun watching those smart bombs on TV, then gloating over the box scores the next day: 250 Americans killed (not all in combat) versus a whopping 100,000 Iraqis. After enticing Bush I to set The Beast loose, the cunning Saddam, recognizing our taste for blood (takes one to know one) built castles while we starved Iraq's children. Drunk with Super Power, we went in for the kill, another major attack against a beaten, helpless "foe." By letting Iraq become such an easy target for our aggression, a weak, hopeless punching bag for the Superest Power on earth, Saddam turned every one of us into a murderer or a murderer's accomplice. He re-created us in his image.

Now comes the clincher: We didn't even win. Sure, Iraqis are dying by the thousands, but who cares? We've been killing them for over a decade, they're used to it. But we're losing at least two Americans a day, and the longer we stay, the worse it's gonna get. And let's not forget about the money! That $87 Billion is merely a down payment. There'll be no improvements in education, infrastructure, the power grid, or anything else—in the U.S. All the tax money Americans fork over to the IRS is going straight to Iraq. Now, if the money were going for reparations after all the damage we've done, it might be excusable in some way (though we should have considered the price tag in lives and treasure before fucking with a country that posed absolutely no threat to "our way of life" in the first place). But George Bush Junior wouldn't give 87 cents, much less $87 Billion to turn a small mideastern train-wreck into a thriving "democracy." No, that money's going to Dubya's oil pals and all the other corporations that make this world such a pleasant place to be. But still, with all these terrorists running around blowing stuff up, Iraq is no place anyone's gonna want to do business. Might have to round up the natives and smoke 'em all. Or at least manage them in camps and ghettos, like the Israelis do with those pesky Palestinians.

So Saddam was indeed a threat to the United States after all. He managed to bankrupt us morally, intellectually, and financially, and the real war has only just begun, for getting rid of him was the easy part. Now we have to take out the Iraqi people. But I have faith in the greed and endurance of the American public. They're not gonna blow hundreds, possibly thousands of young American lives and tens, possibly hundreds of billions of dollars without a fight. "Someday this war's going to end," said Colonel Kilgore, ruefully, in Francis Ford Coppola's timeless Christmas classic, "Apocalypse Now."

It might take some time, but when this war does end, and we've solved the problem of the, uh, Human Element, Iraq's gonna be THE commercial hot-spot. Paris, New York, London have all seen better days. Baghdad is going to be the place to be for the hip, the rich, the beautiful, not to mention arty expatriates, pot-bellied vacationers and tourists greased head to toe with Coppertone 30. Who knows, it might even replace Miami as the college crowd's preferred party destination at Spring Break. I hear the interim dictatorship is already talking to MTV.

If you're smart and have faith in America (you're not un-patriotic, are you?), you'll start investing now. Just think: when the oil's flowing like the river Styx, and the natives have been pacified, you'll be sipping a Pina Colada in your VERY OWN RESTAURANT. "Cafe Purgatory." Or maybe "The Ninth Circle of Shell." Still plenty of time to use that American ingenuity to think up a catchy name. Something to capture the imaginations of vacationers and hipster expatriates alike. Something killer.

**Adam Engel** awoke from he Nightmare of History only to be attacked in his own bed by a rabid, saber-toothed Future. Luckily he keeps a can of pepper spray and a blackjack on his night-table, beside the Morphine Sulfate. Unfortunately, his attacker got away. If you see a dazed Future with blurry red eyes and a large welt on its forehead, please report to: bartlebysamsa65@gmail.com

# TALK DIRTY SCARY MONSTERS

I don't know how these folks get by, make "rational" decisions, operate heavy machinery, vote (hah, hah), or even feed themselves when they let guests at a three-month-old boy's Baptism make a whore outta his five-year-old cousin—not with sticks, genitals, or funny instruments, but with words. Sodomized with sentences. That's not how it happened in The Odyssey. But barbarians that they were, the sackers of Troy had at least some concept of how to behave on social occasions—and how to punish those who didn't. That's how the whole Trojan War thing started, isn't it? Well, leave it to Americans to cheer the burning of cities for the benefit of intangible corporations while their own children are morally defiled in their own damn green-lawn, upper-middle class backyards. During an allegedly "holy" occasion, yet.

So, here we go AGAIN: a passel of adults too baffled by THE MAN inside their heads to know how to behave in a genuine "situation."

The Golf Thugs on the lawn were hanging around in their summer suits, drinking beer, talking about golf and business, business and golf. Economy should bounce back now that "we've" settled the "problem" in Iraq. Something about cleaning a boat for the new season; also stuff about cars and access to certain channels on cable television. They were big. They were fat. They were boring and desperate. They needed something. Dial 1-800-MESSIAH. Or perhaps it was simply a job for Tiger Woods.

I went to where the food was served. There, men and women

ranging from zaftig to rotund, elbowed each other (and me) for first dibs on some kind of mayonnaise-potato glop; frankfurters and sugary beans; limp white coleslaw; sweet sauerkraut and All American Burgers with processed cheese food, fried onions and bleach-flour buns (too late for these folks to worry about mad cow disease, you betcha!). I dropped out of line and grabbed a beer from a cooler and saw little Stephanie talking animatedly to the Golf Thugs on the great lawn. Real show-stopper, that kid. Cute as sin in her party dress. Always the entertainer, I thought. Her five-year-old wit even penetrated the chitinous crania of the Golf Thugs.

I went into the house, the Old Manse, to pee. Upstairs, far from the mumbling crowd, Stephanie was in the room her mother had once lived in as a girl. Face down on the bed. Crying lungful sobs, as little girls do, clutching an old stuffed animal her mother had clutched long ago, I assumed, when in similar distress.

She sat up straight and wiped her eyes as soon as I entered. Very adult-like. Twisted her face into a kind of smile. Pretended she merely had something in her eye.

"What's the matter, kid?"

"How much will you give me to 'talk dirty'?"

Say WHAT?

"I'll charge you a dollar for every naughty word I know."

"What are you, crazy? Where'd you learn such a thing?"

Of course I knew where she learned how to "talk dirty." I guess she'd provided the Golf Thugs with more entertainment than I'd dared assume. I felt like a character in a Salinger story.

"The men outside said they'd give me a dollar for every naughty word I know and I could buy a Barbie with it. They even taught me new words. But I still don't have enough," she started crying again, and laid the money on the bed to show me the extent of her vocabulary. She knew, or was taught, six bucks worth of naughty.

Her grandfather came in, wanted to know what was the matter. I told him, so she wouldn't have to.

"I'm not supposed to use dirty words," Poppy. "I don't like to."

"Of course you don't," he said, looking at me—for what? Help? Advice? I don't know squat about dealing with adults, let alone children.

Stephanie's mother, who may or may not have recognized ghosts of herself in her old room, arrived and held Stephanie as Poppy gave her the low-down.

"Good god," she snapped, and soothed her daughter, who by now was crying quite hysterically. I suppose it was good that she was upset, but maybe not. She's a very smart kid. Might be better if she were less aware of the degenerate world around her.

"It's nothing, baby. They're just ignorant, stupid men."

"They're scary. They're scary monsters," said Stephanie.

Quite right.

"But now I can't get a Barbie!" she began to cry again. Well at least she was still a kid, with kid's priorities.

Her grandfather, staunch supporter of the War Against the Grandchildren of Iraq, did a smart thing. He told her that he would take her, that very moment, in the middle of this big party he was hosting, to buy a Barbie Doll. But first, she had to give him the "dirty" money, and he would replace it with "clean" money. She handed him the six crisp bills in exchange for six rather ragged ones and a twenty. Enough, I assumed, to bag a Barbie at the local Mall. He gave me the "dirty money" and loudly ordered me to get rid of it, that it was worthless. I think the kid caught the drift.

As soon as they left the Mother lit a cigarette, using her can of diet-whatever as an ashtray.

I suggested that now that the kid was gone, I could go look for her husband and some other guys and we could teach the Golf Thugs the protocols of the guest-host relationship (not to mention a few innuendos regarding child abuse, statutory rape, or whatever they might call it). Did her father keep any baseball bats or other "weapons" in the house? I knew he had plenty of golf clubs.

"Are you crazy?" she said.

"Am I crazy?"

"This is my nephew's Baptism celebration."

"I don't care if it's his Second Inaugural Ball. Something really bad went on here and it's gotta be. . . I don't know, the place should be purged. . ."

"So you're going to just go out and start a fight with these men in the middle of my parents' backyard."

"Hell yeah. They tried to turn your five-year-old girl into a prostitute."

"How DARE you say that! Nobody touched Stephanie."

"You don't know that. And even if they didn't, you think paying a five-year-old to 'talk dirty' doesn't fall into the category of buying sexual favors?"

"Mind your own damn business. I don't want to hear this. Nothing happened. Nothing that can't be undone. My husband and I will talk to Stephanie. She'll forget about it. Her grandfather's out buying her a Barbie Doll for god's sake."

"Oh, a Barbie! That'll solve EVERYTHING."

She calmed down and explained she didn't want the kid to have to deal with the naughty word episode of her life ever again, and that any action, especially violent action, would just make it worse, and even if she did something, which would certainly not be violence, at her nephew's baptism, it would be to call the Police and that would entail putting Stephanie through yet further trauma, so why didn't I just be a good guy, butt out, and drop it.

Made sense, but still...

Not even Odysseus had a case this cut and dried (he was away for twenty years; and Penelope was well over eighteen). None of the suitors tried to pervert any five-year-olds in Ithaca, I don't think. What if we did do the "unacceptable" and beat the hell out of the Golf Thugs, or at least humiliated and ejected them? Don't bar bouncers do the same every week-end for far lesser crimes? And what if we broke a few jaws and ribs? Who would they complain to without explaining the uncomfortable fact that they paid a very young girl to "talk dirty to them"? Why is it so hard to punish grown men for abusing a child? Yeah sure, you could go to the cops or a lawyer and press charges or whatever, but that would be "inappropriate," "unseemly." Don't want to drag the kid into some cesspool courtroom drama. But even a decent back-yard drubbing? I suppose that too would have been outré. Don't wanna make waves.

It's THE MAN in us, of course. The Golf Thugs may be merely representatives of THE MAN and his sexual power games, but HE is in all of us. It's one thing to beat on Weird Uncle Harold who works the corner news kiosk and is usually naked beneath his wrinkled trench coat, but patriotic, hard-working Golf Thugs in suits who come from "good families" and are raising "good families" of their own? Nein.

And none of that crap about "they didn't touch her." Five-years is the prime age for learning vocabulary, languages, general concepts. Has THE MAN ever actually poked HIS thing in you? Yet HE'S been in you since always. HE'S still in you.

I imagined Stephanie fifteen, twenty years from now, dressed as Barbie. Then undressed in some old college professor or corporate executive's sweaty bed. Talking naughty. Words that have been in her head so long she hasn't the faintest idea when she learned them, or where.

It began to rain, as usual (it must have rained at least forty days and forty nights this "Spring"; when will the Flood come finally and wash this mess away?), which was a bummer because I'd just stoked up a cigar. I was out front on the driveway. I took out my pen and notebook, wrote "Scary Monsters" on a sheet, wrapped the "dirty" bills in it, and tucked the package under the wiper of an SUV, complete with Old Glory sticker on the windshield. My Salinger moment.

The car might or might not have belonged to one of the Golf Thugs. Probably not. But it doesn't really matter, does it?

# THE DAMNED

I was invited, not long ago, via email, to a Candlelight vigil to stop the invasion of Iraq, or melt the icy heart of Rumsfeld, or short-circuit the electronic ticker of the Veep, I'm not quite sure.

I was thinking more along the lines of angry mobs with pitchforks and torches converging on the Bastille or Castle Frankenstein to rid the country of this plague. Half a dozen madmen slinking out of the Bastille, squinting, confused. The MONSTER, product of dead flesh and high tech wizardry, grunting at the roaring mob (the movie version with Karloff; Mary Shelley's Creature was far too articulate, sensitive, HUMAN, for this show). Guess not.

Then again, maybe it isn't about saving the Iraqi people from carnage at all. Maybe the good folks attending the prayer vigil are out to save their own souls, and ours. Save all our starched WHITE American souls. Too late for all that. Possibly. Probably.

We are about to become the worst generation since Hitler's junky boys stomped around Europe stealing art and wrecking cities. If you're over 18 and of sound mind and body, you will be guilty. No, your little god won't save you, whoever he is. Chances are he already wants to kick your yellow ass for not giving a goddamn about the epic slaughter you're about to pay for with your tax money and soul. The day of the attack he's gonna waggle his giant thing at you "with or without foreskin" and stomp out of your house of worship forever.

Germans paid for the Holocaust and WWII with Dresden, Berlin, and a nation turned to rubble. Not to mention five decades of guilt and infamy. What price America ? The bill's long overdue.

True, most governments are either classical fictions written on paper, or jazz riffs blown out of a gun, but once you get some guy on a gun solo and the hips start swaying and the boots start marching it's usually a show-stopper. Brings down the house. Nevertheless, we still have enough people in and out of uniform who believe this is some sort of democracy, or at least a republic as outlined on that piece of parchment. Chance to overthrow this tin-pot tyranny, as proscribed in that very parchment (amended and revised so many times by now it's done in WordPerfect and translated into PDF for public perusal)?

Possibly. But chances are we won't take it.

The best of us will march in THE MAN's patented non-violent (except for police brutality) licensed parades, like sheep in a pen, often with lambs in tow. They'll get to go home thinking they're lions in wool, only to bleat "Yassah, Bossman!" in school or their sheep jobs the next day. The worst of us are still jerking off over video highlights of Desert Storm. Most don't REALLY give a damn one way or the other. Well, maybe if there's a pollster around they'll vote "yes" instead of "no" or vice versa according to how the poll is worded, but they ain't gonna get off that couch on Sunday for no damn Iraqis. If they're so innocent, those towel heads, why don't they just depose Saddam? Eh? Ever think of that?

"If YOU'RE so innocent, why don't you just depose Bush?" says Mr. B, a native of Baghdad awaiting his first rendezvous with a cruise missile. "We're caught between Saddam and a hard place. You Americans, you're supposed to be a free people, no?"

There's an idea. Maybe it's time for the 250 some-odd million Americans who do not work for the government but rather, pay for it, to call their loans, repossess their property, take matters into their own hands.

I'm not proposing anything VIOLENT (perish the thought), just interesting, and most importantly, effective.

Candlelight vigil my ass. I'm thinking ten million of us converging upon Washington D.C. with torches, like those stalwart monster-movie villagers. With all due respect to the candlelight crowd, prayers ain't gonna do it now. In fact, it seems like a desperate attempt on the part of the damned for some salvation, a balm to their raw-wound spirits. Worse, it's something that pious piss ant Ashcroft might approve of.

Hell, I was a mouse myself in the maze of police barricades set up for Bloomberg Inc.'s experiment in crowd control on February 15th in NYC. Don't get me wrong. It's great that people are displaying enough concern over what is about to happen to light candles and pray, but it's time for a bit more than concern or even marching in the MAN'S orderly, peaceful demonstrations in which the only folks who get hurt are peaceful demonstrators beaten up, brutalized, and arrested on side streets away from the cameras, but not beyond the ken of the well-meaning but ineffectual ACLU.

Civil Disobedience does not mean non-violent obedience to the MAN'S determination of what constitutes a safe, respectable parade. It's gumming up the works by throwing bodies into the gut of the machine; it's putting bodies between THE MAN'S soldiers and their victims. For god's sake, it's being willing to get hurt. That's the problem here. As soon as one mentions any kind of "unconventional" protest or action, the chorus of "non violence" is raised and all it's saying really is "I don't wanna get hurt and I want to be at work on time on Monday."

What about ten million people from all 50 states walking, boating, flying, busing, whatever to Washington D.C. and just shutting the place down? The sheer numbers, a mass movement of unarmed bodies taking over their own capital. Pilgrimage to the "citadel of democracy." How many of us would THE MAN be willing to shoot? And what would be the consequences? Would he nuke HIS own capital?

Malcolm X, MLK, Dorothy Day, Black Elk and Sitting Bull, Gandhi, etc. turned to prayer for strength to help them fight, not as an admission of defeat, for that's what these prayer vigils and "show protests" mean to me: Defeat. "It's all over, but maybe we can console ourselves with prayer." Never mind that whatever gods we're praying to will walk out of their respective houses of worship and gather at Olympus Diner for beer and pizza the minute the first bombs fall on Iraq.

Imagine our friend, Mr. B, in his Baghdad apartment, his wife grieving over the loss of their eldest daughter to some preventable disease made incurable by sanctions, the rest of his five children malnourished and depressed, and all he hears is about how Bush is gonna shock and awe him and turn off his electricity with an e-bomb, and there's a knock at the door. It's his neighbor, Mr. A, who tells him "Good news, good news." "Saddam is dead?" "Better." "Bush is dead?" "Better still: The good people of America are praying for us!"

Oh, who will save us and the rest of the planet from our sorry selves? We've lost everything but our souls, and we may only have a few weeks to hold on to those. Prevent, prevent, prevent. Or REPENT. The choice is still ours. I think. Maybe.

# THE SYSTEM REALLY WORKS: STOP-LIGHT GREEN

In the Summer/Fall of 2000 I decided to Identify myself as a "stop-light green," that is, "if I couldn't vote red, I'd vote green, but never yellow." True, I could have voted red, but I thought that by voting Green and helping them qualify for funding, it would open the way toward making a third party a reality in U.S. politics.

I would hardly call Nader or any of the Greens "radicals." In fact, their most radical proposition was to cut military funding for Israel until it agreed to withdraw from the territories and discuss a genuine two-state solution. The Greens were what people used to call liberals. The flack I got from Democrats—friends, strangers, colleagues, "discussion" groups on the web—actually shocked me.

Worse than the reaction of my nutty old orthodox uncle when I married a "shiksa." In fact, it wasn't worse, it was exactly the same reaction and under parallel circumstances. Just as I'd declared myself an "atheist" at age ten and never followed any religion, I was born Jewish; hence, I had "betrayed" the Jews. Similarly, I had been a socialist/anarchist/libertarian/whatever since I was twenty-two, yet people assumed that, since I was obviously not a Republican, I was a Democrat who'd lost his way. They begged me to "come back" to the Truth, at first, then threatened me with the political equivalent of eternal damnation. I'm sure some of them even followed my Uncle's lead and sat "Shiva."

Many, if not all of these people had the same access to "alternative" media sources as I did, via the Internet. Can Mainstream Media be blamed for such irrational identification with the party that brought us Hiroshima, Vietnam, the persecution of the Sandinistas, the recruitment and training of Bin Laden and his merry Mujahedeen, and the Eisenhower Republicanism of the Democratic Clinton/Gore years?

## Empty Glass?

Okay, so Gore lost, and it was all the fault of Ralph Nader and other traitors like myself (it wasn't actually, but why resort to facts?). But Gore didn't lose. The Presidency was a gift to George Bush, courtesy the Supreme Court. Why didn't they—the Democrats from Gore on down—fight? If Nader had been in Gore's place he'd still be in court demanding, at the very least, the recount that the Supreme Court of Florida had determined was Gore's right (so much for state's rights).

But it gets worse. After the big blowback of 9/11, when Bin Laden (it is assumed—there's been no investigation, so we don't know) handed Bush the SECOND greatest gift he'd received in a lifetime of gifts, allowing the two years of neo-con insanity, murder, graft, war on terror, war on drugs, war on French Fries, what have you. But he couldn't have done any of this without more than a little help from his Democratic friends. For two years the axis of evil (Bush, Sharon, Blair) raged unopposed. With rare exceptions of individuals like Cynthia McKinney, who was deposed by blatant tag-team skullduggery by New York "Israel Firsters" and Republicans in Democrat's clothing (not hard to pull off); Paul Wellstone—disappeared in an accident (??!!)—and a few other liberals (not leftists or radicals by any means; straight liberals) like Kucinich, the Democrats in Congress and the Senate have blatantly lain down and died, at best, or at worst gone out of their way to give Bush unprecedented powers to prosecute war, and stood on the steps of the Capitol and pledged allegiance to god and country, as patriotic ten-year-olds have been doing from time immemorial—as far back as 1954!.

Now this is not arcane knowledge that "the average American" (whoever and wherever he is: He must live somewhere 'cause I've been hearing about him since I was in kindergarten) might not have access to. So-called liberal Democrats conspired with Bush Inc. in full view of the Mainstream cameras for two hellacious years, and once again the faux leftists, or Cruise Missile Leftists (CMLs) from the *Nation*, *In These Times*, *Democracy Now*, etc., are arguing with neither irony nor embarrassment that the Democrats are "different." True, "conservative" Democrats will back "Israel Über Alles" Lieberman, while the "radicals" will court "lefty" war criminals like Wesley Clark. But heaven (the REAL heaven, not that phony

Muslim one) forbid that progressives/leftist/thinking people point out that while Bush proved to be as bad as we thought he'd be, the Democrats are as bad if not worse than we thought they'd be, that the term "Republicrat" is even more appropriate now than it was in 2000. Perhaps there is a small difference between the parties in that the Democrat-leaning Republicrats see the glass being half empty, while Republican-leaning Republicrats see the glass as half full. But what of the rest of us who dare to point out the horrible possibility that THERE'S NOTHING IN THE GLASS AT ALL?

## Bush Single Handedly Destroyed the Light Unto Nations

This is not something, like the War on Terror, the War on the Taliban, the War on Iraq, that the mainstream media drove home so relentlessly that 70% of the U.S. population still believes Saddam was responsible for 9/11, even after Bush admitted to the lie himself (though of course this major, impeachable revelation received minimal coverage). I receive a number of (unsolicited) newsletters from "alternative" and "Indy" media groups who go into long diatribes against the "fascists" in the White House who are destroying the environment, robbing the poor, breaking treaties, pursuing perpetual war, creating a totalitarian police state etc., etc. In short, blaming the Bush Administration for destroying the great citizens' democracy, the hope and envy of the world, that was the United States prior to November 2000.

These aren't fringe lunatics—well, they're lunatics, but not fringe. Many include articles by the usual CML suspects—Gitlin, Moore, Krugman, Kristol, Alterman, Moyers. Whatever these people are, they're not dupes of the corporate media. They often include criticisms of the mainstream and links to sites like *Counterpunch* and Znet. In fact, on more than one occasion, I was surprised to see links to my own articles in "alternative" sites/zines that believe "alternative" means Howard Dean.

How is this possible? It's one thing to have no other access to the news but Fox/CNN and the *New York Times* (though I don't even believe that excuse: people who want to know the truth can find it), but these people are steeped in alternative and foreign media, yet it has no effect on their thinking. Are people so terrified by the fact that the only way to change the world is to dismantle the closed system that is destroying it that, like abused children, they'll deny any and all evidence that "Mommy and Daddy" are insane and must therefore strive for one or the other's love (I see Daddy as being Republican; Mommy a Democrat—a bias drummed into my head God knows when)?

## The Curious Case of Richard M. Nixon

I was only around eight years old when Nixon retired to a life of government subsidized memoir writing, and I spent the next twenty years gobbling the ecstasy of this liberal triumph. It was only in 1994, the 20th year celebration of this great victory for democracy, while reading testimonial after testimonial of how "the system works," that I wised up to the Liberal/Cruise Missile Leftist game. As mainstream liberal pundits like Jimmy Breslin spoke with appropriate awe of how they were waiting in traffic or eating dinner in some posh restaurant when the leadership of the "most powerful Nation the world has ever known" passed hands without a shot being fired, reality slapped me hard and cold as a wet towel.

Here was a man who was directly responsible for the murder of millions in southeast Asia, and indirectly responsible for millions more through his support of killer dictators the world over (Marcos, Pinochet, the Shah of Iran etc.), not to mention countless wounded, bereaved, mentally shattered—and he got busted, like Al Capone, on a technicality. He lied about a petty crime, then covered up the lie and stood fast because even he, Tricky Dick, could not believe that after all the crimes against humanity he'd committed since his first blind date with Senator McCarthy, the liberals would beat him on a misdemeanor. It took the Liberals and "Faux Left" predecessors of today's CMLs to prove what the right could not: the System Really Works.

# WE AND THOU: TRACTATUS RIDICULOUS

## Cheerfulness

1.0 Since Consumer Culture has sucked the marrow of every conceivable pleasure, from eating to fucking to watching the sun rise (without Claritin, thank you), there's nothing left to do but—smile. Smile though you're heart is breaking; smile while you're masturbating, or filling out that questionnaire (though you'd rather be writing poetry and you know it); smile everywhere and always, alone, but especially in public. Smile, smile, smile that shit-eating grin you see in the commercials and magazines and talk-shows. Smile right back at 'em when you're waiting in toxic traffic or riding their dirty trains or walking down their numbing neon streets. Smile until they start to wonder what you're up to.

## Faith

1.0 Trust nobody who believes in anything but nothing.
1.1 Believers can be bamboozled, dumbfounded, snookered, had.
1.2 Those who believe in nothing often do believe in money.

## We Modern Poets

1.0 I celebrate myself and sell myself. What I believe you too shall believe—or I will kill you and enslave your children.

1.1 Sorry. That's just the way it goes.

2.0 Modern American "Literature" is worse than irrelevant, it's boring.

2.1 Be a bug, like Samza. Annoying wrench in the works.

2.2 Wake the easy reader from her snooze.

### G—g generation

1.0 The generation that rose from the ashes of Lennon's first cigarette didn't rise high enough, or at least didn't go anywhere special after their own youth burned out suddenly, and, unexpectedly, they morphed into Clintons and Gores.

2.0 The burning Bush is god? or talks to god? or burns and burns and burns for no reason at all?

### Revolution (sort of) and The Law

1.0 Fighting is all that's left worth fighting for.

1.1 A pie in the sky is hard to eat.

1.2 Occasionally, somebody is right about something; but EVERYONE is ALWAYS wrong about EVERYTHING.

2.0 They took the words out of our mouths, lifted our wallets and built The Law into an edifice of cruelty. We have no choice but to resist—or write our local representatives.

3.0 Fear is terrifying; hence, we must wage war on terror to rid ourselves of fear.

3.1 War is terrifying.

3.2 Bummer.

4.0 The Pen is mightier than the sword or gun.

4.1 But only if you can use that pen to sign fat checks.

4.1.1 Generally, nobody gives a damn what you write unless you're heavily, heavily armed.

5.0 A person with a college degree and no integrity has two places to go in this society: The Cubicle, or The Classroom.

5.1 A person with a college degree and integrity also has two places to go: The Hospital or The Cemetery.

5.2 And the rest? The Street, The Military, Jail or... College.

### Pipe Dream

1.0 Suppose—it's difficult—but suppose we were to become men and women rather than the little boys and girls the plutocratic pedophilic Pharaohs have been shtupping from Day One. What would life be like? Would we still worry more about cholesterol and tooth decay than global warming? Would Real Men still wear ties and dread the possibility of gay genes swishing furtively throughout their DNA? Would women still be too fat or too thin or too something (hairy, maybe?) to be forty without surgery or Photoshop?

## We Reporters

Art is journalism. Dispatches from other zones. That's why it is impossible for us, why there are no great artists—here, now. No one is willing or able to leave this place. Or they think, mistakenly, that they can find another planet here. True, one doesn't have to travel very far physically—Jane Austen in her parlor, Dickinson and Kafka in their fathers' houses; Keats and Marvell in their gardens; Faulkner in his "postage stamp" of a town—but mentally you've got to take great leaps, light years from where you are, where you've always been. Physical travel can't hurt. Henry Miller in Paris (note, not the *Moveable Feast* of Hemingway, but Paris after the crack-up, the Paris less than a decade from Nazi occupation). Gaugin in Tahiti. The Beatles in acidy Indo-Edwardian Pepperland ("Let me take you down. . ."), and after that, in solemn, sober White ("Half of what I say is meaningless. . ."). Even Pynchon, Burroughs, and Delillo traveling through previously uncharted zones of techno-freak Americana. But now. But now. Nobody goes anywhere. Or if they are going, they're not reporting back. Perhaps they find only dead lands, cold moons, rocks. There must be life out there, still, life in the universe to be seen and touched, experienced, even if such life is mad life, or drives you mad, or mute. That is, even if it can't be put in words and pictures or otherwise expressed, it must still be out there to be known (And I'm not talking about *The Corrections*, for god's sake—who has TIME for that shit?).

## The Joyful Wisdom

Hero stood six feet tall, which is just the right height for a protagonist, don't you think? A body of pure earth and feet of clay. He worked at the recycling plant, smashing bottles against a wall. He liked his job. He listened to music while he worked. One day it all seemed so pointless.

After his breakdown Hero read novels in bed. Words marched lock-step in orderly, narrative formation. Which was too bad. The words should have dispersed. Someone should have set them free.

He visited the cemetery for peace and meditative silence, but stumbled accidentally into the life of Rose Vestinger, 1920-1995. A day at the beach when Rose was thirty and tending her husband and two small sons. A clear, warm beautiful afternoon. Small talk. Sun tan lotion. Salty breezes. A day in this stranger's life revealed nothing to Hero, who was still recovering from his nervous breakdown.

Bored, he turned to the computer. World Wide Web. Information Highway. Myriad connections. Big mistake. Flashing whirligigs, mob-ocracy, Flash and JavaScript commercials. The damn thing wouldn't shut up

Morris, the Adjunct Professor, came bearing gifts: tobacco, alcohol, and country music. They smoked and drank and listened to the music of the country. Hank Williams yodeled sadly; Bob Wills quipped as Tommy Duncan crooned. Leadbelly wailed the Truth, but neither man could understand a word.

"What's the matter, Hero? Depressed?"

"Nothing," said Hero. "Nothing."

"'Nothing.' Holy shit. That's really something."

"Nothing from nothing ain't nothing."

"Let's go to Odessa's Diner. Stuffed cabbage. Herring. Poppy cake. The works."

"Think it'll help?"

"Couldn't hurt."

Thus spoke Morris.

## We and Thou

1.0 You can't ask life to be anything other than it is, but you can refuse to be ridiculous.

1.1 I refuse to be ridiculous.

1.2 If everyone refused to be ridiculous, perhaps Seinfeld and Friends would be yanked from syndication and off the air forever.

2.0 Maybe we already are ridiculous, which would be too bad.

2.1 Then again, who's "we?"

2.2 "We" is not me or you, but everything other than you and me.

2.3 "We" is ridiculous.

2.4 Sez I.

# VIDEO JUDAS VIDEO

My wife and I were playing cards with four old friends (CAUTION #1: Old friends should be remembered as they were; seen in memory, but not heard; like nudie photographs of old lovers, NOT to be revisited except in moments of utmost nostalgia/despair), and this one woman was losing pretty bad, Sore Loser, I'll call her though I'd rather call her something else—in fact, that's what I will call her, "Something Else." I guess some of us were ragging on Something Else—you know how nasty old friends in their cups can be. I was just trying to lose so I could go home.

Unfortunately, my wife was doing okay, and anyway she wouldn't just up and leave because she suddenly decided she hated the company she was keeping. Just not that type. So, Something Else was losing and some of us were needling her and she said, "Fine. That's okay. I make twice as much money as anyone here," and I thought of those portraits of Jesus and the Apostles and imagined a cartoon bubble over Judas Iscariot with the words "Fine. That's okay. I make twice as money as anyone here."

I would have said something appropriately nasty to Something Else, but since I probably made half as much money as anyone there—if that—I had no ground to stand on, no VALUE beyond the dwindling pile of chips beside my folded hand.

Once the game was over, the whole gang, or a "democratic majority," decided to do something cultural. So we parked ourselves in the "TV Room." Can you imagine? Not the kids' room or the parents' room or even the dog's room; it's the TV's room; that 50-something-inch box lived better than most people on this earth—and rent free!

What was on TV? Everything about nothing, and folks selling a lot of nothing nobody needs to everyone. But that's irrelevant, I assume. The designated Channel Zapper—our host, of course—finally stopped at one of the five hundred blind destinations—really I didn't care if he stopped on the Lawrence Welk show. I hate that channel surfing shit it bugs me out I'm sorry I'm just an anxious guy and there's only so many Xanax the body can withstand with out turning to aspic.

It was the Snoop Channel or the Snitch Channel or the USA/PATRIOT GOTCHA channel, I forget. This particular show was called the "Most Outrageous, Embarrassing Shit Caught On Video." Whatever.

Just Plain Old Folks all over this great land indulging in chemically induced monkey-shines: college "kids" fucking on the beach after a drinking bout (Spring Break orgy shades of Dionysus—or Rome)—and getting busted; a Bride fondling the Best Man as The Groom is walking down a bush-lined path not twenty yards away—and getting busted; roommates picking their noses and peeing on their roomie's bed—and getting busted; a chartered plane full of decadent party goers, the women submitting to a wet t-shirt contest in mid-fight and the pilots obliging—and getting busted; a bunch of cafeteria workers stoned probably hanging out showing some T and A—and getting busted; and a bunch of other assholes videoed doing more or less harmless stuff and the videos unnecessarily handed over to THE AUTHORITIES (after all, that's the moral imperative of video stalkers/snitches, isn't it? hand the evidence over to THE AUTHORITIES like good little rats).

It was ever so embarrassing for me to be human, watching this show, but the rest of our little group were laughing so hard I thought they'd piss their pants—which could have been dangerous if one of us had a video cam and decided to hand the tape over to THE AUTHORITIES or the Snitch Channel (somehow they're not one and the same, but it's never explained how).

Of course the scenes of "regular folks" doing stupid embarrassing stuff segued into the cops busting people for doing not necessarily stupid, but "irregular" stuff ( a man, dressed in expensive women's clothing, driving a rusty old convertible), the narrator's voice-over telling us "and if there's one bunch of guys who KNOW ALL ABOUT OUTRAGEOUS BEHAVIOR it's the police" and something started to click, of course (workers in some nightmare cafeteria kitchen job getting snooped on and sacked for kidding around, trying to add a few minutes of—red alert!—amusement to their nightmare jobs?

what gives?), but the wheels weren't grinding full speed—damn sedatives!—and my wife was quicker to the draw.

"So that's what these shows are about," said she.

"What?" I asked, after a pause, since the rest of our gang of merrymakers were too agog at the sex- and violence-based humiliations to answer (of course they never showed any real T and A or genitalia, it was all blurred out, but you got the overall "idea," and of course the faces were quite clear). "Assholes doing ridiculous shit so we can feel superior?"

"No," she said. "Surveillance. It's not about these morons exposing themselves—half of them don't even know they're on camera, or don't think the videos will cause them trouble. It's about not having any privacy anywhere, ever. I saw one of these shows before and the first thing I felt afterwards was not embarrassment for those women who degrade themselves, or even repulsion at the freaky men, but 'this could be me.' This isn't such weird stuff they're doing. Some of these people are just getting caught peeing in the woods or having sex in a 'forbidden' zone. Trying to be human and have fun, basically. The thing I think about when I come away from these shows is that they're trying to tell us 'we're everywhere; you can't hide; you are always being watched.'"

Yeah. Shit, yeah. I became more than a tad paranoid. What hidden gadgets did these "old friends" of mine have socked away in their seemingly innocuous TV Room? Was the television ITSELF recording me? And if so, was my fly unzipped?

"See, look," my wife said, pointing to the EMBARRASSING and OUTRAGEOUS moment when a guy tries using a mirror to look under a girl's skirt but gets nailed by the security guards, who of course handed the video over to THE AUTHORITIES, which in this case happened to be the Fink Channel. "They'll make me think I should be sympathizing with the woman, and I do, that guy with the mirror's a creep, but the real message is that NOBODY can get away with anything ever. We're always on camera."

"Oh, are you two at it again?" said Something Else, who had as much money as Judas Iscariot but probably not as much as Pontius Pilate. "We're trying to have fun here. Can't you just lighten up?"

By then my synapses were juiced enough by my wife's astute observation to overcome the Xanax haze, and I was able to make small but significant connections between Something Else, Judas Iscariot, and the evening's after-poker entertainment in the TV Room:

FINK. RAT. STOOL PIGEON. TIPS. SQUEALER. TATTLE TALE. AGENT. NARC. 24/7 SURVEILLANCE. PANOPTICON. POLICE STATE. CALL THIS NUMBER NOW! STRICTLY CONFIDENTIAL. VIDEO DIDN'T KILL THE RADIO STAR, IT SOLD HIM OUT TO

THE AUTHORITIES.

Excellent book on all this, I remembered. "*Snitch Culture*," by Jim Redden (Feral House).

I don't think I'll be going out much anymore, regardless of the company. It's not safe. You never know who's watching, or if you'll end up on TV with your gonads blurred, your face revealed, and your name on someone's, or perhaps everyone's, black list.

CAUTION #2: Anyone wielding a recording device—analog or digital—is to be considered armed and extremely dangerous. If Judas had had a camcorder Jesus never even would have had a last supper. They would have bagged him early on for some "outrageous, embarrassing act" like walking on water, resurrecting dead guys, cloning fish...

**Adam Engel** carries no recording equipment but is something of a Narc himself: When in the midst of Rats, TIPS, Finks, Something Else, etc. he takes notes. One day, these notes might be quite valuable. After all, eventually Robespierre himself lost his head and Mussolini wound up hanging upside down dead like a stuck pig. If you suspect Rats in your basement, contact the AH HA! Hotline at bartlebysamsa65@gmail.com

# WAL-MART AND PEACE: WHAT IS THEIR PROBLEM? WHAT MORE DO THEY WANT FROM US?

I'm all man and only man. I work and weep at Wal-Mart. Our new "town hall." What was that poem from high school? "In Xanadu did Kublai Khan yadda yadda yadda pleasure dome decree..." Well I'd bet my bottom dollar that under that pleasure dome was a bright, shiny Wal-Mart. We have no clue as to why our boys are overseas again, but the President says they must be to defend our freedoms. Smash those WMD's. Liberate the downtrodden people starved half to death by Saddam's sanctions.

> "It is springtime, and so all the Wal-Marts around the country have plastic flowers in the crafts aisle and chocolate eggs in the candy section. But it is also wartime, and at Wal-Mart, which sometimes functions in its vastness as a kind of substitute town square, the impact of the war in Iraq is on display around the clock. For Wal-Mart, the country's biggest company and employer of more people than any entity except the government, only something like a war could force the kinds of changes it has made since the fighting began. Computers normally used for gift registry now send e-mail greetings to the military. On the internal Wal-Mart television network, the usual loop of giddy promotions for Mary Kate and Ashley apparel, garden tools and DVD's is interrupted twice a day for live briefings from the White House and the Pentagon."
> —*New York Times*, "Wartime Grief at Wal-Mart," April 4, 2003

We congregate on breaks to hear the latest. About our boys, our fiancés, our brothers. Over there, over there. We tie yellow ribbons to our flags. Management gives us time to grieve when the television spits bad news down on our muddled heads. We can't put two and two together. But we can work the register, it's computerized and self-correcting, in case we mess up, or let greed get the best of us.

> "In the beginning, someone at Wal-Mart headquarters decided that it would be a good idea to broadcast war coverage, via CNN, into its stores around the clock. The monitors, which exist mainly to advertise Wal-Mart wares, are everywhere, from the front of the stores to the infant, sporting goods, electronics and grocery sections. . . The round-the-clock coverage was not well received at stores where the American forces represented real people, not just images on a screen. Under Wal-Mart policy, stores are not allowed to turn the monitors off, and because it is a closed system, they cannot change the channel to something else. Before long, Ms. Stallings was on the phone to Wal-Mart headquarters in Bentonville, Ark., asking the Wal-Mart brass to do something about the broadcasts. By March 22, the format was scaled back nationwide to include only the two daily briefings."
> —*New York Times*, "Wartime Grief at Wal-Mart," April 4, 2003

Wal-Mart is good to us. We are allowed to read emails during breaks, and when the television-always-on delivered too much worry, Management agreed to keep it tuned to CNN only some of the time, not all of the time, so as not to upset us, but at the same time show the customers, or "guests" as we refer to them, that Wal-Mart is as patriotic as the next super store.

> "At the store in Jacksonville, N.C., near Camp Lejeune, practically all the employees and customers are related to someone in the Marines. Ms. Stallings spends her days and nights on an emotional shore patrol, up and down the aisles of her store, a 200,000-square-foot 'supercenter' that sells everything from baby clothes to Bloody Mary mix. She and her co-manager, Terry Branton, seek out the unusually quiet, the drawn-looking and the people who are openly in tears—mostly their employees, sometimes their customers, too. They console them as best they can."
> —*New York Times*,"Wartime Grief at Wal-Mart," April 4, 2003

Some of us have read radical nonsense about the Walton family that owns Wal-Mart and their being one of the wealthiest families on the planet, the top one tenth of one percent of the population that owns 80 percent of everything. But they give us work. Honest day's work for an honest day's pay. Put food on our tables. Discounts on Wal-Mart items with company scrip—I mean, dollars, strong U.S. currency.

And if one of our boys makes the Ultimate Sacrifice, why, we all pitch in, like one big family, we meet and grieve together, in shifts, in the employee lounge, but only for as much time as is necessary, we have guests to wait on, we can't smoke cigarettes in there but we break out a box of nicotine gum, courtesy the Pharmacy, this being war time, and we console each other and the bereaved, and promise to be there for each other always, we are family.

Yeah I once had my own business, a little discount store the family owned since grandpa came to America, a "general store" really, nothing much, it's better this way. Wal-Mart has so much of everything to offer its guests, while we had so little and didn't even have the sense to call 'em "guests" we called 'em "customers," what hicks we were. But when Wal-Mart came in and the family business tanked, the Company was kind enough to give me a uniform and, taking my years into consideration, make me a "greeter," which is an easy gig, and I'm part of the Wal-Mart family here in this shopper's paradise where the guests have everything available for their purchasing needs.

> "The store's break rooms have become repositories for sorrow, the places where Wal-Mart workers go to cope privately. None of the store managers interviewed said they had brought in extra grief counselors or other specialists. 'Fortunately, the military has very good counseling services,' Mr. Branton said. Although full-time employees can call a counseling line for help as part of their benefits, others tend to rely on their friends at work."
> —*New York Times*, "Wartime Grief at Wal-Mart," April 4, 2003

Really they've been good to us. And were else can we go to support each other, the town going the way of my old discount shop, and the boys off to war again?

We need Wal-Mart just like we need each other, come business or pleasure, cause there's no place else to go. And we have everything we need including Mexican, Chinese, Pizza, Hamburgers and soda, and a pharmacy (sometimes the folks with loved ones over THERE go in for sedatives: Valium, Xanax, and whatnot. I see nothing wrong with that in stressful times like this so long as it doesn't become a habit or anything illegal.

> "Many of the employees, whom Wal-Mart prefers to call associates, are wearing yellow ribbons to work."
> —*New York Times*, "Wartime Grief at Wal-Mart," April 4, 2003

That girl, what's her name, Stella, for instance, lost her husband the first week.

If anyone needed medicating. . . though you're not supposed to drink on that stuff but oh, hell. . . sometimes anything to kill the pain. Chewed that nicotine gum 24/7, smoked like a chimney too out in the parking lot.

Only 20 years old. Her husband 21, now, for the ages. She had some problems not two months ago, miscarriage. I suppose no kid left behind without a dad and for her a haunting loving spitting image face. Maybe better this way, financially. And she's still so very young, in a few years maybe someone else. Start life new. She already used up her personal days for her pregnancy problems, but Management understands, what with the stress of him being sent off maybe that's what caused the abor—the miscarriage. Point I'm trying to make is when she got the news from that nice Army chaplain she had no personal days left. But as I said we're family, we pitched in, everyone a few hours here and there. And Blanche, an older gal needed the money, took extra shifts in Stella's place while she settled into the, her new situation.

> "There are two stages of major upset: first, when e-mail messages and phone calls are cut off because a military unit is heading into combat, and again when reports of casualties come in and mention a military unit stationed nearby. But people inside the Wal-Marts seem to share more general fears, as well: About their children, and about the future."
> —*New York Times*, "Wartime Grief at Wal-Mart," April 4, 2003

One day Stella went in to talk to Management, then hugged and kissed us all good-bye, said, "Nothing left for me here, nothing." But she'll be taken care of. She did good work here. I'm sure Management has only fine things to say, and her being a war widow and all she'll find a position in any town. Wal-Mart's a big chain all over the country nothing bigger. And again she's a gold star widow. The higher ups in the Central Office, wherever that is, will take that into account. No problem anywhere she goes. A hard-working pretty girl; she's young.

> "Many workers also have pictures of their husbands or wives stationed in the gulf pinned to their smocks alongside the name tags adorned with smiley faces, a Wal-Mart staple. . . Some stores have organized collections of food, toiletries, clothing and other items for the troops and their families left back home. In Atlanta, contributions gathered with the help of a radio appeal filled four 18-wheel tractor-trailers and included bottles of Listerine and boxes of Girl Scout cookies on which donors scribbled messages like 'Thanks for keeping us free.'"
> —*New York Times*, "Wartime Grief at Wal-Mart," April 4, 2003

This war will be over soon and most of our boys will come home safe and sound. I've been in the Army myself and I know they take care of their own. And we didn't have smart bombs and computer cruise missiles to protect us, only napalm. And now I hear they have a MOAB bomb to put Saddam in his place once and for all. Goddam Saddam and all his crew, when will they leave us alone? Why must we Americans be the only people of conscience to take out these dictators and put this crazy world in order?

All they know is force, the only language they know. When I saw those towers in NYC, though I've never been to that particular city myself, when I saw them fall like mounds of gray snow, I wept, oh yes, I wept and all I wanted was revenge. All I wanted was to kill Saddam with my bare hands for doing that—wait, it wasn't Saddam, it was that other guy—but hell I wanted to kill 'em all for bringing their evil to this clean country, our beautiful, free land.

> "Back at the stores, the talk of war continues, and employees get through their shifts hoping for the best. Mr. Branton, 36, said he had some experience with his employees' feelings: his father spent 25 years in the military, including lengthy tours in Vietnam. 'So I was a little boy on the front steps waiting for Daddy to come home a couple of times,' he said. His store is decorated for Easter, he added, and he is planning to conduct business as usual. 'We have to carry on,' he said. 'That's important for our whole nation. That's one of the things that makes America America.'"
> —*New York Times*, "Wartime Grief at Wal-Mart," April 4, 2003

Those tall tales about how all our boys are gonna die of depleted uranium and what not: pure propaganda put out by the anti-war crowd and the trouble-makers. I remember those parasites well. In my day they were communists and hippie drug peaceniks not terrorists. What, I ask you, WHAT is their problem? What do they want from us hard-working, life-loving Americans who only want to do what's right; who only want to feed our families; who only want our children to make grandchildren; who only want to live in peace?

**Adam Engel** would rather scrape the blood, shit, vomit, teeth, hair and other human matter from the torture chambers of Camp X-Ray with a tooth brush than work for either Wal-Mart or the *New York Times*. Flags, yellow ribbons and conjectures as to what excuse Bush Inc. will use to bomb Syria can be sent to bartlebysamsa65@gmail.com

# WHAT IT IS

*(Winner of the Jericho Junior High School Essay Contest)*

Topic: But when you say you neither love nor hate "America," what do you mean? What is "America?"

America is a joint-stock company shared by various transnational corporations.

America is a brutal hyper-state (of mind?) that won't accept Tragedy unless it falls out of a plane.

America is a saber-toothed beast gobbling resources and farting poison into an already exhausted environment, the death of which will mean the death of America.

America is my Grandmother's home-made matzo balls and Hungarian Stuffed Cabbage.

America stole my heart and mailed it to my wife (she keeps it hidden and won't say where—this is the only secret between us).

America killed my mother with Darvocet and lawyers.

America called me a "dirty Jew" then sent 3 billion dollars to a guy named Eretz Israel. I don't care what America calls me I just wish it would stop confusing me with that gun nut, Eretz, who stole my Grandma's matzo balls then claimed the recipe wasn't hers at all: It belonged to God, who left the box of index cards containing ALL of grandma's recipes (including the Marshmallow Rice Krispy Treats) to Eretz Israel when He died..

America let me finger her that week my parents went away and left me to baby sit my sweet, demented Grandfather the Summer of 1980. My first encounter with a GENUINE REAL LIVE PUSSY came quite unexpectedly and afterwards we ordered in Chinese (mooshu chicken, I think, and egg rolls).

One colorful late Spring evening in America I pitched a shut-out in the Little League play-offs and they let me keep the game ball (I have it still).

America fooled me into thinking I needed yet more education and more and more and now I owe the bank my life. Thank you America for teaching me hard lessons (I guess that's what you meant by "education").

America raped my girlfriend in high school. (I knew it was you America so I beat you bloody in the hallway it took two Gym Instructors and the Football Coach to pull me off—I would have killed you, America—but really, did beating you change anything at all?)

America wouldn't print my article and I got scooped by the "rival" paper and demanded to know why so the editor opened the morning edition to the advertisement paid for by the company I was investigating and America laughed so hard it fell out of its chair.

I loved getting drunk back of the Datsun listening to "Get Yer Ya Ya's Out" real loud while manic, coked-out America sped down Jericho Turnpike at eighty-something miles an hour and did "do-nuts" in the parking lot.

America applauded when I shot a duck, a sparrow, a rabbit, a gardener and a two door Fiat with my pellet gun (age twelve).

America taught me to throw a wicked curve when I was thirteen; I struck out batter after batter till my arm blew out. "You know, you shouldn't be throwing curve balls at least until you're seventeen," said America. "Your body's not developed yet."

America opened her innermost to me when I was seventeen. It felt weird because of the rubber—like a cold, dead fish between me and America.

America is a huge chunk of stolen property on which 280 million people live along with animals and plant life. The plants and animals are disappearing.

America's so angry and depressed it's killing itself and the world.

**America** can be reached at bartlebysamsa65@gmail.com

# THE WAR AGAINST TOYS AND PHARMA-GANDA

The only way outta town tonight is Santa Claus. Kris Kringle. The Man in the Red Suit.

Couldn't think anything but bad thoughts Sunday when I heard it in the other room: "Santa Claus is Coming To Town." Clay-mation or stop-action-mation or however they made those cool Christmas specials featuring lights and snow and joyous elfin jesters back in the day.

This was the original, the story of how it all began, the story of the Revolution in Somberville and the War Against Toys.

Kris, a subversive young man with extremely bright red hair, is raised in the woods by rebel elves called "Kringles." Kringles are artisans, craftsmen, who reject the authoritarian regime of nearby City of Somberville. They and their leader, a woman known as "Tanta," teach Kris readin' writin' 'rithmetic' and how to make toys.

And get this: Kris makes friends with animals in the woods, develops this noble savage/Rousseau/Sioux medicine-man thing with squirrels, birds, rabbits, reindeer and a little penguin who looks remarkably like the universal Linux logo. (Is this where Linus Torvalds and Richard Stallman got the idea?) They teach him to run, jump, think and LAUGH like an animal. He grows up and sets out to distribute the Kringles' toys because —because the Kringles want children to enjoy them.

So the Man in the Red Suit saunters into Somberville, a dark ghetto full of depressed, oppressed, repressed white people (well, not EXACTLY white: looks like a shtetl out of a Shalom Aleichem story, real Fiddler On The Roof stuff) run by this mean old Nazi, the Burgher Meister Meister Burgher, who prohibits toys or fun of any kind. It's A War Against Toys.

But Kringle manages to corrupt the children and their pretty, young, extremely red-haired school marm, Jessica, by getting 'em all high on fun. He melts the icy heart of the Winter Warlock with the gift of a toy Choo-choo train. He even gets the Burgher Meister off with a psychedelic yo-yo until one of the Meister's henchmen reminds him he's breaking his own law, so The Man In The Red Suit splits and—

—commercial break. Grim reality, so called.

This woman says to me, "You've got a yeast infection."

I say, "No way."

She says, "Yeah you do, and you use greasy, gooey topical creams."

"Bullshit."

"You've got a yeast infection and you cover it with cream to hide the shame of your stanky cooter. Admit it. It's okay."

"NO!"

But there's a way outta this mess, she tells me. I don't need to rub this wretched, thick cream on my itchy labia if I just swallow this little pill. Don't smear. Swallow.

"Wait a minute, Lady, what's in that little pill?"

But poof she's gone, and some old fart with a face like a scrotum tells me he can cure my hemorrhoids with—guess what?—a little pill.

"Hold on there, old-timer. What's in that little pill?"

But back to the story:

Something obviously subversive about a guy (in red, no less) sneaking into a town full of oppressed repressed and depressed workers who work morning to night every damn day till the weekend during which they work on looking busy, and the Burgher Meister says so.

"You are a radical unt a non-conformist!" the Meister barks to Kringle mit heavy Deutsch gutturals.

Musta been written by lefty Jews, this Christmas special, what with the dark-haired ghetto folk lorded over by a fat German autocrat, and red-haired, red-suited Kringle, like the slap-happy fool we wish Schindler had been, distributing colorful, hand-crafted artifacts created solely for the health and enjoyment of children—for free! Kringle actually shouts out joyously, "I love my job!" ARREST THAT MAN!

And the authorities sure try, but Kringle's got a whole support network, including Jessica, the school-marm; the now kindly but impotent Winter Warlock (no more magic powers what're they saying here about wickedness and power I'm confused); the children; the animals and the Kringle elves who make the toys and actually ENJOY their work and were only sad because no one else could enjoy the fruits of their labor until Kris became their fence, their middle man, their bag man (literally) to distribute PRODUCT.

Of course he ends up in the slammer—how can he not, with that nasty burgher king and his goons always on his case? But he busts out by feeding the reindeer these magic seeds that make them fly (can we get in any MORE drug culture versus authority references here? I don't know whether to refer to a Oliver Stone's NIXON or Euripides' THE BACCHAE).

And there's all SORTS of subversive goings on: Rebel kids on the circuit leaving their doors open (and getting caught); kids hanging stockings for Kris to stuff with toys at night (and getting caught); Kris climbing down the chimneys cause the doors have all been locked (and getting caught).

And every time THE MAN tries to crack down, the network of rebel thrill-seekers grows until Kris—who grows a Che Guevara beard and changes his name to "Claus" after a wanted poster names the clean-shaven Kris Kringle PUBLIC ENEMY NUMBER ONE—is welcome among fellow travelers and creatures of the woods like Che himself among the peasants.

Santa and Jessica marry outdoors amid trees decked out with sparkling trinkets galore. They exchange vows and gifts among their friends—animal, vegetable and mineral—before god, but they don't say which god, and it's implied by the ceremony we're dealing with Dionysus or the Green Man or some polytheistic party god/goddess, not pissed off Yahweh or his Hippy Son (nice guy, but so damn serious—all those issues with Dad, I guess).

Cut to yet ANOTHER commercial:

"You're depressed," a somber but not-too-blue lady (might scare consumers if she looks too bummed) tells me.

"Not anymore, man. Santa Claus is COOL!"

"It's nothing to be ashamed of. Millions of Americans are depressed."

"That's cause they work too much, play too little, and have to deal with a farbisseneh like you! Beat it."

So she goes on to tell me how I can stop being depressed by asking my doctor to prescribe me a dandy little pill.

"But what, I ask you, what IS IN THAT FUCKING PILL?"

Poof she's gone and a guy comes on singing about how he's so happy (must have taken a fistful of those pills: He's wearing a tie and in the middle of an office-suite labyrinth of corpse-gray cubicles) cause he bought this PDA (personal digital annoyance) palm pilot thingy to help him organize his work and be not twice but thrice as productive—DOING WHAT? WHAT ARE YOU MAKING? TOYS? AT LEAST THE FUCKING ELVES CAME THROUGH WITH PRODUCT!—and he bought it on Ebay right before the digital gavel closed the bid. He beat the competition so he could get a good deal on this pain-in-the-ass gadget he plans to use to help his employer beat the competition. Gadzooks! Get away from me you freak, get off my screen before I turn zap yer ass with the remote

—but back to Christmas. Santa and his posse realize Somberville's just too hot with the TEA (Toy Enforcement Authority), so they start this free commune in the North Pole where they make toys all year round and Santa revs up his sleigh on Christmas eve and distributes hand-crafted playthings among the good children of the world. He has this "naughty and nice" clause—it's why they call him "Claus"—but it's only a formality. As long as you don't pout and whine all the time and instead use your energy creatively to buck authority, you're cool with him. You may not get a super-electronic "KILL TERROR" computer game like you wanted, cause that's not his thing—Santa and the elves are into craftsmanship, the personal touch, everything handmade—but you sure as shit won't get a lump of coal.

Finally the narrator—who's Fred Astaire by the way, Hollywood's own Nijinsky tippy-tap-tap-tapping his holiday rendition of the Rites of Spring—tells us that though Santa's not an outlaw anymore, and the Burgher Meister and his crowd died away and were replaced by a more liberal administration (we'll see how long THAT lasts), there are some folks who still hate Santa Claus, and damned if they didn't cut to:

A HARASSED SALESCLERK in a department store getting yelled at, poked and prodded by adult CONSUMERS who want SERVICE, like, IMMEDIATELY

and THEN to

A CIGAR-CHOMPING EXECUTIVE in his depressing office through the window of which we see a horrible sooty filthy goddamn factory with smokestacks burping toxic smoke into the pure pink lungs of Christmas. And this guy, who's obviously stacked (no pun), but miserable, says, "Who can think of Christmas in a world like THIS?"

I mean, who wrote the script for this baby, Herbert Marcuse?

Man what a lesson, what a show! I remembered the first time I saw "Santa Clause is Coming to Town," (goddamn!) thirty years ago. I was working on this wood-burning set my parents got me for Hanukah—of course—and it seemed so apropos, the craft I was working on and the craft of the elves, and even now, remembering, I could smell the sweet smoke rising from the wood when once again—

cut to a commercial for yet another little pill to stop my farts from making noise or god knows what, and yet another adult dancing—like a puppet, not a pagan—through the isles of some department store, Stuff-Fer-YOU, or whatever, and the stuff was a bunch of doohickeys with which to thrill your kids, if you can afford kids, and the batteries are not included and there's no guarantee they won't be obsolete two days outta the box and say, you look DEPRESSED, anxious, stressed—what you need is this little ol' pill that's GUARANTEED to burn that Holiday fever right outta yer Yiddisher Kupf. . . .

Oh Youth! Oh Santa—get me outta town!

# WHAT?

Bush is an aberration . Unlike more skillful Republican front men—Ronald Reagan, Bill Clinton—he does not know how to say one thing and do the other. He says what he means and means what he says. Which is terrifying. He believes in all that crap about God and Democracy, etc, whereas Clinton—a Republican by any definition of the term—knew how to make the folks feel good while prosecuting the grim business of Empire.

For instance, in the thoroughly illegal and counter productive bombing of Serbia , which confirmed his place as a murderer and war criminal (yawn), he played the media, the numbers (body counts, body-part counts; how many cleansed, how many totally wiped clean etc.) and the "good-intentioned yet hopelessly righteous Boobus Americanus for all he was worth. Whereas Bush and his team don't care. Bring 'em on. Put 'em down. Shock 'em. Aw 'em. Democratize 'em. What are YOU gonna do about it? Really, they just don't care. Then again, why should they?

Clinton's "Effective Death Penalty and Anti-Terrorism Act" was the first sledgehammer blow to the Bill or Rights and paved the way for the USA PATRIOT ACT, yet it was subtler, and necessarily less dramatic if more far-seeing. Then again, Clinton hadn't had the luxury of the 9/11 hysteria, the greatest gift given to Bush since the Supreme Court handed him the Presidency itself.

Where were the Democrats then? It was their duty to fight tooth and nail for the people who voted for Gore, those patriotic voters who had to drive all the way to the local high school and push a button for the "candidate of their choice." Coke, Pepsi or Nader Green Tea.

Similarly, where have the Democrats been for the past 3 years? With the exception of Kucinich, who was the only candidate I might have voted for without feeling I was contributing to the system's never-ending cycle of never ending, every candidate proposed by the Democrats—the usual suspects, by the way; interesting, no?—supported the Patriot Act, The War against Drugs, The War against Afghanistan, The War against Iraq, the War Against Tooth Decay and what not. Furthermore, them fightin' Dems let their Republican colleagues give Bush unprecedented powers to instigate further ridiculous, useless, bloody and illegal wars in the future, not to mention supporting many of his pro-corporate, anti-environment, anti-cerebral cortex initiatives.

Wars have been going on for at least six thousand years, and so long as no one resorts to nukes again (like in Hiroshima), they probably won't affect the ultimate destiny of all life on the planet. The absolute destruction of the air, water, land, forests and other "biological necessities" on this planet by corporations whose legal duty is to ignore such damage in pursuit of profits for their share-holders, means that "we" and most of the other species alive today, won't make it another 100 years. But the Earth will be around for at least another 5 billion. In ten thousand years or so, the mess will be cleaned and the cities and stadiums buried and new life will grow.

Still, after months of "Kucinich is our only hope" followed by "Greens for Dean" and other SPAM flooding my IN BOX at a rate not even the best hacker Knights of Norton and McAfee could contend with, is it even interesting that after all the hoopla it turns out to be Skull-and-Bones Kerry, pre-selected long before Kucinich and Dean put on their little side-shows, who "won" the candidacy, or simply so predictable as to be merely ridiculous. Beyond ridiculous. Stupefying. One can only watch such long, pathetic spectacles play themselves out so many times before being reduced to spending days in one's pajamas, uncleansed, ethnically or otherwise, unshaven, unkempt, muttering "what? What? What?"

I really can't see a way out of this. It will have to play itself out, like most historical follies. Waves, set in motion by the power elite, that eventually crash to the surf of the masses who take their hits like the good grains of sand that they are, have always been, and it seems, always will be.

# AMERICAN PIE (IN YOUR FACE)

"OneTwoThree: F—"
—the Beatles

"What's that spell?"
—Country Joe and the Fish

"There came a voice from over the sea. . . "
— Percy Bysshe Shelley

My, my, she was just seventeen hello, hello good finger pie, and then John Lennon died and President-elect Reagan bitched about how anybody un-American enough to get himself shot and killed must be on drugs and ought to be shot and killed; after all, he himself was popped plenty of times and just picked himself up by his bootstraps and walked away; anyway, folks know how to play it cool with guns in Californucopia, where he was hatched like Athena from Knute Rockne's golden calf. . . . And that's all I remember of America. . .

(Ante Dubius: A few days after the First Caricature narco-ambulated through his coronation like Boris Karloff—Frankenstein? The Mummy?—in Edwardian drag, a friend, Ivan, appropriately named, asked me if I knew that "the letters of the name 'Ronald Wilson Reagan' signify '666?'" Come on, he didn't believe in Revelations, did he? No, but apparently Ronnie did, and had the Defense Budget to make the big score. Armageddon: Jesus—the nice Nordic one, not the real one, who probably looked more like Arafat, or Nelson Mandela, or those Sephardic Israelis you don't see on TV—leads the faithful in the rumble of all Manichean rumbles; the Jews are gathered in the Holy Land so the former carpenter can finish what the former painter started. Unfortunately, Godless Gorby delayed this Second Coming. But Emperor Georgius Dubius has no bona-fide Lucifer to sucker him into peace. Did you know the letters of the name "George Dubya Bush" signify nothing?)

Where were we?

Oh yes: those were the days, my friends, when poets were as unacknowledged as the legislators of the world (at least in Washington), before Amiri Baraka called Jews a spade, and New Jersey seceded from the Union whistling "Born to Run." Mighty lucky of Waylon Jennings to finally join his buddies, Holly, Valens and the Big Bopper in Death (Oh, Baby, that's what we like!) because such goings on under these (RedWhiteAnd) blue skies would surely make him puke. Hell, we used to wanna be Bugs Bunny, not Yosemite Sam. Now even Tweety sings for TIPS and Tony Blair flitter-flutter-and-frets openly:

"What's we gonna do massa George? What's we gonna do?"

"What do you mean, 'we'?"

Plain as the blood on your boots, me Limey Lackey; plain as the tooth in your shorts, plain as Summer in October (Summer of brown skies gray skies beige skies. Global warming and environmental stress caused by, say, the murder of two very tall buildings? Fuggetaboutit!). We'll kick terror's fearsome ass. And Emperor Dubius said as much, more or less:

"Off-ense is the best dee-fence, (next to non-sense). So we'll be offensive!"

True, this chicken hawk in the henhouse defended (offended?) the Nation on 9/11/01 the way he defended it during Nam as an FFF (Fleeing Fire Fast): In an airplane high over god blessed America. Nevertheless, though Emperor Dubius wore no combat clothes, he sure caught Congress with its proverbial pant(ies) down:

"Of course, you can use the citizens' tax money to defend the Empire from the ever-scheming barbarian hordes, Georgius Dubius. We just wanted you to ask, is all. We like to feel like we're, well, you know, we like to feel needed."

Honestly, why do we bother to pay for a large, gelatinous Congress (true, some pay more than others, but now's not the time to beggar GE's right to free speech) when we can use that tax money to buy good, solid firepower? And why should Emperor Dubius waste time, that is, money, explaining the obvious to the dim-witted UN that we couldn't have bombed the Soviets because they'd have bombed us back, big time, but we can bomb Iraq because they have weapons of mass destruction and might. . . . well, again, why should the Emperor of America have to explain anything to anyone when we're the biggest best-est number one-est super-powerful-est democracy ever, and the best place for anyone in his right(wing) mind to live since Santa busted the elves' union, thereby liberating the North Pole from Communism and ending the cold war? Being America means never having to say you're sorry (cause the folks you'd be apologizing to have disappeared, their stories, grievances, whatever, long forgotten).

You Can't Stay the Course Till Your Feet Start Runnin'

What I'm getting at is this: when will we finally bomb Saddam, just blast the black outta his fat stock-villain mustache? When will we do what Emperor Poppy (Oh, Father Totem of the great Taboo, if you'd only stayed the course and not withdrawn so. . . prematurely, we could have, we would have made that Jezebel come!) should have done? I'm going mad with impatience—I've been waiting since yesterday! So where will you go my blue-collared sons? Where will you go, my dark-skinned young ones birthed after Bruce sang ruefully of others unfortunate enough to be Born (into the wrong class, at the wrong time) In The U.S.A.? Fear not. There be ditties yet unsung. So. All together now:

Leviathan swallowed Miss American Pie. Poor old woman I fear she'll die (refrain).

Gorilla Warfare

(A Value Added Warning Fable—yours free for reading the above)

The Top Banana (TB) entered the assembly of Unctuous Hominids (UH), towers burning in the darkness of his eyes, and said to himself aloud, aloud:

"Why are there so many damn simianese baboons in here and why must they grunt like, like apes?"

Many simians (and simianese), wondering if the Alpha Male was carrying some sort of "peace-keeping" device, closed their eyes and prayed their godless monkey prayers; others bit their nails and nervously crunched lice between their teeth and day-dreamed of justice and opposable thumbs. Sighs and applause resounded through the UH assembly when the TB was through saying whatever he had meant to say but didn't really have to because it was well understood. The assembly, thankful the TB withheld his heater for another chump chimp in whose obliteration he'd graciously welcomed them assist, or at least not resist—or risk the same and then some!

The hominids began to rise, but the Top Banana arched his ridged brow, thumped his chest and bellowed:

"Pain can be killed by Poppy and Fear can be killed by Poppy. Yet what can kill better than Poppy, but the end of days, the end of pain, both so easily arranged. Thank you, and god bless US, but not them. You neither. Night."

## American Vampire In New York

I died for your sins—almost. I never quite died complete. But still. You didn't notice either way. It's been a year, more or less. You didn't call my wife. You didn't send a card.

I don't know why I stay on. Something in me clings to this wretched place. I refuse to leave. Perhaps I feel I deserve something. I broke my back carrying the burden of America. They gave me painkillers (pills, not Marines). Oxycontin, oxycodone. Now I'm addicted and must pay and pay and pay for more. Lucky my wife works.

I can't sleep, but I'm clear, clear in the head. I need blood. I read the articles on the Web. So many writing, nobody doing. I look at clips of children stained with blood, or jetting blood from severed limbs, and think: Waste, waste, waste.

All that blood and none for me. Do you think it's a coincidence, me being a vampire and all, with all this blood around, everywhere I turn, and not drop for me, unless I pay and pay and pay?

It should be free, but the medical establishment, the ones who hooked me on the painkillers (pills, not Marines) won't give me my fix unless I go to a Pain Management Specialist, and of course they don't take insurance, so I must pay and pay and pay. Do you think an internist in a "troubled" neighborhood could get away with that?

These Pain Management Specialists are drug dealers to the rich. If you wonder why there's a war on drugs that's why. So doctors can get rich and the rich can have their drugs. Also, America is insane, which means if you're not insane, you must be mad.

I need strong, organic hashish for this TERRIBLE NAUSEA, but all I can score is "synthetic cannaboids," "plastic pot" for $30 a pill. It wasn't the war "against" drugs, it was the war "versus" drugs, and BigPharma won, in the short term, over nature. Hasn't anyone read "Frankenstein?" A vampire must feed on life, not "synthetic consumables."

But the blood, the blood. Doctors call my condition Diamond Blackfan Anemia, a rare disease, 600 known cases worldwide. Mostly children who die well before thirty. I'm forty, ten years overdue.[4] I'm dead but not dead.

Undead.

The undead (surely I am not alone: My comrades are vampires, not the other 599 sufferers of this mythical disease) are condemned to night hours glued to screens. Gush of words (same old, same old) and blood, blood, blood. Worlds of blood untouchable. Life divided from death by screens.

If you only knew how frustrated a vampire becomes when he is restrained, restricted, under government control, corporate control, medical control, that is, control of the medical profession, the medical industry, the medical establishment, whose purpose is not to heal, but to make heel.

I need blood and all I see are torrents of blood the painkillers (not pills, Marines) unleash daily; tidal waves of ruby nourishment seep into the earth a world away, wasted. By right that blood belongs to me.

---

[4] As of the publication of this book, Adam Engel is forty-five.

For some, the living, this war is about oil. I won't dispute that. But for me and my kind it is a harvest of blood, a bounty of blood—wasted, discarded, like a sour coleslaw at a bitter family picnic.

"Why?" I ask. Why can't they fill their canteens with blood or capture it in containers and freeze it and send it to the clinic and disperse it, without charge, so I can live and work and be sociable with my countrymen who relish the blood almost as much as I? Though, wasteful Americans, they see it not as their salvation, merely their due. Like the oil meant to sustain their "way of life." A gusher of oil would make them cringe if the liquid was not harnessed and contained and purified and shipped in barrels back to the Homeland to fuel their cars and heat their homes.

But the blood is wasted, splattered on clothes, on walls, on streets, or seeping into sand. There's so much sand there, all of it rich with iron. "To see hematocrit in a grain of sand, hold hemoglobin in the palm of your hand. . . "

They think nothing of the vampire who needs this blood to live like them, to work like them, to be insane like them, to sleep the night away, wake up refreshed, ready for work: The cubicle work, the Mega store work, the retail fast food convenience store counter work.

What would they be without their oil and healthy blood and energy to work, work, work? So much they take for granted, they think only for themselves and their strong backs not broken by the burden of America.

Why me? Why must I be burdened? Why did my back break under the strain?

They don't care about the vampires who need blood, the broken ones who need painkillers (not Marines, pills) but are too tired from lack of blood to cross the street for a prescription, too tired to wait for the pharmaceutical chain to fill it—they don't carry painkillers (pills, not Marines) in stock you know, they must order them special. Why is this? I'll tell you: Spite. They love to see a vampire writhe in pain; they love the misery of the weak ones whose backs break under the burdens they themselves bear with alacrity and ease. They love to see the blood seep into sand instead of my veins because. . . because. . . they are insane, not mad, like me, from lack of sleep, lack of blood, undead yet in pain; they are insane, and wasteful and selfish to send their pain-killers (not pills, Marines) to harvest blood by the barrel-full and dump it on the ground or paint the clothes and shattered homes of donors.

But if so much as a drop of oil is spilt, heads will roll because oil is their poison, simple as that. So they think little or nothing of blood for the bloodless or painkillers (pills, not Marines) for backs broken under their burden.

The only painkillers they recognize are the soldiers who harvest blood yet leave it there to desiccate and rot, for their homes are heated and their tanks are full. They can rest cozy on the couch or drive to the mall, while I am cold, and tired, and in pain.

What would it cost them? Who would it harm, if they stopped to think, even for a moment, of the vampire, and opened the spigots of blood, and let the pharmacists deliver painkillers (drugs, not Marines) and bags of real, organic Marijuana, free of charge... to me?

# SUPPORT OUR ROBOTS

> "BALAD AIR BASE, Iraq–The airplane is the size of a jet fighter, powered by a turboprop engine, able to fly at 300 mph and reach 50,000 feet. It's outfitted with infrared, laser, and radar targeting, and with a ton and a half of guided bombs and missiles.
>
> The Reaper is loaded, but there's no one on board. Its pilot, as it bombs targets in Iraq, will sit at a video console 7,000 miles away in Nevada.
>
> The arrival of these outsize U.S. "hunter-killer" drones, in aviation history's first robot attack squadron, will be a watershed moment even in an Iraq that has seen too many innovative ways to hunt and kill."
> —Associated Press, July 16, 2007.

So BushCo solved the PR problem that might possibly have grown into a credible anti-war movement by alleging to guarantee fewer American casualties which, let's face it, is all Americans really care about anyway. Otherwise, we would have protested the massacre of the first "Gulf War" in which Iraqi soldiers and civilians were slaughtered in their cars while trying to escape Baghdad.

Forget all that "military honor" nonsense. What kind of monsters fire on retreating troops AND fleeing civilians? Despite all the movies and TV shows referring to "American casualties" in 1991, including that movie with Meg Ryan, only about 200 Americans died in that war as opposed to 150,000-plus Iraqis, mostly civilian. The movie, JARHEAD, unique among Gulf I movies, depicts burnt corpses on a highway crammed with cars and trucks bombed while fleeing American air power and "smart bombs."

Gulf War Syndrome... that's a different story. Poisoning our own troops is not very heroic. But the Pentagon doubts GWS is a real disease, much less caused by our own poisonous artillery, DU and all the rest. And so the Pentagon thinks these alleged "GWS sufferers" are really a bunch of lay-abouts looking for a hand-out merely because they "risked their lives" for their country. But again, the Pentagon knows they didn't really risk much of anything; it was an air war for chrissake. Well just because the Government has treated war veterans like doo-doo ever since Vietnam doesn't mean. . . well, forget it. Who am I, who is anybody, war-veteran or not, to question the U.S. Government?

But let's imagine for a moment that Iraqis are actually human beings. Or better yet, imagine a country 100 times more powerful than the U.S. bombing all our major cities, then slaughtering the survivors as they attempted to escape in their cars (stuck in traffic jams; literally sitting ducks). Imagine if after this three-week nightmare resulting in the equivalent of millions of American casualties, the Attackers forced an embargo for twelve years, in which hospitals could not get medicine, vehicles could not receive spare parts, and food and water were scarce, not to mention the destruction of the infrastructure and occasional air raid. THEN imagine that after twelve years of this, the ATTACKERS struck again, this time with the intention of taking over the country, stealing its natural and cultural resources, and basically leaving the U.S. not a society, but a chunk of bombed-out land populated by sick, hungry, wounded, terrified walking zombies. Would we fight back, like the "insurgents?" Or would we throw flowers at our ATTACKER? Would we even call those Americans who, like many French in WWII, resisted, "insurgents" or "Patriots?"

In a high school history class I opined that if I could go back to 1938, strapped with explosives, enter an event populated by Hitler, his top officials, and even their WIVES AND CHILDREN, I would willingly "give my life" to blow up the building and prevent WWII. The teacher applauded my bravery and self-sacrifice. But that was 22 years ago. Today, I suppose I'd be labeled a "terrorist" for even contemplating such a thing. Especially against our friends the Nazis!

Honestly, did anyone, even in the planning stages of 2001-2002, expect that the Iraqis might not appreciate the wholesale destruction of their country? Because "we" didn't like their government (which "our" CIA helped put in place)? People all over the world condemned our invasion of Viet Nam and Cambodia. If they had the means to "change our government" and punish U.S. citizens for the mistakes of that government, would it not be more or less the same thing?

Did anyone really believe the BushCo's arguments for war in the first place? I remember several large demonstrations against the war before it started in April, 2003. But even so, we don't give a damn about the Iraqis, only "our troops," an invading force, including torturers and psycho-killers. For all of Cindy Sheehan's anti-war work, we didn't hear much from her until her son was killed while attempting to kill Iraqis. Perhaps, before he was killed, he killed many Iraqis. Did Cindy fly to Iraq to bring him home before he did any more damage?

Well, I suppose we won't have to worry as much about the safety of our invading, marauding army. We can "support our Robots" instead, as unmanned planes, named, appropriately, The Reaper, murder Iraqis, destroy more homes and "secret insurgent hideouts" (along with their families, friends and other non-combatants), and secure the area for Truth, Justice, and the American Way (massive oil consumption, militarism, predatory Corporatism, racism and all the rest).

This is not about "honor or bravery or sacrifice," any more than Hiroshima or Nagasaki were. It's pure cowardice, killing without having to put "our" troops in harm's way. "Support our troops," indeed. But we know what we are, so why fight with our own selfish, cowardly, murderous intent? Must a dog learn to meow or a cat bark? Why pretend we're something we're not? "We" didn't create the largest military on earth because we're decent, peace-loving, democratic do-gooders.

We're afraid. Very afraid. Fortunately, the wicked cunning of our scientists allows us to have our oil and choke on it too.

I feel safer already knowing our patriotic killer-robots are in Iraq, a button-push, dial-turn or lever-switch away from blasting those evil, freedom-hating prepubescent terrorists back to the. . . uh . . . antebellum stone-age.

JULY 26TH, 2007

# QUESTIONS OF EMPIRE

What do you do if you're a minority and "everyone" hates you? What if you realize that lots of people like or even love you, actually, but none of them are ever on TV? And the TV was the one that told you that you were a minority and everyone hated you in the first place?

What if your country were not the land of opportunity, merely of opportunists?

What if you had not an enemy in the world capable of harming you, and a trillion dollars to spend on housing, schools, hospitals, transportation, and, most important of all, preventing as best as possible the dire consequences of a compromised environment?

What if "The Environment" were just the green fields and mountains and stuff you know from postcards, ads, and TV, but have never actually experienced with your other four senses?

What if someone lied to you in order to prevent you from spending the trillion dollars on the aforementioned public necessities and amenities so they could spend it on a war against a foreign country that had neither ability nor intention of ever attacking you, but that did harbor a great supply of the oil that is destroying your planet?

What if someone told you that the war was of immediate necessity because the Enemy harbored weapons of mass destruction (just like your country and its "allies")?

What if thousands of your "countrymen" were wounded, dying, or dead?

What if hundreds of thousands, probably millions, of The Enemy's children had been killed by bullet or embargo, thousands killed daily or dying in barren hospitals since your daughter, now in college, was born?

How come the number of offenses by Corporate/Military/Political elites against the people outside the Nation and the Nation's own people cannot be counted by mere men in real time, but, like the fractal, must undergo millions of iterations by computer, to reach completion?

Why are people dying of cancer in the street, or if not on the street in hospitals or homes and why is everyone always dying of cancer?

Why won't the Nation treat its cancerized citizens who don't have health insurance? Why do sick people have no homes? Why does anyone have no home?

Why is the "National Institute of Health" (NIH) taking government money to do research to create drugs that will be sold back to the taxpayer at exorbitant prices? Is there a "National Free Clinic?" Is there a "National Free Aspirin?"

Why is my friend dying because he doesn't have health insurance? Why am I dying because I don't have health insurance?

Is that why the "Indians" died, because they didn't have health insurance? Is that how Lincoln died?

If we're the "good guys," why does everyone want to kill us? Are we lone cowboys like Gary Cooper and John Wayne?

What if all these questions were asked of a ten-year-old, the age at which, it seems, the Modern American Mind closes, shutting down all alternatives to racism, corporatism, imperialism, and savage, restless violence?

How many questions about America are there? Enough to fill every database on the Internet?

JULY 16TH, 2007

# TUNE OUT, TURN OFF, UN-PLUG

Radical problems demand radical, not "bipartisan," solutions. If we don't change, the climate will. It already is changing with more rapidity than anyone dared imagine twenty years ago.

No time for Main Stream politics now, NONE AT ALL. Either we come up with radical solutions to this radical problem of Climate Change, or we swab the deck while the Corporate Elite (Republicans AND Democrats) and their aristocratic equivalents around the world, man the life-boats—Billionaires, Silicon-enhanced Women, and Pure-Born Royalty first.

I don't believe for a minute that a) humanity and all of life can sustain itself under the current system. However, the current system will use anything in its power, including Nukes and WMD, to stop the threat of even the slightest change. That's why the whip came down in Seattle in 1999, during the halcyon days of Democrats, because the activists, however ingenuous and trusting AND unarmed, had gotten way too close to the real and only issue: Accept Capitalist Civilization's planned reduction of all living things, all wildlife into dead consumer goods, or die.

We've learned what damage a fist-full of Republicans can do in a few years, and it's only marginally worse than damage done in the "good old days" by droves of Democrats.

We've NO TIME for Democrats! They gave up the 2000 and 2004 elections to Bush; the Democrats in Congress voted for the war and nearly every other nefarious attack on civil rights and public assistance proposed by their Republican "colleagues" or Bush himself.

And just when were the "good old days?"

Democrats were in charge during both the Korean and Vietnamese wars, the McCarthy Period, and gave Bush nearly unanimous support after the panic unleashed by 9/11, when critical thinking, important questions, and balanced observation were in order. Democrats dropped two nuclear weapons on real people, set up legislation that allowed Bush to score the "goal" of the PATRIOT ACT, not to mention killing almost a million Iraqis "softly" with sanctions. So we're supposed to worship Roosevelt for the pennies he threw to the poor and working classes—which then, as they do again today, formed a far higher, wider base of the economic pyramid than ever before or since—earning him scorn from the "business class," though his welfare Trojan Horse effectively neutralized all "third-party threats" such as socialists and communists from the "national debate," which comprised, essentially, his "fire-side chats," answered by countless letters from "citizens" voicing their opinions, which were always inspiring though irrelevant on all such occasions, when Power wins the battle, then generously allows you to keep your wasted farm and half-dead mule.

It might be a good idea to stop and think about things before accepting, rejecting or even responding to your next web article or blog piece, this one included (perhaps in particular).

What has this "System" called "Civilization" actually achieved beyond baubles for the very rich and famous? What has this "Civilization," now 6000 years old or so and not about to change, brought to humanity? After it slaughtered and/or enslaved ALL indigenous peoples, Asians, Africans, Native Americans, fought a few Holy Wars after burning many "lesser" religions out of History's prayer-book, and even after "god was dead" managed two world wars in one particularly bloody century?

Here in the "land of the free," after a bloody civil war, the chattel slave was converted into the wage slave just in time for the factories to begin "production." See, the Civil War wasn't about "freeing" black chattel slaves so much as ensuring the corporate wage state would be large and powerful enough to enslave YOU (if you happen to be black, that's double-jeopardy).

For merely tinkering with the System to ensure that people, in general, had at least a small income from Public Works and social security and the rest, Roosevelt was called a "communist" and a "traitor to his class." Meanwhile, it's the old MLK/Malcolm X split: would MLK have gotten any concessions at all if the possibility of Malcolm X and other more militant, more violent radicals wasn't waiting in the wings?

There were a lot of angry, desperate people during the 1930s, many of them veterans demanding rightful benefits; Communists demanding revolution; even socialists demanding permanent government sponsored food, shelter and health care (now that's REALLY sick). According to former Marine General Smedley Butler, one of the most "decorated" soldiers in American military history and author of War is a Racket, some super rich people, you know, the folks who really run America, wanted him to lead a coup against Roosevelt, turn America into a true plutocratic oligarchy.

You can get the basics about the Climate Change issue, the ultimate and only issue at this time, by reading Rand Clifford's three-part essay, "Perspectives on a Changing Climate,"[5] or search the WEB for any number of articles. Or if you want to go deep into the whole shebang, read Derek Jenson's two-volume End Game, or Lewis Mumford's Myth of the Machine. Or read "alternative" magazines, like the ones these pieces appeared in to get a broader perspective than you can get from Mainstream Media. I hear Mainstream Media is starting to admit, here and there, that there "may" be a problem with the Environment that sustains all life, from the Redwood Forests to the Lower East Side. There's really not a lot one needs to know, now that there's one issue that must be dealt with before others, though it helps to be as knowledgeable as possible, to get a sense of the facts we're not supposed to know, facts that make it ever more difficult for the Imperial government to pull the wool over our eyes—again. But if we remain in our state of arrested development (most American minds close in what, the fifth grade? sixth grade?), another Katrina will blow by, this time taking NYC or LA with it, and FEMA will send in the Marines—or better yet, a "private" security firm—to restore order to the desperate, starving, homeless masses. Well, I hope citizens in "high risk" areas get their gats while the gettin's good.

Again, it all depends on whether you do or don't want to check out the evils of the hierarchical, plutocratic, patriarchal order that we've called "civilization" for the past 6,000 years. (Big irony: It all began in Iraq or thereabouts; can't say THE MAN doesn't have a sense of humor!) It's a mind-blower, how the broad range of greed, corruption and waste, beginning from the top down in civilization, has turned 90 percent of the planet into urban wasteland and suburban sprawl. The Natives of North America lived in the same regions for at least ten thousand years; and we've managed to destroy 90 percent of the earth in six centuries, mostly in the last 150 years of Corporate Capitalism. And America, the "New World," soiled its own didies, perhaps irrevocably, in a mere 500 years. If even the remaining ten

[5] http://www.starchiefpress.com/search.php?q=perspectives%20on%20a%20changing%20climate

percent of the "Natural World" were saved for some possible future generation who would learn to live with Nature, not against it, the struggle will be fierce; hundreds of millions, including yours truly, will die, perhaps Billions, to get the population of humans down to a sustainable level. The Native Americans, who were almost made extinct by the "American Dream," were a model of sustainability and ecology. Again, they lived in the same regions for over ten thousand years, always replacing, in some way, what they took from the land.

Compare the at-least-ten-thousand to the "almost 500" (really the past 150: the Industrial Revolution) and you gotta wonder: which of the "fittest" were meant to survive, or even, what exactly does the word "fittest" imply. . . .

We're in serious, serious trouble. "Debate" with Mainstream representatives of the Corporate/Military state was unsuccessful even in the late sixties (remember the Chicago riots, the Chicago Seven, COINTELPRO, FBI harassment of U.S. citizens?), when the business class, realizing Vietnam would ultimately be costly unless it were turned into some kind of cheap market or production site—which is exactly what happened: Ask the women who work in its sweatshops)—and when the Military class, realizing it was not equipped to fight an "invisible" indigenous population, and deciding that it would have to take a holiday and regroup, pulled the plug on the war.

Speaking of which. . . . I STILL see bumper-stickers urging us to "support our troops!" You think Germans and Japanese didn't "support" their troops during WWII? What did that "support" amount to? A desire to kill Americans, if only to "get them before they got your son." Then again, just cause they're murdering people who posed no threat to them BEFORE they landed in Iraq (we invaded a foreign country; what did we expect, to be greeted with flowers? Oh yeah, we DID expect that, didn't we?), and we know now what we pretended not to know before the war, that Iraq had no WMD and posed about as much a threat to us as the Sandinistas allegedly posed to Texas in the 1980s. It doesn't mean that we should stop "supporting our troops," even though some of the more faint-hearted among us might "condemn" the war itself. If we stopped supporting "our" troops, why, they might get all depressed and start reading books and smoking marijuana and learn about all the terrible things our addiction to oil is doing—the most important of which is the global climate change destroying every living thing on the planet. They might even put down their guns and stop fighting and go against ALL orders and join the surviving men women and children of Iraq in rebuilding their culture into the "cradle of civilization" it once was. As soon as that happens, who knows what'll fall next? If their older bothers and sisters stop obeying the dictates of a deranged, psychotic "Commander-in-Chief" who eats our Aunt Jemima frozen bleached white-flour waffles slathered in white corn syrup with artificial maple flavoring and caramel coloring, not to mention also wolfing down Uncle Ben's plantation style White-Wash rice?

What's so horrible is that if the Iraq war ends tomorrow, and peace is declared around the globe, with all oppressors giving aid and retribution to the oppressed, and all territories being shared etc., etc., we'd STILL be doomed 'cause someone was stupid enough to declare a war against Nature (like the war against drugs, war against smoking, war against poverty, war against racism, terrorism, ismism—wow, we've lost a lot of wars, haven't we—and to keep burning the gas in greater and greater quantities and burning plants and animals to extinction, so that now Nature is incomprehensibly pissed. Think about all the "odd weather" and natural disasters we've had in the past 20 years, then multiply it by orders of magnitude, and that's the inheritance you're leaving your children and, if they survive, grand children, great grandchildren, etc.

No more compromise with Corporations whose basic function is to turn life—plants, animals—into death—"products, merchandise." We need radical action. We need a worldwide commitment to keep the population down, feed the living, and clean up. Rebuild sustainable housing, replant whatever near-gone plants we can salvage, turn this planet into something livable and beautiful again. There will be organizers, engineers, various "officials" and plain old laborers. But even the unskilled laborers—among whom I'll be—picking up litter, will know their work is meaningful, as opposed to upping productivity of widgets for MegaCorps so that powerful Casino called the stock market can give it a higher "earning potential" and return on Investment (appropriately acronymed ROI). If humans can organize for this one 100-plus year task, perhaps the balance between humans and nature (which means all other species and plant life) will be restored.

Of course, reaching the ideals expressed in the previous paragraph is a long shot, possibly just short of fantasy. But that's the situation we're in. Either the "people of the earth" take down the Current System immediately and put everything they have into cleaning the earth, air, and water, and into planning and creating a sustainable life—or their progeny won't survive and the last sunset humanity will enjoy will come down in about 100 years, maybe less.

This article was posted on Sunday, May 13th, 2007 at 5:00am

# LAST EXIT TO DISNEYLAND

It's a long story... then again, aren't they all...

So I thought I was subletting an apartment, "rent stabilized" at $1350 from my sister, who was recently married, without realizing the absentee "landlord," BSG Management Inc. (duh!) is trying to squeeze out such ne'er do-wells as my sister, who's lived here and paid them rent for FIFTEEN YEARS, so they can charge the current "market value" of $3600/month for said shit-hole (well, I've been in worse shit-holes; this is a "doorman" building; but still, I'm living in essentially a studio for what should be the price of a mortgage). So they've been "calling" my sister, who, though a well-intentioned, kind person—to me, at least—lives in their bourgeois world, and like the bourgeois, is in total denial of the impending total collapse and imminent police-state (did I say imminent? We've been under occupation since October 1st, officially, haven't we?),[6] still believing they're in Disneyland where everything works out to their advantage as long as they pay through the nose. We don' need no steenkeen Second Law of Thermodynamics...

My sister, of course, has a friend who's a real estate lawyer who's threatening THEM with "harassment" etc. etc. etc.

Like I NEED this shit? I just wanted a place to read and think for the winter and hopefully figure a way outta this One-trick Magic

---

6 "Brigade Homeland Tours Start October 1," *Army Times*: http://www.armytimes.com/news/2008/09/army_homeland_090708w/

Kingdom, or deeper into it—living off credit cards going "home" to my wife and dog on week-ends. (Note: I intend to pay back every penny—at the minimum rate, regardless of "interest" accrued, once the economy gets back on its feet again—wink, wink; nudge, nudge. It's a waiting game: sooner or later one of us is gonna fall, me or the Bank; who knows, maybe I'll play the Lottery like the folks at the Deli next door, who drop $20, $30, even $50 a day of money they don't have for millions they'll never see—well one lucky person might "win," but "they" won't, and certainly not "we." Anyway, what does it say about the value of work, when those who work hate their lives so much they'll gladly piss away hundreds of "honest wages" for fantasy millions of ill-gotten gain—gambling? At least in Vegas, though the house always wins, the rube gets to win sometimes...)

So as I said, the "Super," a rat for management who keeps meticulous records of who comes in and out, found that my parents—last name: Engel—stayed TWO week-ends and my wife—last name: Engel—stays every Tuesday night. Uh OH! These bums are trying to screw management by allowing family members to stay as guests while paying a mere $1350 a month when the CORPORATION can easily get $3600 from bigger, wealthier bums!!!

So as I said, they've been calling my sister, who sells "green" spin control to Corporations via her PR COMPANY (READ: The Pursuit of Pure Talk). She said she and her lawyer friend, her best pal from high school, smart, competent woman, but surely not one to inspire terror at close range, are "handling it."

Call me sexist, but in cases like these, that is, face-to-face combat among us peons, the best kind of lawyer/representative one can have, if one is aware of one's surroundings, is an intelligent, articulate, experienced six-foot-two-inch 210 pound Alpha Male Gorilla, like my own high school "pal" Dave, a millionaire foreclosure lawyer—allegedly with a "conscience"; he feels "bad" about forcing families from their homes—whose inherent violence, though sublimated by the byzantine "legal process," is palpable in such "personal situations." If you're doing corporate law, where no one really sees you except occasionally at a meeting, it doesn't matter—"unisex" situation; if you're doing courtroom law, where you want to win over a jury, it helps to be an attractive, petite, sympathetic, articulate woman; if you're doing dirt-work confronting Corporate thugs and thuggettes, it sure as hell helps to have "body language" and a body capable of "speaking" loud and clear...

Nevertheless, in this make-shift case, my five-seven 150 lb. outraged, un-sublimated, "presence," stoked with righteous indignation, had to do. Also, I was wearing my "Homeland Security... Fighting Terrorism Since 1492" t-shirt, complete with large photo-image of Geronimo and associates.

So. . .the "super" asked, as I was walking out, stick (cane, but I hate to call it that; makes me sound crippled or old) in hand, and asked me where "Your Sister" is. I asked him "Who wants to know?" Somewhat less truculently, he put on the ingratiating, "Hi, I'm the Superintendent, Bena," routine. He held out his hand, which I didn't shake, and I said, "Why do you want to reach my sister?"

"I tried calling, she didn't answer," he muttered.

Anyway, after some mild "harassment" on his part, I said, "OH! You mean you're the JANITOR! Well, I got a doorbell that needs fixing. You're not doing your job."

So then the puckered up thuggette slave said "I'm mmghsmdsh of BSG Management. He doesn't have to fix anything until the 'tenant of record' fills out a form. I tried calling the tenant of record, but she refused the courtesy of a return call."

"Oh, did she? Maybe you're harassing her," says I ("harassing" seems to be a big word among these systems administrators/enablers, or what Malcolm X called "house slaves" as opposed to us—soon to be house-less?—"field slaves").

"WE'RE not harassing her!" says Ms. BSG.

WE????

"WE know what she's up to."

"Oh? What might that be?" I asked.

"WE know she's married and she has no right to give this place to you."

I didn't want to get involved with bullshit, so I told her to call 'the tenant of record' and walked away. But damned if my "inner voice" didn't start HARASSING ME, forcing me to remember every situation in which I'd backed down from a fight and how each one haunted me always and forever.

Soooo. . . I returned, and started to explain to the Janitor that he was a rat, a serf, a kapo, and a minion—politely, of course. When the woman piped in "I'm his supervisor, and I say. . ."

"—I don't care who the FUCK you are, Ms. BSG. I'm talking to Bena the Janitor."

Bena, being "chivalrous"—ass-kissing, actually— started in about how I shouldn't be acting "like this" and cursing in front of a "woman." So I said, in just so many words, "You mean, your Master."

"Yes she is my Mast—no! My Supervisor!"

Then Ms. BSG got on her cell-phone and called HER supervisor and told him she spoke to "the brother" who was rude and "cursed her out."

THAT'S cursing somebody out? I'd hate to imagine her idea of a full-blown rebellion.

Well. Derrick Jensen is right. Violence can only flow smoothly downwards, NOT upstream. Here I am, defending myself, and I daresay, my sister, against the accusations of this hierarchy of toadies vying for the approval of supervisor, hauptsupervisor, uberhauptsupervisor, etc., so BSG can kick out a tenant of fifteen years for an extra $2150/month, and I DARED speak "violent language." Really now, what on earth can be MORE VIOLENT than harassing someone to leave their home so that The Lords of the Manor (etymology of "landlord?") can profit from his/her vacancy? Didn't the "settlers" do that to the Indians? The Israelis to the Palestinians? The KKK to "freed" black people?

So as not to be out-shined, the doorman, whose supervisor, I assume, is Bena, the janitor, mumbled something about I shouldn't be behaving this way he can't understand what's happening to people these days what are they losing their minds (as well as they're homes) etc. etc. etc.? What was I supposed to do, coax him from his New York Post to debate him about the Corporate State, Systems, Hierarchies, Class Warfare?

Once, a long, long, long time ago (East Village, 1993; 10th between B&C, where Ginsberg once lived, right across the street from where Charlie Parker once lived, and the place hadn't been "improved" since, though I was paying an outrageous, for the time, $620/month: it now goes for about $2000. Just what kind of MORONS would pay that for a shit-hole? Even if I were Bill Gates I wouldn't pay that much for an old tenement studio, which is why "HE'S Bill Gates, and WE'RE NOT")...uh...where was I?

...oh yeah, once, when me and the other tenants got fed up with the garbage strewn elevator with bullet holes in it; the broken front door that allowed junkies to hang out in the halls 24/7; the numerous repairs needed in various apartments and the building in general that were never made, we organized a RENT STRIKE, assisted by a lawyer from GOLES (Good Old Lower East Side), a non-profit tenants' rights organization. We held the rent in an escrow account, and refused to pay until our "demands" (stated above) were met. The GOLES lawyer told us that the "absentee landlord" was actually a Corporation running slums in Harlem and the Bronx, had lawsuits out the wazoo and didn't want any more bad publicity.

SlumLords Inc. eventually gave in. More importantly, me and my fellow paranoid tenants got to know one another, and talk, and become actual friends and neighbors. A community united by common purpose. But that was long, long, long ago, when rat-and-roach infested tenement studios went for a "mere" $620/month.

As I was leaving, Bena told HIS serf, the doorman, to "call the police if anything—"

"If WHAT? Why don't you call the police right NOW?"

"I say call police if you do anything stupid," Bena replied, careful to avoid eye contact.

"I don't do stupid things," I said.

"Why, you're being stupid right NOW, cursing in front of a woman and all," said the Door Mouse.

Now I see how the phony Hillary/Palin "feminism"—as opposed to the true feminism, which is of course the antithesis of this hierarchy of Beta male baboons trying to 'make it' with the invisible Corporate Alpha, who of course doesn't exist, in a palpable sense—works to the advantage of the "Alpha Males" (cowering in collective Corporation).

They hire a female serf, who can insinuate that merely by living there and paying an outrageous rent, I'm "pulling something," and moreover, my sister who's lived in the place for almost two decades, and my wife and parents who stayed as guests, were in on the racket, and I'm not "behaving" if I talk back. Hmmm. My sister's lawyer said something about a "family clause" in these things, but I don't give a fuck. I'd rather just have it out with the serfs than live among them.

Also, my "unofficial" approach does have its benefits. No matter how "rational" "cool" and "professional" these types try to be, they are still—somewhat—human. They do not like real confrontation anymore than "we free spirits" do. I assume most of the folks they deal with don't challenge them outright, or their day-to-day "jobs" would be hell. Hence, somewhat rattled, she FUCKED UP. She took out the "official sheet" which said my sister was supposed to vacate by November 3, pending a new lease—which she did receive anyway, but as I said, fuck all that.

My first thought was, "well, thanks for the heads up. Now I know I have at least three weeks to leave and be a most unpleasant tenant."

THEN it occurred to me. How do they know I'm a "tenant" at all? How do they know I'm not just staying for a few weeks as my sister's guest before she vacates on November 3rd?

So if I'm cool to split by November 3—which I am—Ms. BSG fucked up royally.

So, I'm just a guest, and they were VERY rude to me.

They were, in fact, STUPID.

OCTOBER 2008

"WHAT? Why don't you call the police right NOW?"

"Lady, I'll [illegible] if you do my time [illegible]," [illegible] replied, careful to avoid eye contact.

"I don't do stupid things," I said.

"Why you not [illegible] stupid right NOW, [illegible] look of a [illegible] and all," said the [illegible].

Now I see how the phony Hillary/Palin [illegible] was [illegible] to the true feminism, which is because [illegible] he deems "inferior." Her female behind is trying to "make it" with the [illegible], who [illegible] her [illegible] to the [illegible] of the "Alpha Males" [illegible] competition.

[illegible]

# POWER DOWN

We really make me sick.

I used to think we were all a bunch of clowns.

Where did I get the arrogance, the audacity, the sheer chutzpah to believe we were equal to clowns, who after all, are entertainers, in their own way, make-up artists, acrobats, performers who get paid at the end of the night, scrub off their grease-paint, twist off their rubber noses, and sleep well, while we, we are merely children in the audience bedazzled and beguiled by the clowns while outside the big top, under the benevolent watch of the Strong Man, The Knife-Thrower and Lobster Boy ("support our freaks") our parents are signing away the family farm, our inheritance, and that of our children, to the Ringmaster, who orders the Strongman to bugger Dad while Lobster Boy and Knife-Thrower do unspeakable things to Mom, for after all, they got paid for the gig, gotta make 'em earn their freak. Otherwise, it just wouldn't be natural.

That we dare flatter ourselves with such attributes as clown, buffoon, jester, jackanapes, lummox, oaf. . . another testimony to our unmitigated gall.

### Communication Breakdown in the Great Beyond (Apropos Fox, not Cox)

How telling that the television ghost-hunters (all right, we'll go along with it: "there are more things in heaven and on earth, Horatio," yadda yadda yadda) were worried about entering the haunted basement because of the POWER PROBLEM. That is, there was no place to hook up their fancy high-tech ghost hunting doo-dads, so they had to bring down a generator. Interesting that even in the "other world" communication depends on non-renewable—or re-incarnation-able—energy sources.

### Cox Says "No!" to Unmarketable Drugs

We paranoids don't do well with hallucinogenics. Then again, maybe it's the epoch; it's not like I'm hanging out with Grace Slick on a warm June night in San Francisco, circa 1967. The sixties had pot and acid; the seventies had heroin and Quaaludes; the eighties cocaine and Ecstasy; the nineties anti-depressants; and our current era a mishmash of anti-depressants, benzodiazepams, and highly caffeinated "soft drinks." Booze and nicotine throughout, of course; the timeless "legal" drugs we are actually encouraged not to "say no" to—don't let the anti-smoking ads fool you; besides encouraging smoking as an act of rebellion via corn-ball reverse-propaganda, the hardest drug of all to kick is Nicotine gum. It's like chewing cocaine.

### We're All Better Now: The Post-Election Irrelevance of Cox

The modern president is like a systems administrator of a system that's been fixed for years with minor "patches" and "upgrades," only making it even more complex and subsequently closer to chaos, a system that can only be "fixed" by a complete "power down" and rewrite of the kernel and OS code; no matter how colorful and dazzling the screen-saver, it'll only save what it's meant to save—the screen; thousands of lines of code between pressing a key and the instant appearance of a letter or number on the screen.

I wouldn't be surprised if The Board of Trustees (whoever they really are) sat McCain and Obama in a room and said,

"We need an articulate, relatively young, black man to take off some of the heat, ease tension, bring back that Kennedy/MLK sense of hope and 'change.' Sorry, John, you represent the so-called 'old school.' Barack, you're in. Congratulations. No hard feelings, John. Our men at Diebold have been instructed to give you a number of 'red states' so it won't be an embarrassment."

"Yes. I understand, sir. Congratulations, Barack."

"Thanks, John. If there's anything I can do, you let me know."

## Comedians as Letter "C"

Ten pies-in-the-face "to-go" for the clowns who managed to take a once outrageous weekly (5 minute) skit on the real Saturday Night Live 1975-80 (imagine if, after 1970, they'd hired four new guys every couple of years to write and play crappy music and called them The Beatles or The Doors? What's in a name?) into hour-long ACTUAL mainstream "news shows" with ACTUAL mainstream guests (who they josh around with with all the investigative chops of Jay Leno) and call it "comedy." For some reason this pisses me off even more than the fucking election, which is at least a "sort of" funny joke. This "Fake News" using "actual mainstream news" with some limp, sponsor-approved "satire" would make Lenny Bruce, George Carlin, Richard Pryor and the real "SNL NEWS" satirists WISH they were dead, if they weren't already dead, and therefore, most of them being dead, damn proud of it. What did I just say?

## Modrun Media Medicine: a Possible (Mis?)Reading of Cox

Actors, formerly lowest of life forms, became icons—literally–once their owners had the technology to reproduce their images so they could earn money off the actors not merely from one or two stage performances a day, but from thousands of movie screenings a day throughout the world, not to mention magazines, memorabilia, free media publicity, etc. Unfortunately, the actors, never the brightest of the lot, took this to mean that they themselves were somehow more important.

Surgeries don't matter anyway, especially for women, who once they pass 40 have to wait till they're over sixty or so to play 40-year-olds and such. Cheaper for celebrities to dress in diapers as a means toward regaining lost youth and more effective than surgery; also, they can "grow into them" as they age...

But the surgeries made them look like teenagers strung out on heroin. So the Owners began to harvest real old people, the ones who still had enough memory left to remember lines (not that it mattered much; in film, you only have to say one or two lines between 'takes'); also, the old people died before they became annoying; so the owners told the filmmakers to make movies about old people; but the young people weren't interested in seeing such films; so the Owners had Big Media churn out magazines, websites, television shows, etc., portraying the old people as desirable, THE PEOPLE to be; so the young people began buying fanzines and going to films starring old people. Soon the young people wanted to be like their heroes. They tried heroin, but that didn't work well for more than a few weeks, or minutes, for most; so the stores began selling old people masks and props to make the young folks look old with sagging breasts and low scrotums like melting wax; and the wealthy young people had this done via surgery; so everyone, even the doctors who lost so much business making old people look young—which was way passé—were happy...

### To Paraphrase Cox...

Capitalists and their "enablers" cannot be reasoned with or "talked to." There is no dialog. If there were enough space, and a lot fewer people, that would be fine with me. They stay where they are, I stay where I am, and we're happy as pigs in poop with our own peculiar notions about what "is" is. However, Capitalism, which began as a malignant tumor some 500 years ago (some would say it began as "Civilization" itself, which started around 8000 years ago), has metastasized to engulf the globe. There is no "escape" unless you're rich enough to buy a temporary Disneyland off the coast of some third world "paradise" which will, ultimately, be engulfed by the tidal waves of climate change "inspired by" industrialism and post-industrialism—whatever that is. We are what we eat, (i.e., the planet).

The ultimate goal of capitalism is one "legal" Man—the Chief Executives and Board—celebrating absolute monopoly over the wasteland, all the while eying each other hungrily and wondering "gee, who will 'we' exploit next?"

### ...and Add My Own Two Cents

That said, once someone crosses the "line" into my "space," and worse, threatens to eliminate me in order to occupy said "space," I don't think "love" or "tolerance," as preached by capitalist clergy, are the affectations that are in my "best interest." In such situations, an absolute devotion to defending "one of god's creatures" (i.e. moi) BY ANY MEANS NECESSARY, is in order. Just a thought.

### American Bards and Cox Reviewers

Of course, Cox's *Sick Planet*,[7] if it's read, as it certainly should be, will probably generate all sorts of "opinions" among the millions floating around "the information super highway that's gonna bring us all together" these days, including this one. But I prefer to think of opinions not "like assholes, but like original minds; not everybody has one."

---

[7] http://www.amazon.com/exec/obidos/ASIN/0745327400/counterpunchmaga

## Beyond Cox and Evil

Maybe all that mumbo-jumbo (see Ishmael Reed)[8] mythopoaeic poppycock about the "dead king" sacrifice which culminated in Jesus appeasing his mean old dad for the sins of mankind in order to save mankind was not as wickedly conceived as the mind of mankind is capable of and consistent in conceiving.

Men hate and fear god. The way they hate and fear THE CORPORATION. But like THE CORPORATION, the old testament god, Yahweh, is invisible, immortal, untouchable. But Jesus, his "representative" on earth, was quite mortal, visible and touchable. Better yet, he was capable of being harmed.

Men nailed him to the cross in vengeance, their only means of redress, against the merciless, implacable, unreachable Yahweh.

So what might this mean in terms of seeking "redress" against THE CORPORATION?

In an EMERGENCY SITUATION, such as ours, one must come to terms with whatever interpretation of the cosmic order one may have, then put a lid on it and let's get down to brass tacks—and use them...

## Concluding Unscientific Post-It™

those who can't do, leach
those who can't sing, preach
those who can't grab, reach
if agent manage sale then
 go to beach
else if
agent manage fail
then
prayer (pitch)=beseech

NOVEMBER 2008

[8] http://www.amazon.com/Mumbo-Jumbo-Ishmael-Reed/dp/0684824779/ref=sr_1_1?s=books&ie=UTF8&qid=1282570049&sr=1-1

# THE IRONY OF THE ECSTASY

Maybe we can—but why bother?

Personally, I viewed the whole thing as if it were a boxing match (CNN or FOX, anyplace that even had an advertisement for election coverage featuring McInsane and Bareback Obama faced off in profile, like fighters). Say, Holyfield versus Tyson (the re-match, after Holyfield's ear was sewed back on). I ignored the hype qua hype, but once the "bout" began, consciously or unconsciously I "took sides." Just like I wanted Holyfield to give Tyson his "come-uppance" (and just like I wanted the similar thing when Clinton took away the twelve-year Reign of Terror by Reagan/Bush I for the heavyweight title in '92), I "rooted" for Obama.

Then I had second thoughts. Since, like any other sports event/entertainment, the outcome wouldn't make much of a difference to this huge sick planet, I thought it might be funnier, more hysterical, just for kicks and guffaws, if McCain was actually "elected"—then succumbed to his melanoma after a few months to issue in the "Palin era." Also, I actually prefer an outright bully/gangster/thug, like Dubya or John Gotti, who lays his trick cards on the table, to a "friendly executive" like Clinton or the fictional Michael Corleone, who'll "let you win" then stab you in the back as you're leaving the Casino.

Then again, what do I know? Maybe Obama represents the latter.

Regardless, the whole circus reminds me of '92, when I was still "green under the apple boughs..."

"Nobel Laureate" (I read that Nobel created the prize because he didn't want his legacy to be that of the inventor of the then ultimate weapon, Dynamite, although I now think the "Nobel Propaganda Prize" is more of a danger to living things than TNT) Al Gore, warming up the crowd as opening act for Bill Clinton, announcing, point-by-pithy-sound-byte-point, various failures of the Reagan/Bush era, then pausing as the "home crowd" in Madison Square Garden (broadcast to the world) repeated the refrain, chanting over and over, "it's TIME for CHANGE."

Yeah. Tell that to one of the dead Iraqis whose murder was "worth it." Or a Palestinian in Camp Gaza. Or a Serbian in the once-beautiful city of Belgrade. Or a "welfare queen" forced to leave her kids alone so she could be an indentured servant to "work-fare" when the whole reason she went on "welfare" was cause she couldn't both support and nurture her kids while working 60 hrs a week for "minimum wage" at McDonalds etc., etc., etc.

Meanwhile. MEANWHILE...

Dionysus reigned supreme last night in Union Square park. They—mostly NYU students—were partying till 4 AM. Thousands jammed the park, chanting, singing, whooing, hooing and hee-ing and haw-ing (imagine if "they" had done that four years ago, but in protest, when BushCo. stole the election). Worse, the cars, trucks, buses, honking horns as they passed to the delight of the drunken crowd. I guess I don't blame them, in a way. I remember being young and stupid and so fucking happy when Clinton ended the Reagan/Bush Reign of Terror that so dominated my entire young adulthood. They'll sober up when Obama cancels their guaranteed student loans to help pay for the Wall Street bail-out, the noble "wars" in Iraq, Afghanistan, and soon Iran. As for the car-truck-bus crowd: Their oil has peaked, I think, or is damn close to it. Again, I understand people's need to feel part of a "group," a "celebration" of "change" and the "official end of racism," etc. But I couldn't help thinking how ironic it was that thousands of people expressed "political commitment" not by gathering together to soberly plan the Next Move (i.e. putting the president elect in the hot seat), but by behaving like a bunch of typically arrogant, indulgent, selfish, drunk, overbearing Americans....

I mean, my wife had to get up for work at eight, and I had to DO work—I do both my "paid" writing—hack copywriting, ghost-writing, etc.—and "leisurely" work, such as this here, at night. WE sure felt the ramifications of "change..."

The irony is...

My wife works at the Digital Animation Center at the NYU Film School. Those were some of her own students keeping her up all night. While she, like me, is a "gym rat" and in better shape than most 20 year olds, she, like me, is in her early 40s and just can't "party like it's 1999" til 4 AM and get up "for class" at 8 AM like her students, who will no doubt be full of pep and energy and good cheer, awaiting "change" as I was when Clinton ended the Reagan/Bush nightmare to create his own. Well, I wish them well. But I wouldn't wish on anyone the kind of "change" Obama (now the number one corporeal representative of the invisible, immortal corporate body known as THE MAN) will be bringing. . . .

Bad news that the New Prince-in-Waiting made some unfortunate veiled threats to the REST of the planet in his Live-from-Chicago acceptance speech, a more corporate, user-friendly, lawyer-ish version of "yer either with us, or against us."

Often think of the millions of people who lived entire lifetimes—70, 80 years—thousands of years before Homer was in baby booties. Moments of love, fear, happiness, pleasure, pain, etc. experienced by REAL people, who just didn't have camcorders to record it all for the infinite boredom of posterity—Humanity's Home Movie; interesting if you've never seen any type of movie before, or suddenly found a 30,000 year old DVD and spent an evening watching "a day in the life" of our ancestors, but if passed along like our own over-recorded/photographed/digitized antics, a yawner for sure. . . .

Ah, for the (allegedly) good ol' days of Matriarchy, before some dudes got together with a bunch of sharp objects and realized, with some verbal acrobatics, they could "rule forever and ever look on these works ye mighty and despair." On the other hand, there are non-matriarchal tribal cultures like the Sioux, Navajo etc. in which men and women were "separate but equal," each having their own work, responsibilities and value. The whole Judeo-Christian-Islam (and other "civilization" religions) scam is a waste of life-energy and a royal pain in the ass for all involved. Not to mention the near absolute exploitation of women either as phony Hillary/Palin type "feminists" (absolute opposite of what my friend Barbara Mor wrote about in *The Great Cosmic Mother*—terrible title; Harper-Collins' idea; her real title was the excellent: *The First God*—trying to be like men (who themselves have long since become "machines" or cogs in THE MACHINE) or remaining generally downtrodden sex slaves, house-keepers and/or shielded from all light in burkhas. Why would any heterosexual man want women to be dressed in lampshades? Then again, why would any sentient being want women with plastic breasts, silicon buttocks and faces "re-invented" by surgery????

On the other hand: "Yawn."

NOVEMBER 7TH, 2008

www.ingramcontent.com/pod-product-compliance
Ingram Content Group UK Ltd.
Pitfield, Milton Keynes, MK11 3LW, UK
UKHW020131250726
13967UKWH00002B/594